SPACE COMERCIALISATION

Prospects, Challenges and Way Forward

SPACE COMERCIALISATION

Prospects, Challenges and Way Forward

Gurbachan Singh Sachdeva, Ph.D.

PENTAGON PRESS LLP

Space Comercialisation: Prospects, Challenges and Way Forward
Gurbachan Singh Sachdeva

First Published in 2019

ISBN 978-93-86618-69-6

Published by
PENTAGON PRESS LLP
206, Peacock Lane, Shahpur Jat
New Delhi-110049
Phones: 011-64706243, 26491568
Telefax: 011-26490600
email: rajan@pentagonpress.in
website: www.pentagonpress.in

Printed at Aegean Offset Printers, Greater Noida, U.P.

Dedicated to

MY STUDENTS

who have

TAUGHT ME SO MUCH

Contents

Preface

Man has reached the final frontier and breached it too. Historically, the advent into outer space was a spin-off of military adventurism, yet it has laid bare myriad opportunities for scientific exploration, peaceful uses, and excavation of natural resources. Each aspect offers great potential for the benefit of mankind and improvement in quality of terrestrial life and welfare of humanity. As a result, nations are now becoming dependent on outer space assets for a wide array of utilities and functions in both civilian usages and military domains. But each activity has its own challenges of technical feasibility, desired standards of operational safety, inclination for investment, as well as permissibility under the legal regime of outer space.

Till lately, most of the space activities were carried out within the public domain and mostly by military personnel with governmental civil agencies gradually taking over. This trend has since abated and now private enterprise has entered the arena in a big way; in telecommunications, broadcasting, remote-sensing, shuttle service, space travel, as well as commercial exploitation of celestial natural resources. Many other fields, like gravity-free manufacturing, vaccines in sterile environment, super-conductors in extreme cold ambience, space tourism and hospitality, and colonisation of the Moon and Mars are waiting in the wings, with viable technologies, to be commercially exploited. Possibilities in the future seem endless.

At the same time, the number of players (state and non-state) utilizing outer space for these purposes is fast increasing and is set to escalate dramatically making outer space highly congested, prone to accidents in space navigation, and thus potentially leading to conflicts . Issues such as density of space objects, rampant space debris, arms race in space, radio frequency interference with resultant disputes are also likely to become impediments for the long-term sustainability of outer space. These factors underline the need for proper governance to regulate launches, particularly mini, micro and small satellites as also put in place a legal regime for exploitation of celestial natural resources and sharing of benefits globally as promised in the Outer Space Treaty (OST).

The corpus of space law, so far, in the form of Conventions, Treaties and Agreements has come about more out of necessity and urgency consequent to the circumstances or to remedy contingent situations. It has not evolved systematically with experience or over relatively long period of time. For example, the OST, however laudable, is a medley of compromises with advertent loopholes. The Moon Treaty, despite enshrining the espoused principles, has found little acceptance and fewer ratifications. The Rescue Agreement was an exigent measure for the then space powers. The UN guidelines on remote-sensing and prevention of debris are not mandatory and hence their abidance is suspect due to economic implications of such measures.

Commercialization of outer space by private corporations has already begun and is galloping. But the existing law hardly provides impetus to this trend, in fact, it is obstructive. Evidently, space law, as in the past, has lagged behind technology and needs to be proactive enough to prance hand in hand with technology in outer space for peace and commerce. This book addresses some of the lacunae and shortcomings in space law relating to commercial exploitation of celestial natural resources with some pointers to contemporary problems as well. It also offers suggestions for prudent, harmonious and ethical exploitation of mineral resources of outer space and celestial bodies. Given that more nations than ever before are today poised at the threshold of space activities, space travel, tourism, and space habitation are in the offing; this book is thought-provoking, urgent and urges for timely revision of germane law, regulatory regimen, and governing mechanisms.

This book focuses on and addresses incumbent legal issues, regulatory problems and suggests an appropriate governing body in the form of World Space Organisation (WSO) to handle commercial aspects of exploitative space applications concerning non-renewable celestial natural resources. Each chapter aims to highlight an attempt at commercial exploitation of outer space and points towards some lacunae and shortcomings while at the same time offering some viable suggestions. It further establishes an imperative necessity to create global platforms for exchanging views on the workable recommendations for eventual implementation of WSO as an empowered organ for space governance.

As the subjects covered in different chapters are cognate in content and have been discussed on the same template of International Space Law (ISL) and with relevance to the established tenets of International Law, there is bound to be certain repetition of texts, arguments, authors and analysis. This was unavoidable to enable the reader to understand the argument in context rather than refer to other chapters and pages for a part of the logic and rationale. The citations to other pages would have distracted the attention and focus could be lost. Hence, it has been considered advisable in the interest of the reader to treat the complete argument in each place of discourse.

Thus, this book is a wakeup call on a couple of challenges and unresolved contingencies that failed consensus during negotiations but today stare us in the face to be addressed suitably. One example can be absence of legal regimen governing commercial mining on the asteroids and other celestial bodies by private enterprise, in competitive business environment. Another example could be lack of explication of the concepts of Province of Mankind and Common Heritage of Mankind (CHM); as well as modalities for sharing of benefits between nations. The ambiguity on policy and governance issues seeks urgent resolution.

The book has come to the conclusion that effective public order in outer space, good governance of celestial resources, and regulation of space activities through law can lead to progressively better welfare and perpetual growth in prosperity of humanity. However, some of the issues analysed may appear controversial or solutions offered seemingly unviable, here a debate would be desirable to generate greater thought process by scholars to mull over the issues and arrive at judicious consensus. The author, in due humility, acknowledges his failings in research content, fallacies in analysis, and frailties in the style of presentation. Nevertheless, he is frank in his arguments and sincere in his approach.

I owe sincere gratitude to Dr Manpreet Sethi for constant help in my research to hone finer details that have substantially improved the quality and content; and her prodding encouragement to complete this work. I must also acknowledge the invaluable help of Mr Y. P. Madan in my research on certain issues.

Profuse thanks are genuinely due to Shri Rajan Arya of Pentagon Publishers for his sincere efforts in meeting the deadlines for publication of this book. Shri Sharad Tiwari also deserves my personal gratitude for painstaking efforts to achieve a commendable copy-editing.

5 September, 2018 ***Gurbachan Singh Sachdeva***

Introduction

The fact that there lies a limitless bounty of mineral resources in outer space has been proved by remote sensing and close observation through space probes and analysis of samples. And that these are useful to humanity and can augment the depleting natural resources of Earth is also established beyond doubt. Further, the technology to excavate and, to some extent, process the same *in situ* also promises feasibility. The end product that would make for a smaller quantum of high utility metals can be used for other activities on the mined planet or transported to Earth in economical capsules. Possibility can also be envisaged where processed material and procured water can be recycled in some manner for use and manufacturing on the celestial body itself or to replenish probe vehicles on deep-space missions. Thus, the utility of celestial natural resources, including water, to mankind is affirmative but the algorithms of comparative economics of excavation, processing, transportation or use *in situ* are not yet clear to convince of commercial viability and reasonable profits. But prospects appear positive and business sentiment is bullish.

Attention to space resources has been attracted due to depleting natural resources on the earth, the growing scarcity and consequently escalating prices. The pinch has been felt rather acutely that has diverted attention to prospects for other probable sources, the viability of excavation, the quality of the excavated ore, and the cost parameters. One such source zeroed onto asteroids which were long known for their mineral richness but technological viability for exploitability on commercial scale was lacking. Technology has progressed to challenge this opportunity and viability knocks at our door. Some countries, through non-governmental organizations, are making frantic efforts to actualize this possibility soonest.

Considering the trend of state agencies selectively withdrawing from space activities, except those of strategic importance or deep space exploration, it seems certain that such an activity as mining in space is of commercial nature and import and will not be undertaken by any governmental space agency nor would public exchequer funds be allocated for this purpose.[1] Perforce, such activity will have to depend upon a business initiative from private enterprise, whether for commercial adventurism or entrepreneurial vanity or business aggrandizement. And given the present standing and competence of private enterprises, which can harness complex space technology, are willing to invest huge funds in space projects and patiently wait during the gestation period. It would, therefore, not be presumptuous to believe that Space-X, Virgin Galactic, Blue Origin, Boeing Aerospace, Lockheed Martin etc. or a consortium of willing and enterprising astro-preneurs would venture into this nascent yet promising segment for prestige or profit irrespective of the attendant financial risks or hazards of space activities. Hope prevails with positivity.

The legality of private enterprise undertaking activities relating to use and exploration in outer space can be validly derived from Article VI of Outer Space Treaty (OST)[2] which permits non-governmental entities for such ventures. There is, however, a rider in the same article of the Treaty that these activities "shall require authorization and continuing supervision by the appropriate State Party to the Treaty". Thus, whatever may be the nature of conditionality, a basic permission exists for private enterprise to enter this domain for legitimate and *bonafide* activities within the ambit of the Treaty. In fact, this is happening already and satellites owned and operated by the private sector are already in outer space. Even mining for *in-situ* utilization of space mineral resources, raw or processed, can be justified on existing law. Hence, the US Commercial Space Launch Competitiveness Act, 2015[3] is valid and benign to this extent.

The problem would arise at 'commercial recovery of space resources'. Perhaps, quantum of recovery could be relevant here. Small quantities as samples may be obtained from celestial bodies and recovered for distribution or may be sale to interested parties for scientific investigation as urged under the Treaty. But the clause that "United States citizens engaged in commercial recovery of an asteroid resource or space resource obtained, including to possess, own, transport, use and sell the asteroid resources or space resources obtained in accordance with applicable law, including the international obligations of the United States" is tricky. This provision contains a syllogistic fallacy and lacks legal synchronicity with the Treaty.

Articles I and II of the OST clearly omit permission for such an attempt at commercialization. The US, in an act of 'business populomacy', has made domestic law to overcome this obstacle that impinges on the OST as this guarantees enlarged rights to its citizen than bestowed by the Treaty. In a way, the US enactment has strains of negativity against established legal position and is not as innocuous as is made to appear. But there is no need to be dismissive of the motivated narrative of the enactment. The matter deserves to be rationally debated to find best amends to the situation within the gamut of space law and explore viable solution in the common interest of humanity. This chapter is basically a concept paper on the subject, yet also attempts a case study of the US laws relating to commercial exploitation and private appropriation of space mineral resources. In the ultimate, there appears a need for a revised and modern construct of OST because the narrative must change with technological developments and business initiatives.

In my opinion, OST is a symbol of global trust and any infringement of the Treaty would be inappropriate and set a bad precedent. Such a violative action will be highly embarrassing to a space-leader like the US. Hence, there is need to find an unimpeachable legal solution because existing regimen of OST offers no concession. And, amendment to treaties is painfully arduous in diplomacy and time-consuming in negotiations. One plausible solution is to initiate and conclude a *specialis* protocol to the Treaty or an amending resolution in the UN General Assembly. The proposal can be nuanced for success by offering bait of benefits. Further, if an agreed portion of accruing profits from such activity can be shared to benefit all states in some ratio and weightage as Space Benefits Fund (SBF) on the lines of Corporate Social Responsibility (CSR), then a broad agreement may be easier, if not true consensus. This would thus satisfy the inclusive spirit of the Treaty as well as pacify non-stakeholders.

The Moon Agreement (MA)[4], however, is more permissive and liberal in this regard. In Article 8, the Agreement permits excavation on the Moon, on or below the surface, and allows for free movement of equipment and personnel etc. Further, provisions of this Agreement '...shall also apply to other celestial bodies within the solar system…'.So near-Earth asteroids get covered by this provision. But as regards natural resources of outer space, Article 11 (1) of the MA treats these as 'Common Heritage of Mankind (CHM)'. Under this concept, celestial natural resources are treated as *res communis omnium* which defies proprietary individualization in any manner. It is felt that it may be more prudent to ratify this Agreement and initiate a suitably modified legal regime for exploitation of natural resources under Article 11(5) and get this negotiated by the requisite number of state parties to the Agreement by a majority vote. Even otherwise also, MA deserves to be mainstreamed and is ripe for revision under Article 18.

Another field of commercialization of celestial bodies concerns space travel and space tourism. This activity adds value to the real estate of planetary bodies for establishing space-ports for travel and tourism infra-structure in the form of hotels and resorts that offer thrills and pleasures to the tourists. Space tourism would be expected to be innovative and novel, to impart life-time memories and out-of-the-world experience that adequately pays back the value of the trip. Some of the ideas being touted are honey-mooning in near-zero-gravity environment or an exhilarating view of the mother earth in lights at night or *lumiere* splendour of the universe. Once this industry picks up in right earnest, the commercial value of celestial realty will soar tremendously.

There is a trend metamorphosing rather fast with claims of humans wanting to settle down on the planetary bodies with permanent residence and are willing to go to space on a one-way ticket. The Moon Village and Mars Colony are favourite townships to reside and live permanently. The prospective residents believe that they can sever their nationality affiliation to the global state and can survive as citizens of the planet of emigration. Though technically the idea is not weird and designs of residential accommodation and provision of utilities and conveniences are on the anvil yet, it appears a distant vision. But dreams do come true also.

A group of Asgardians, who claim themselves to be a Space Nation, are also striving for a place in space that they can call as their own. Their competition with commercial usages by global astro-preneurs is possibly going to be fierce because global corporates will be governed by the UN regulations while the Asgardians will have no such legal shackles. Adherents of the Church of Scientology profess faith in the belief that they are descendants from a Space Confederacy of King Xenu and have the first right on planetary bodies of the confederacy. Conflict is again on the horizon.

Logic and rationality may dismiss these claims on whatever reasoning or lack of justification from the other side yet, an endemic conflict resides in the situation that may adversely affect the commercial ventures on celestial bodies. At present, the existing law of space treaties is silent on this aspect of commercialization of space resources. Frankly, it could not have been anticipate half century back that man would achieve progress on space technology in diverse application and, that too, so fast. But this development is on us and we cannot shut off a treasure trove of spatial natural resources for sheer lack of legal solutions, which have to be found and equally fast. Some short-term and long-term legal measures and policy expedients have been proposed for the space-faring nations to take initiative and resolve issues on the legal canvas keeping in view the principles of common benefit, inclusiveness and equity.

Apart from legal and policy solutions, it has been commented that humanity has not covered itself with glory in its business activities. No doubt, the motivation for any commercial or industrial activity is profit but the business agenda has been to squeeze profit by means, legal, pseudo-legal, or even illegal. This does not behove well and has created inequity, acrimony and discord among the participants for production of wealth. Management-labour disputes have existed for over centuries and sharing of wealth has been disproportionate to contribution for production. It needs no citations or statistics because the economic milieu is open to empirical observation and daily comment.

It will deem desirable not to carry such a baggage of business mind-set and commercial culture to the outer space activities, even if it needs a corrective surgery of foul beliefs to induce purity of thoughts for space activities. First, the OST mandates use of space to be 'the province of all mankind' and that such use 'shall be carried out for the benefit and in the interest of all countries' (Article I). The principles espoused are egalitarianism, altruism and inclusiveness. Hence, the accrued total profits cannot be privately appropriated. There is, of course, a theory of unearned profits and unfair enrichment that foils this stand. But OST still constitutes law on the subject and its provisions stand valid. Of course, the sharing principle and proportions are yet to be stipulated and promulgated but that does not permit violation of the basic law. There are, however, temporary expedients that have been discussed and proposed so that the dignity of law is respected.

Commercialization of outer space activities, in particular, space travel and tourism as also exploitation of celestial natural resources, whether renewable or non-renewable, by private corporate sector, needs a new set of rules under Private Space Law, e.g. leasing for excavation or regulation of 'space-lines' and tourist facilities vis-à-vis the tourist; in contra-distinction to Public Space Law that governs and regulates public order in the space domain. The differences can be broadly treated as analogous to International Law (Public and Private). A chapter in the book also explores ethical values for space business and evolves basic tenets for adoption in private commercial activities in the outer space. These, in nutshell, are principles of natural justice, equity and fair play, corporate social responsibility, and sensitivity towards space workforce.

It is further emphasized that diversification of space activities and commercial exploitation of space resources brings humanity to a different threshold and ushers in a new era. No operator in space is fully self-sufficient in all respects to operate independently; and his dependence on other space players is manifest in normal operations as well as in emergencies. Therefore, new space age will be an 'Era of Cooperation and Responsibility' among space players. The law of international responsibility, and consequent liability, is well established and only needs to be adapted *mutatis mutandis*. More specifics on this aspect have been stipulated in the Liability Convention, 1972.[5] Similarly, international cooperation between space players has been repeatedly urged in the OST and more specifically enunciated in the Declaration on International Cooperation, 1996.[6] It will be in the mutual and reciprocal interests of all space actors to abide by this declaration and respect its exhortation.

In nutshell, it may be concluded that the era of commercialization of outer space and its celestial bodies is right on us with technological capabilities, economic viability, and corporate eagerness to exploit the opportunities lying in wait. The pioneer will be the winner in business terms. At the same time the legality of such activities and total appropriation of profits by the engaging private enterprise is under penumbra of doubt in relation to the OST and allied international instruments that seem braided together for synergy and for public order in space. Business motivations should not overpower the law. The majesty of OST must be upheld and changes that are required to revise and contemporise the treaty should be taken as per procedure. Some suggestions have been made in the relevant chapters. This treatise also proposes short-term measures and expedients so that law does not appear a handicap in the welfare of humanity and betterment of humankind.

I must concede that some of the concepts and possibilities visualized in this book relating to technical creativity and space applications may appear futuristic but it is no oneiric vision. Science of today is the technology of tomorrow that may become operational ground reality sooner than later. The purpose is that law should not be a laggard and not 'look an ass' when it confronts a new situation or reality. The law scholars also need to be pro-active in identifying impending issues, initiate healthy discussions, and create valid opinions on such issues so that law is not caught napping. In fact, in the absence of direct and relevant provisions, ingenious constructions and devious interpretations motivated by national policy or devoted to vested interests start doing the rounds. A current example of lacunae in law confronts us is in exploitation of celestial mineral resources by corporations, who are almost ready with wherewithal, for private appropriation. This is least desirable and only debated solutions with substantial congruence should be accepted for the emerging space economic order.

Therefore, let's herald a new space revolution and welcome it with open arms for its expected benefits but with a caveat. The acceptance of infraction of established space law by these activities will come at a cost that will be hard to pay in the future. Ergo, caution beckons us to adapt and adjust the laws in conformity to contemporary challenges rather than disrespect the OST and land ourselves in legal chaos and disorder in space. The interests of posterity can also not be sacrificed. Therefore, treaty-member-states owe a duty *erga omnes* to usher the development process and simultaneously introduce desired upgrade of Treaty law and other adaptive legal changes to maintain peace and stability in the public order of outer space.

NOTES

1. It is likely that certain countries like China and India may not involve private enterprise in strategic or commercial space activities for a long time. Yet a small beginning has been made by China which permitted establishment of a private company in 2015 to undertake space activities. It is planning a rocket launch in 2019. Nevertheless, state-owned companies will remain the main players in Chinese space activities for quite some time.

2. Treaty on Principles Governing the Activities of States in the Exploration and Use of Outer Space, including the Moon and other Celestial Bodies, 1967. 610 UNTS 205 (1967); 18 UST 2410, TIAS No 6347, 6 ILM 386.Often referred to as Outer Space Treaty or the Treaty or OST.
3. HR 2262. The President of the US signed it into law on 25 November, 2015.
4. Agreement Governing the Activities of the States on the Moon and other Celestial Bodies, 1979, available at <https://treaties.un.org/pages/ViewDetails.aspx?src=TREATY&mtdsg_no=XXIV-2& chapter=24&clang=_en>

   It entered into force on 11 July, 1984. It has received 17 ratifications till February, 2017.
5. Convention on International Liability for Damage Caused by Space Objects, 1972. UNTS.
6. Declaration on International Cooperation in the Exploration and Use of Outer Space for the Benefit and in the Interest of All States, Taking into Particular Account the Needs of Developing Countries, 1996. Adopted by the UN General Assembly in its Resolution 51/122 0f 13 December, 1996.

CHAPTER ONE

Commercial Mining of Celestial Natural Resources

Legal Challenges and Viable Solutions

INTRODUCTION

The fact that there lies a cornucopian bounty of mineral resources in outer space has been proved by remote sensing and close observation through space probes and analysis of samples obtained through robotics. And that these are useful to humanity and can augment the depleting natural resources of Earth is also established beyond doubt. Further, the technology to excavate and to some extent process the same *in situ* also promises feasibility. The end product that would make for a smaller quantum of high utility metals can be used for other activities on the mined planet or transported to Earth in economical capsules. Possibility can also be envisaged where processed material and procured water can be recycled in some manner for use and manufacturing on the celestial body itself or to replenish probe vehicles on deep-space missions. Thus, the utility of celestial natural resources, including water, to mankind is affirmative but the algorithms of comparative economics of excavation, processing, transportation, or use *in situ* are not yet clear to convince of commercial viability and reasonable profits. But prospects appear positive and business sentiment is bullish.

Considering the trend of state-agencies selectively withdrawing from space activities except those of strategic importance or deep space exploration, it seems certain that such an activity as mining in space is of commercial nature and import and will not be undertaken by any governmental space agency nor would public exchequer funds be allocated for this purpose.[1]

Perforce such activity will have to depend upon a business initiative from private enterprise whether for commercial adventurism or entrepreneurial vanity or business aggrandizement. And given the present standing and competence of private enterprise, it can harness complex space technology, is willing to invest huge funds in space projects and patiently wait during the gestation period. It would, therefore, not be presumptuous to believe that Space-X, Virgin Galactic, Blue Origin, Deep Space Industries, Boeing Aerospace, Lockheed Martin, etc. or a consortium of willing and enterprising 'astro-preneurs' would venture into this nascent yet promising segment for prestige or profit irrespective of the attendant financial risks or hazards of space activities. Hope prevails with positivity.

The legality of private enterprise undertaking activities relating to use and exploration in outer space can be validly derived from Article VI of Outer Space Treaty (OST)[2] which permits non-governmental entities for such ventures. There is, however, a rider in the same article of the Treaty that these activities 'shall require authorisation and continuing supervision by the appropriate State Party to the Treaty'. Thus, whatever may be the nature of conditionality, a basic permission exists for private enterprise to enter this domain for legitimate and *bonafide* activities within the ambit of the Treaty. In fact, this is happening already and satellites owned and operated by the private sector are already in outer space. Even mining for *in situ* utilisation of space mineral resources, raw or processed, can be justified on existing law. Hence, the US Commercial Space Launch Competitiveness Act, 2015[3] is valid and benign to this extent.

The problem would arise at 'commercial recovery of space resources'. Perhaps, quantum of recovery could be relevant here. Small quantities as samples may be obtained from celestial bodies and recovered for distribution or even sale to interested parties for scientific investigation as urged under the Treaty. But the clause that 'United States citizens engaged in commercial recovery of an asteroid resource or space resource obtained, including to possess, own, transport, use and sell the asteroid resources or space resources obtained in accordance with applicable law, including the international obligations of the United States' is tricky and remains suspect. This provision seems to contain a syllogistic fallacy and lacks legal synchronicity with the Treaty.

Articles I and II of the OST clearly omit permission for such an attempt at commercialisation. In a way, the US enactment has strains of negativity against established legal position and is not as innocuous as is made out to appear. But there is no need to be dismissive of the motivated narrative of the enactment nor unduly reactive or paranoid. The matter deserves to be rationally debated to find best amends to the situation within the gamut of space law and explore viable solution in the common interest of humanity. This chapter is basically a concept paper on the subject, yet also attempts a case study of the US laws relating to commercial exploitation and private appropriation of space mineral resources.

In my opinion, infringement of the Treaty would be inappropriate and condemnable that would set a bad precedent. Such a violative action will be highly embarrassing to a space-leader like the US. Hence, there is a need to find an unimpeachable legal solution because existing regimen of OST offers no concession and no amount of legal sophistry or verbal tautology may be able to vindicate this move. Yet, we cannot afford a moribund situation of outright denial. So stakeholders must partner together in quest of an acceptable solution for a secure, sustainable and profitable commercial mining of celestial mineral resources for the common benefit of humanity.

In search for solutions, amendment to treaties is painfully arduous in diplomacy and time-consuming in negotiations. One plausible solution is to initiate and conclude a *specialis* protocol to the Treaty or an amending resolution in the UN General Assembly. Precedents of latter action do already exist and the proposal can be nuanced for success by offering bait of benefits. Further, if an agreed portion of accruing profits from such activity can be shared with and to benefit all states in some ratio and weightage as Space Benefits Fund (SBF) on the lines of Corporate Social Responsibility (CSR), then a broad agreement may be easier, if not true consensus. This would thus satisfy the inclusive spirit of the Treaty as well as pacify non-stakeholders.

The Moon Agreement[4], however, is more permissive and liberal in this regard. In Article 8, the Agreement permits excavation on the Moon, on or below the surface, and allows for free movement of equipment and personnel, etc. Further, provisions of this Agreement "...shall also apply to other celestial bodies within the solar system..." So near-Earth asteroids get covered by this provision. But as regards natural resources of outer space, Article 11 (1) of the Moon Agreement treats these as 'Common Heritage of Mankind'. Under this concept, celestial natural resources are treated as *res communis omnium* which defies proprietary individualisation in any manner. It is felt that it may be more prudent to ratify this Agreement and initiate a suitably modified legal regime for exploitation of natural resources under Article 11(5) and get this negotiated by the requisite number of State Parties to the Agreement by a majority vote which is likely to be small. Even otherwise also, Moon Agreement deserves to be mainstreamed for relevance and is ripe for revision under Article 18.

NATIONAL ENACTMENTS FOR SPACE COMMERCIALISATION

A Case Study of the US Legislations

The private corporate sector in the US has been eyeing opportunities in outer space that are techno-economically viable and could be commercially harnessed. This lobby has been pressurizing the US government for permission to participate in space activities, at least in partnership with National Aeronautics and Space Administration (NASA). Thus in the US, a debate has raged for over a decade on the subject and opinion has been crystallised. This objective has been partially achieved and NASA has withdrawn shuttle facilities from public funding; and private participation of Space X and other space giants has commenced cargo replenishments to the International Space Station (ISS). This partnership is being further expanded to manned flights which may also begin to operate shortly. Thus, the US overtures in this direction of public-private partnership are growing bold to pick up speed and variety. So far so good, as it does not contradict any legal mandate; and so long as these activities are being properly regulated, continuously overseen, and kept under constant vigil by the state in accordance with the relevant OST provisions, the enactments would be innocuous and conformist.

Now having tasted success, the private sector lobby is aggressive to grab other commercial opportunities that are becoming progressively techno-feasible in outer space.[5] This stance is natural as it is believed to offer billion-dollar business in next decade with attractive profit margins. No wonder, competition is building up and the lobby gaining in vocal strength with corresponding pressure on the government due to sheer proximity and economic influence to open up this space segment to private sector. Of course, the Administration has to put in place a proper perspective of obligations and evolve a stable and facilitative legal and regulatory structure to inform and guide commercial activities in the neo-market of space domain. This has translated itself into legislative initiatives through House Committee Reports that have led to presentation of bills in the House, of which three are specifically discussed.

All these statutory measures have apparently encouraged private sector to openly compete and confidently invest in space activities of commercial nature. Earlier, the US stakeholders were not fully aware and conscious of legal imponderables and regulatory uncertainties that in a way impeded their development efforts or tended to disrupt their continued investment and delay eventual activities in the outer space. Bills presented in the House have progressively tried to set at rest apprehensions and allay doubts of the corporate sector about the future of their research investments and developmental outlays assuring stability of returns thereon, though with some promises of national protection and assurances beyond competence of the state.

The impetus documents of legislative import have been carefully worded under the façade of OST and compliance of international obligations of the state. But the texts do not afford enough clarity or carry conviction to match the reality of the space legal regime. The suspected provision, with whatever its meaning or implication, hardly exudes an earnest commitment to the intent and spirit of OST. And, at times, seem hollow in practice and defiant in offered assurances. Overall, it smacks of tokenism. May be, the US is building an opinion fund around its overtures to evaluate international reaction, or proverbial testing of waters before the actual plunge. Either way, it is a great tactical move to attract some followers, with or without stakes in the outer space.

Space Resources Exploration and Utilization Act, 2015

Let's be more specific and factual on the history of this initiative. Apart from informal opinionated influences, the earliest effort towards this end was the sponsoring of Space Resources Exploration and Utilization Act of 2015. This was introduced as a Bill in the 114th Congress and after preliminary discussion, the House referred it to the Committee on Science, Space and Technology. The Committee submitted its Report, numbered HR-1508, on 15 June 2015 with dissenting minority opinion. This bill, however, was not passed by the end of the same Congress session and it lapsed and is cleared from the books.[6] Even if this proposed legislation could not be enacted, the lobby behind this, its motivations and text of the Bill are revealing of its intent and the extent to which the US can succumb to business influence and be defiant of the international instruments to which it is a signatory. Hence, it will be interesting to discuss this proposed Act in some detail.

This bill was aimed to 'facilitate commercial exploration and utilisation of space resources to meet national needs' by "enabling this new industry and providing clarity for future entrepreneurs"[7] by addressing doubts and concerns. The object of this legislation is to "promote the right of US commercial entities to explore outer space and utilise space resources...and to transfer and sell such resources".[8] For this purpose, the Bill tends 'to expand Presidential powers regarding space resources and to regulate US based space exploration companies'. Thus, the proposed Act aimed to 'establish a legal framework to govern property rights of resources obtained from asteroids'.

The proposed Act, therefore, permits commercial utilisation and national appropriation in removing, taking possession, and using in situ celestial resources so mined or excavated. It also declares property rights for entities that obtain such asteroid resources and the text of the Bill reads, "Any asteroid resources obtained in outer space are the property of the entity that obtained such resources, which shall be entitled to all property rights thereto, consistent with applicable provisions of Federal Law and existing international obligations".[9] There is a further rider to this provision which requires that such entity 'shall avoid causing harmful interference in outer space'.[10] Despite their inclusion, the riders appear as toothless as paper tigers.

Interestingly, it flagrantly holds out that this is not to be construed as an act of national appropriation by claim of sovereignty, by means of use or occupation or by other means. Irrespective of the text, context or its intent, it fouls with the letter and spirit of the OST. There is, however, another rider in the proposed Act that this be 'in accordance with all existing international obligations of the United States'. This compliance raises a moot question and the intrinsic inconsistency stares us in the face. This clause hardly carries believable conviction to abide by the OST or other international obligations.

The drafters of the proposed Act and the Committee report HR-1508, however, have tried to offer some explanations and justification which are hardly valid or convincing. First escape suggested by the Committee is that the Title of the legislation does not violate existing international obligations or claim sovereignty over outer space or celestial bodies. This is least of an argument. Secondly, the Report asserts that 'removing, taking possession, and using in situ celestial resources is not to be construed as an act of national appropriation by claim of sovereignty, by means of use or occupation or by any other means'.[11] The argument appears a sheer statement devoid of legal acumen and the veil seems too thin for effect and hardly needs piercing. In fact, the obvious becomes too obvious to remain well-meaning or innocuous and the farce of façade can hardly be sustained.

Later in the Report, the Committee itself obliquely concedes and records that this view is not shared by all states and many legal scholars. It again specifically mentions, 'The non-appropriation clause in Article II of the 1967 Treaty precludes exploitation of celestial natural resources and the reduction to private property'.[12] Nevertheless, it continues with the contrarian argument that 'state practice is consistent to treat exploration and use with the right to remove, take possession and use in situ natural resources from celestial bodies'.[13] It cites instances of US, Russia and Japan having removed, taken possession and/or used *in situ* such resources and these appropriative activities have never been protested by any state.[14] But this argument hides the other part of the truth that these removals were primarily for scientific investigation, were extracted in small quantities and were shared among nations desirous of such investigative pursuits. The Treaty explicitly permits such purposeful removals.

Some legal scholars have resented the 'non-appropriation clause' as well as Common Heritage principle and criticized *res communis omnium* status of the outer space on the plea that it denies mankind the rewards from the bountiful universe for no cogent reasons.[15] They maintain that granting to the citizen entities the right to commercial appropriation of space resources does not tantamount to claiming sovereignty over them.[16] It is also argued that this provision does not extend sovereignty; it is rather exercising of jurisdiction over their citizen and entities in outer space and protecting their interests and assets against third parties.[17] Hence, it does not conflict with the Space Treaty. Somehow, the argument is weak on logic and appears rather simplistic and contrived.

The Report also cites cases where courts have given verdict upholding property rights of the buyer or possessor of moon-rock or sundry articles related to such activity. In US v. Lucite Ball case, the US District Court upheld the right of Honduras to assert national property ownership over a Moon rock.[18] To arrive at the judgment, the Court discussed two cases of sale of lunar samples involving private parties. The first related to a slide of lunar dust sold at Sotheby's auction and the second involved the giving of plaque for a lunar sample to Nicaragua that was purchased by a private buyer from the Middle East.[19]

Based on another report from NASA concerning Moon rock and Astro-material loaned for research, education and public display, the Committee Report reiterates, "Lunar material retrieved from the Moon during the Apollo program is US government property".[20] The House Report then quotes a parallel to vindicate its stand that a part of lunar samples brought under Luna programme were sold as private property to a private bidder at a Sotheby's auction in 1993 for the cost of $ 422,500.[21] Wisdom seldom accepts that two wrongs make one right.

Based on above citations and instances, the Report craftily words an assertion, 'Exploration and use of outer space includes the right to remove, take possession, and use in situ natural resources from celestial bodies'. And this seems devoid of logic and fails the test of ordinary meaning in good faith under the Vienna Convention on the Law of Treaties.[22] The Report further amplifies that 'whether or not the end-use of such resources is for private purposes does not qualify the right to explore and use outer space'.[23] This argument, too, remains questionable because aberrations do not justify the disregard of law or condone the offence.

The Minority View and Specialist Legal Opinion appended to the Report seem more objective and neutral to the business motivations and exploitable opportunities. At the very outset, it points out that the Bill is in conflict with OST and adding consistency clause to abide by the Treaty does not make the inconsistency go away; on the contrary, it highlights the contradiction more conspicuously. Further, Prof Joanne Gabrynowicz opines that the right to possess and dispose of excavated natural resources, in ultimate analysis, is a form of appropriation by other means under Article II of the Treaty.[24] She further raises an objection in her opinion that, whether such a right can exist even if the excavated material is not brought to Earth and is used in situ; and under such circumstances, how or under what process would the original and exclusive jurisdictional powers vest in the US Courts or derived by them.[25] The anomaly in conferment of jurisdiction is glaring and irreconcilable.

Another criticism against the proposed Act is that it provides a Rule of Decision to the Courts to enable verdict in favour of a plaintiff on 'first come first owned' basis and without regard to quantity in the controversy.[26] This simplistic criteria, though facilitative, yet is pre-judgmental and 'prescriptive' to the extent of ignoring merits of the case and thus putting curb on judicial freedom and interfering with the due process of law. Secondly, it implicitly permits occupation and private appropriation of natural resources from celestial bodies to the first miner entity or private company on mistakenly assumed, undeclared pseudo-sovereignty that constitutes negation of the Treaty.

US Commercial Space Launch Competitiveness Act, 2015

The next serious attempt in this direction resulted in the US Commercial Space Launch Competitiveness Act, 2015.[27] This legislation is based on the Report of House Committee on Science, Space and Technology and Senate Committee on Commerce, Science and Transportation, HR-2262. The Bill under this Report was passed by 114th Congress (2015-2016) and has come into force consequent to the signing of the same by the US President on 25 November 2015. Incidentally, this Act appears to have been modelled on an earlier US legislation, Deep Seabed Hard Mineral Resources Act, 1980.

The Act aims "to facilitate a pro-growth environment for the developing commercial space industry by encouraging private sector investment and creating more stable and predictable regulatory conditions and for other purposes".[28] The title and aim of the Act primarily encourage a legitimate activity as a basic responsibility of the state and should be welcome. It is a usual practice of the states to spur and protect investments, offer legal stability and predictability for investments towards innovation and development in the hope of attracting larger outlays and longer commitments to the national economy.[29] The initiative is, of course laudable but not under existing legal regimen.

It consists of four Titles, namely, Spurring Private Aerospace Competitiveness and Entrepreneurship; Commercial Remote Sensing; Office of Space Commerce; and Space Resource Exploration and Utilization. In nutshell, it facilitates 'commercial exploitation for and commercial recovery of space resources by United States Citizens'. And in a way promotes 'the right of United States citizens to engage in commercial exploration for and commercial recovery of space resources free from harmful interference...'. The first three Titles of this Act relate to genuine concerns of any state and fall well within the purview of domestic legislation to address the same.

However, controversial and contentious issues are contained in Title IV of the Act with the heading, 'Space Resource Exploration and Utilization'. The text reads, "A United States citizen engaged in commercial recovery of an asteroid resource or space resource under this chapter shall be entitled to any asteroid resource or space resource obtained, including to possess, own, transport, use and sell the asteroid resource or space resource obtained in accordance with applicable law, including the international obligations of the United States".[30] Despite the overt disclaimer, this clause is pregnant with moot issues of great consequence which do not match the template of OST. In all probability, it may over time, lead to inter-state conflicts due to competing mining operations being located close to each other thus affecting global security; and may also through its incursive provisions foster legal instability in the OST regimen.

Interestingly however, under the definitions of both the resources, asteroid and celestial, the Act portrays great vision. It defines an asteroid resource as that found within a single asteroid.[31] And a space resource is defined as "an 'abiotic' resource *in situ* in outer space" yet explicitly includes both minerals of all kinds and water in any form that are believed to exist on celestial bodies.[32] Thus space resource is any material that does not qualify as being biotic or alive. This provision is futuristic yet hypothetical and caters only to the odd chance of a significant find of such biotic material or living organisms that may invalidate our established views and challenge existing beliefs regarding origins of life.

Another perplexing issue raised by the text of this Title is the right to minerals but at what stage is it secured whether by sheer discovery, by remote sensing or by merely detecting a potentially rich celestial body and virtually claiming it or on actual extraction and physical possession of the material resource? This dilemma has been explained by the Chairman, Committee Report in following words, "The term "obtain" was ultimately chosen because it carried no presumption about technical means with which the resource was to be recovered.... Only through physical recovery does this right manifest".[33] In nutshell, it explicates that the right granted "to possess, own, transport, use or sell a space resource' can only stand on physical acquisition and actual control facilitated through human labour or robot effort.

There is, however, an important caveat to this right which asserts that commercial recovery of space resources should be free from harmful interference. This term can don different meaning and interpretations yet for our purpose it implies carrying of any exo-biological contamination to Earth and vice versa,[34] as well as causing pollution or communicating any organic contamination from one mined celestial body to any other. This obligation under the US law would require Environment Impact Assessment (EIA) of launch facilities and activities from all angles to ensure biological containment and microbial reduction for every mining project.[35]

COSPAR[36] has worked rather sufficiently on the issue of extra-terrestrial biological contamination that may be brought to Earth or in reverse carried to the celestial bodies and has analysed a broad array of possibilities. The basic fundamentals, cautionary practices, and guidelines are contained in a recommendatory document called Policy for Planetary Protection. This, though not legally binding yet, acts in tandem to Article IX of the OST to impel compliance. Its normative value is enormous.

The Policy categorises the risk threshold where, as on today, Mars carries the highest risk potential and small asteroids, the least possibility and accordingly the proposed standard of hardware sterilization. Similar guidance tips and mandatory rules are also contained in NASA Planetary Protection Policy that applies internally and specifically to the named organisation. But it must be extended to regulate and control the commercial space players with strict monitoring and continuing supervision as required by the OST. For this purpose, the US President has been empowered under the Act to use full force of his office to facilitate space mining and enforce the rights guaranteed to the space miners.[37]

American Space Commerce Free Enterprise Act, 2017

The latest attempt in this direction has been through the Report of House Committee on Science, Space and Technology (HR-2809) that has led to this Act. This was introduced as a Bill in 115th Congress on 7 June 2017 and was passed by voice vote on 15 June 2017.[38] This Act seeks to amend Title 51, US Code to provide for authorisation and supervision of non-governmental space entities and their activities and for other allied purposes.

The objects of the Act record that the US has a robust and innovative private sector that is investing in, developing and placing into outer space objects and payloads. Further, private exploration and use of outer space by non-governmental entities will further the national security, foreign policy, and economic interests of the US. And, that the private sector has certain apprehensions and misperceptions about legal uncertainty that deserve to be addressed in national interest so that space activities are carried out in conformity with international obligations under the OST. This necessitates certain mechanism to regulate and assure that new space actors are relieved of administrative burden. However, for constant and continuous interaction between stakeholders, the Act provides for Private Space Activity Advisory Committee.[39]

This Act declares, as a matter of policy, that US citizens and entities are free to explore and use outer space including resources contained therein without conditions or limitations. However, this freedom is only to be curtailed in national security interest, to protect physical safety of US space assets or to conform to international obligations of the US under the OST. Thus, the US policy is to maximise freedom and minimise regulations that will operate in a transparent, timely and predictable manner to impart greater efficiency with minimal administrative and cost burdens on private space players. This is aimed to ensure that the US remains world leader in commercial space activities.[40]

Despite assurances and disclaimers to abide by the OST obligations, the Act, in the end, reserves the right to the federal government to interpret, determine and fulfill its obligations under the OST in a manner that promotes free enterprise in outer space. This acceptance appears skewed and belies conviction because treaties may not "...be interpreted in good faith in accordance with the ordinary meaning to be given to the terms of the treaty in their context and in the light of its object and purpose".[41] The apprehension arises because the meaning imputed or interpretation will be of the US government that may not be impartial or objective.

This Act has been widely welcomed in space business sector as "it brilliantly resolves contradictions inherent in more traditional models and removes outdated provisions of remote sensing law and regulatory system thus providing an effective legal structure for future space activities by private enterprise".[42] Other responses are also positive and salutary to the governmental action and it seems that the US is ready to hand over outer space enterprise to the private and corporate sector for commercial appropriation. But the legal position seems dented.

Overall, the US must make conscious and informed choice whether to vote for legal stability and integrity of the OST or buck up the national trend of business profiteering and political defiance or succumb to business 'populomacy'. The world community is presently showing a decent sense of restraint or resigned acceptance towards US legislations and incursions into the realm of OST but it may soon reach the end of strategic patience and the foisted wrongs may not be acquiesced into any longer and international remonstration may become vocal and visible.

A Case Study of Luxembourg Legislation

Perhaps, the example of Grand-Duchy de Luxembourg is apt and pertinent here. This tiny European island state, having an area of 2568 km square and a total population of 600 thousands inhabitants but with the second highest in the world per capita GDP of $ 104,000, has also passed a similar act with zilch technological capabilities to take advantage of the legislated measure. This signals Luxembourg's intention to persist with bold pro-space strategy after reaping immense rewards from its first initiative when it founded SES that launched ASTRA in 1985 and today this company operates a fleet of 42 satellites.[43]

Luxembourg has a stable government and visionary leadership ready to pounce at lucrative opportunities in whichever segment or in whatever manner. Now it is dubiously encouraging prospecting and mining of celestial natural resources by foreign corporations. Towards this end, it has passed a draft version of the law in November 2016. It is called the Luxembourg Space Act and is patterned on the US Space Act tending to promote mining on asteroids. It recognises and vests legal ownership of mineral resources in outer space that are mined and harvested by the private companies unto themselves. In fact, it goes a step farther than the US enactments and promises national protection not only to native companies that are headquartered in the country and qualify as juridical nationals but also those that have only a representative office and merely flaunt the resident address of the country.[44]

Despite its overt act, Luxembourg is still not clear on the national and international implications of its legislation. One such aspect relates to planting of flag on the mined celestial body and whose, of the country or the private company. This conundrum still remains unsolved. Another aspect relates to its façade of no claim of sovereignty on celestial bodies; only exploitation of natural resources that is not specifically prohibited under the OST. Anyway, as per proposed law, the miners would be permitted to claim ownership on the material excavated and Luxembourg believes that there is no legal framework within which a government could be called upon to defend the company's claim or, perhaps, be liable for its acts of omission or commission on a multi-lateral forum. This seems a highly mistaken notion and irresponsible understanding of the OST and international law.

Nevertheless, consequent to this initiative, two American companies, viz. Deep Space Industries (DSI) and Planetary Resources, one Japanese company and Blue Horizon of Germany are planning relocation or establish a resident office in Luxembourg to ultimately take advantage of this legislative measure. The companies are confident of assured state patronage and protection to their actions, and intoxicated with this trust have failed to comprehend legal implications and seem utterly unaware of the possible consequences.[45] Anyway, plans have yet to be actualized.

Be that as it may, on the part of Luxembourg also, the offers and promises to the private sector companies are beyond their legislative competence and outright defiance of established treaties of space law. To borrow the comments of Gbenga Oduntan of Kent University, it is another face of 'audacity of greed' despite international remonstration.[46] Therefore, it will be interesting to see if Luxembourg will be able to attract the right type of 'astro-preneurs' on mere legislative promises without the requisite infrastructure and technical knowhow within the country.

The Possible Trend

These two nations have set in motion a dangerous trend, that may possibly snowball, of defiance of international space law and unilateral usurpation of assets from 'a province of mankind', also reverentially treated as 'Common Heritage of Mankind' without explicit approval or even tacit concurrence of the international comity representing mankind. This tantamount to daring the international order to act against the impingement as well as a breach of the established law that was voluntarily acceded to by the states in large measure and has assumed customary status. The *pacta* is fouled and the humanity is humbled.

This pro-exploitation tribe may solicit support from the Lockean philosophy of individual's right to property.[47] In a way, he propounded the concept of common heritage of mankind on the reasoning that 'man' (or humankind), in general, had been bestowed with the world (or planet Earth) in common and any man who used the labour of his body and the work of his hands to appropriate an un-owned land, he was entitled solely to the fruits of the same. The idea appears analogous to space mining, yet carries a syllogistic fallacy in that celestial bodies are not 'un-owned' but *res communis omnium* and the Treaty bars any national claims of property rights or ownership 'by occupation or by any other means'. It can thus be logically argued that no individual rights can subsist because the 'state' of nationality of a citizen grants or subsumes the individual rights consequent to its sovereignty.

Sooner or later, more countries may emerge as US supporters and opt for this view volitionally or be coaxed to sprint to this rally point for tangible or intangible benefits whether already accepted or duly promised. The game has just started and is far from over as yet. It seems to carry endemic seeds of strife and dispute due to competition over lucrative sites, proximity of digging areas, and corporate vested interests that may spill over globally as well as on astro-realty. This undesirable trend must be stemmed or corrected at the earliest.

Be that as it may, the swelling number of this defiant guild or non-stakeholder community will not 'set right' a wrong. The core credentials of the Treaty have been assailed and it will only perpetuate the wrong by destabilizing public order and disturbing good governance in outer space domain. This may turn as sure recipe for international discord as well as an ominous risk to global security; and may even pose an existential threat to the OST.

ANALYSIS OF LEGAL POSITION

The content and intent of the US legislations, proposed and enacted, lead to three hypotheses under the scenario that need to be validated against the existing provisions of the OST to vindicate permissibility or identify conflicts and contradictions that need to be smoothened. Based on this analysis some possible solutions can be evolved and their viability for general acceptance and universal implementation can be evaluated. However, this specific problem and its prospects can be discussed in generality, independent of the US enactments, to provide for the future needs and aspirations of humanity. The issues can be rationally analysed to identify legal challenges that need solution in our search for legitimacy and treaty compliance.

The First Hypothesis

The first hypothesis emerges whether private enterprise can undertake activities relating to exploration and use of outer space. This assumes importance because space activities in almost all countries for almost four decades were primarily and solely undertaken by governmental agencies directly under state direction and control. However, the OST is permissive on this issue of private entrepreneurial excursions into outer space and deems governments as facilitator, regulator and supervisor for their conduct. Additionally, international liability vests in the state irrespective of the entity whose actions incur this liability.

The above contention draws strength from Para 2 of Article I of the OST that states, 'Outer space, including the Moon and other celestial bodies, shall be free for exploration and use by all States without discrimination of any kind, on basis of equality...and there shall be free access to all areas of celestial bodies'. This right of the US is sacrosanct under the Treaty as state-party and this freedom cannot be denied or abridged. For our purpose, the strongest recognition of participation by private enterprise emanates from Article VI of the Treaty that states, "...national activities [may be] carried on by governmental agencies or by non-governmental entities...and are [to be] carried out in conformity with provisions set forth in the present Treaty".[48] And this provision is amply permissive to admit of space activities by corporate enterprise as well as public-private partnership models.

However, some scholars are more liberal in their understanding of this clause. For example, Gerardine Goh interprets this article as an "affirmation of commercial utilisation of space...and that such commercialisation was conceived with utmost regard to these founding principles of space law".[49] Another scholar asserts that the unqualified expression in the Treaty 'to use outer space including the Moon and celestial bodies' has wider content and connotation. Its meaning cannot be restricted for explorative and scientific purposes only; it denotes inclusivity of "commercial use" and even beyond to make it synonymous with any exploitation.[50] But one would be hesitant to fully subscribe to this liberal, elongated view because commercialisation has many ramifications while this Article is specific in purpose and precise in content about permissibility of private entities engaging in space activities under control of the state.

However, a proviso in the same Article of OST further specifies, 'The activities of non-governmental entities in outer space, including the Moon and other celestial bodies shall require authorisation and continuing supervision by the appropriate State Party to the Treaty'. The OST thus being a state-centric international instrument creates a *vinculum juris* in that the state "shall bear international responsibility for national activities in outer space, including the Moon and other celestial bodies..."[51] International responsibility, therefore, is an active obligation of the state and makes it fully accountable and internationally liable for all national activities, whether in consonance or aberrant to the OST.

To this extent the US enactments that strive to encourage US citizens to competitively engage in exploration and use of outer space and celestial bodies are legally tenable and foul with no international law. Even its facilitative, promotive and regulatory efforts aimed at simplification of bureaucratic procedures, clarifications on business uncertainties, rectification of contradictions, vigilance of ventures, etc. for engaging in space activities that are viable, safe and stable are in consonance with the thrust of OST and legitimately fall within the domestic jurisdiction and national legislative domain.

The Second Hypothesis

The second hypothesis relates to permissibility of mining of celestial resources on a commercial scale, implying excavations beyond digging of rock and dust samples for scientific analysis by the state-parties to the Treaty or other nations. This leads us to serious doubts. In the past crust samples have been brought from the Moon and shared among desirous nations and later surpluses have even been sold in the open market by auction. But this does not truly equate with commercial scales or quantum of excavation envisaged in the US enactments and proffered assurances to the business community deem inconsistent with space law.

Further the US Commercial Space Launch Competitiveness Act, 2015 (USCSLCA) encourages US citizens to engage in commercial exploration for and commercial recovery of space resources.[52] This persuasion goes beyond the ambit of legal permissibility under OST irrespective of the riders to the provisions or ostensive safeguards or legislative disclaimers provided in the Act. In fact, OST is silently vocal on the issue which it has not considered to conclusion. Hence, lack of negative mention or explicit prohibition cannot be contrarily construed as permission. This will be travesty of the spirit of the OST.

However, the expression "exploration and use" of celestial bodies under the OST would allow mining and excavation, irrespective of the scale so long as these space activities "... shall be carried out for the benefit and in the interest of all countries...".[53] This intention is reinforced and amplified by provisions of the Moon Agreement[54] that applies to all celestial bodies within the solar system, except the Earth.[55] Article 8 (1) of Moon Agreement (MA) permits '...exploration and use of the Moon anywhere on or below the surface...' This clearly implies excavation or mining activity.

Further, MA also grants freedom that, "States Parties may in the course of scientific investigations also use minerals and other substances of the Moon in quantities appropriate for the support of their missions".[56] This is indicative of permission for *in-situ* use of space natural resources, or in processed form, for space probe missions, e.g. fuel for space vehicles; and for projects to create human habitations like envisaged Moon villages and Mars colonies with their construction supplemented by locally available material resources.

The Third Hypothesis

The third hypothesis concerns Para 51303 of USCSLCA that legally guarantees that the US citizens engaged in commercial recovery of an asteroid resource or a space resource (under this chapter), "shall be entitled to any asteroid resource or space resource obtained, including to possess, own, transport, use and sell the asteroid resource or space resource obtained in accordance with applicable law, including the international obligations of the United States".[57] On the very face of it, this authorisation is patently illegal and goes beyond the sovereign rights and legislative competence of the state.

The inherent fallacy in the Act relates to commercial appropriation of celestial natural resources in business interest or private profit that becomes so obvious even on a cursory reading. Further, the phrase referring to the requirement of compliance of international obligation appears hollow in force, inconsistent with content, and untenable in practice. No amount of legal sophistry may be able to vindicate this stand because one cannot wish away an actual infraction by a mere disclaimer. Perhaps, when faced with litigation, the US court of competence may deem this Act *ultra-vires* and unenforceable.[58]

THE LEGAL SCENARIO

Having exhausted earth's natural resources through indiscreet mining globally and asymmetrical industrial usage of such assets, the developed nations are again scrambling to other celestial bodies in a proverbial 'gold rush'. With more credible information about the usefulness of the asteroid rocks and crust of the Moon and physical composition of other celestial bodies as well as increasing technological possibility of mining their natural resources and economic viability of their use *in situ* or transportation to the nearest processing facility on an another celestial body or Earth has aroused commercial interest for business profits.

There is need for reality check here. Space mining is not going to be as easy as the Gold Rush of California or Yukon in Canada where one could just walk the streets and pick up pieces of shiny metal without any let or hindrance. In the beginning, here on celestial bodies also, useful material will be relatively abundant and easy to excavate from the crust and collect the ore. But with time and gradual depletion, the space mines will lapse into proverbial economics of diminishing returns with deep-pit low-grade ores requiring excavation of large quantities at increased costs yet yielding reduced quantity of resultant product at higher per unit cost and consequently leading to low appropriable profits. On the other hand, establishing supply chain at off-planet sites is going to be expensive and hazardous and may necessitate ever continuous prospecting and shifting of infra-structure. It is thus a costly game. The word of caution may, therefore, be well taken for its advisory worth.

Be that as it may, the private enterprise is lobbying for permissions and assurances even against the established law and US government is progressively succumbing to this pressure. This has resulted in enactments that have been discussed in earlier paragraphs. The enactments are only partially valid on law to the extent that non-governmental entities can undertake space activities under state regulation and continued supervision. Yet, there are some clauses that are patently violative and infractions stare us in the face.

It will be prudent to honestly accept that the corpus of substantive space law comprising a Treaty, two Conventions, and two Agreements is hardly adequate for its avowed purpose of regulation of space activities, governance of space domain, and preservation of sustainability. Of course, these international instruments have the backing of the UN and are further supported by a subaltern structure of normative guidelines and principles. This, of course, constitutes large corpus with wide gamut yet reveals growing inadequacy for the purpose with ever advancing technology and its applications.

Under this architecture, space law is state-centric and mostly comprises rules of political interaction and principles of governance and public order in outer space. Space law as originally drafted and accepted had no commercial orientation and thus did not directly allude to or cater for the interests of liberal economies and motivations of entrepreneurial players. Economics and commerce are a different ball game that requires hard core assurances of stable market conditions, an impetus of sustained incentives and legitimization of free market practices to enable business fraternity to take strategic business decisions.

Commercial implication of use of outer space and celestial bodies is a critical and sensitive matter. Simplistic assumptions and false riders to enacted provisions cannot vindicate either the professed assurances or the true intent of the legislation. Commercial use of outer space in the form of communications, broadcasting, etc. from geo-synchronous slots has been in existence but the slots were allotted and cooperatively accepted. There are no sovereign or proprietary rights to these slots, despite possible permanence in use. Similarly, remote-sensing from orbiting satellites have commercial applications but with no property rights to the specific defined orbit or orbital space. These are uses of 'non-invasive' nature and do not physically or materially disturb the celestial environment for the present as well as future generations. On the other hand, mining of mineral resources from celestial bodies is outright invasive, possibly polluting, non-renewable and depleting activity. The OST has a reasonably elaborate provision on this subject.[59]

In fact, the legal character of US enactments is repugnant to the tenets of space law. The conflictive provision relates to the US citizens, through the instrumentality of public corporations, being entitled to the celestial resources so obtained and this right extends to 'including to possess, own, transport, use and sell' in any manner in commercial interest. This clause is alarming in the face of explicit prohibition on appropriation in any manner under the OST. Such rights can originate only from the Doctrine of Eminent Domain[60] and 'such eminence' of the state does not prevail over the real estate of the celestial bodies.

The Treaty in Article II unambiguously iterates, 'Outer space, including the Moon and other celestial bodies, is not subject to national appropriation by claim of sovereignty, by means of use or occupation, or by any other means'. This provision outright rules out any existence or semblance of national sovereignty in outer space or on realty of celestial bodies and hence no state, party or non-party to the OST, can grant any spatial property rights on celestial bodies to its individual citizen, legal or natural. In fact, individual property rights stem from state sovereignty and wisdom says that you cannot give what you do not have.

Let's look at it in another way. Article I of the Treaty exhorts, "The exploration and use of outer space, including the Moon and celestial bodies, shall be carried out for the benefit and in the interest of all countries...and shall be the province of all mankind". This means that the use of celestial bodies, whether for mining of natural resources or for other purposes, shall benefit all countries and the benefits cannot be individualised or 'discretised' in the face of province of mankind nor profits fully and totally appropriated by the private enterprise.

Agreed that modalities for sharing as yet do not exist but the principle of sharing of benefits of use is unassailable because 'exploration and use' is 'the province of all mankind'. In a sense, the outer space and celestial bodies are *res communis* and not discrete, distinct or definable properties that can be individualised and separately used or commercially appropriated solely for private benefit or personal profit. Hence, the US legislation authorising US citizens for commercial mining of celestial mineral resources and 'to possess, own, transport, use and sell' goes way beyond international legality.

The above contention gets ample clarification and clear support from the Moon Agreement,[61] which though not ratified by many states, is a rational iteration and visionary expression of conditionalities for the exploration and use of celestial bodies and their resources. The MA also "recognizes the great prospects opening up before the mankind as a result of man's entry into outer space".[62] It further emphasises the common interest of humanity in "[T]he exploration and use of the Moon shall be the province of all mankind..."[63] Thus it reiterates the essential core element of the Article I of the OST and with better wisdom.

This contention is further stressed and reinforced in Article 11 (1) of the MA that declares, 'The Moon and its natural resources are the common heritage of mankind,...' and unambiguously maintains, 'Neither the surface or the subsurface of the Moon, nor any part thereof or natural resources in place, shall become the property of any state, international intergovernmental or non-governmental organisation, national organisation or non-governmental entity or any natural person'. The mandate is loud and clear and applies to all celestial bodies in the solar system. Functional co-existence and international cooperation are the cardinal principles of space law. Therefore, seeking refuge and hiding under non-ratification of the MA would be unethical when the US has participated in discussions and the passing of the germane UN resolution. To say the least, even normative law has certain binding force and obligatory tradition for compliance that responsible states usually respect and abide by.[64]

Another aspect that arouses doubts relates to the invasive nature of mining natural resources, *in-situ* processing operations, and transportation travails of excavated material that may induct pollution in crushing, pulverization and other processes, the long-term impact of which may not be apparent at present. All these activities are beset with apprehensions about environmental degradation in space and alien contamination on Earth. It is likely that the act of physical excavation and processing of raw minerals from the celestial bodies may potentially cause dust and pollution that may adversely affect the sustainability of the outer space environment for posterity and possibly bring contaminants to our planet. Here COSPAR Planetary Protection Policy of 2002 that governs exploratory activities in outer space for prevention of carriage of microbial contaminations to the celestial bodies or back to Earth may also be relevant.[65] Yet, more scientific investigations in collaboration with other states are necessary on these ensuing experiments to study of possible harmful interference, changes or exchanges and their impact.

The necessity for such cooperation and consultation is ordained in Article IX of the OST where even other member states 'may request consultation concerning the activity or experiment'. The principle of due regard is relevant and can be invoked as mining and processing activities could 'cause potentially harmful interference'. But the international space-faring fraternity is unmindful of and silent on possible impending risks. Perhaps, they are not fully conscious of the consequences and the resultant impact that may manifest itself over a period of time. Therefore, an initiative to engage in consultations to disseminate awareness about the safety of mining experiments and allay lurking fears about real or imagined risks associated therewith certainly appears an affirmative duty and a vicarious responsibility of the US as undisputed space leader, if not a substantive obligation. Arrogance of aloofness by the US is neither the right attitude nor righteous approach.

In the end, certain apprehensions of a political mindset need to be relieved. History has a lesson or two that are important and empirical to deserve a proper consideration. Firstly, memory haunts back to the era of colonization, wakes up a feeling of paranoia and harps on circumstances analogous to prospective celestial mining. History reminds that it was East India Company in 1600 AD that laid the foundation for subjugation of

India as dominion and ultimately as a colony of the British Empire.[66] This colonial rule had, incidentally, spread over most of Asia.

Similar modus operandi was deployed on the African continent, where inroads were made by the Royal Niger Company. This company was taken over by the British government in 1899 and Niger was declared a British protectorate.[67] Thus the common factor identified is that the respective companies laid down the foundations of the future British Empire and this factum cannot be disregarded.[68] Further, the commonalities are neither incidental nor accidental but deliberate as a part of overall expansionist policy and political strategy.

A dictum wisely puts that smart rulers always send their traders first to unknown lands and responsibly protect trade interests of their nationals using their military might.[69] Thus, powerful nations sponsor corporations as a façade of informal influence which crystallizes over time and results in colonisation which is worse than sovereignty. The sufferings of over half of the world for almost three centuries are testimony to the process of consolidation and colonial rule. Humanity still carries and can exhibit in evidence the scars of the times.

Other scholars too have expressed similar and yet more serious apprehensions visualising that a state that successfully colonizes in outer space will undoubtedly not only extract pride from the accomplishment but also, in all probability, realise easy and enhanced resources, spin-off technologies as well as military power. "If it uses that accomplishment or the increase in wealth it can expect from so doing, then dictums of *Astropolitik* are invoked."[70]

The US initiatives through these legislations are surprisingly similar in motive, almost identical in approach and analogous in circumstances. The space mining companies to be authorised by the US (and Luxembourg) could usher in an era of space colonisation because usurpation will be practically complete on occupation which cannot be interfered with even by other space faring states under the clause of "due regard to the corresponding interests of all other states".[71] This legitimate territorial use over passage of time will consolidate itself and convert to illegitimate possession amounting to undeclared sovereignty. The cycle of colonisation of space would have thus run a complete circle. And law knows that it is always legal possession that turns into illegitimate occupation. No wonder, the paranoia that grips is real and genuine.

AN APPRAISAL OF CHALLENGES OF NEO-OUTER SPACE

Having analysed the legal position and discussed the legal scenario, it is now incumbent to make an honest appraisal of the developments so far. Space observation and scientific investigation with spectrometry studies and remotely sensed data analyses have revealed that celestial natural resources contain copious content of several minerals and metals that are rare or fast depleting on the earth. One such element, Helium-3 detected in the surface crust of the Moon is a concentrated and powerful energy source usable on the earth. The asteroid family by their known taxonomy and definitive mineralogy studies is equally rich in mineral deposits of precious or scarce metals. Asteroid Psyche has been discovered to have a treasure trove of iron and nickel. Another asteroid Nereus has very low gravity but is believed to have an abundance of precious ores. Recent probes have established the specifics of minerals and volatiles like titanium, platinum, cobalt and gold. The US has landed a robotic probe on asteroid Eros for exploration and investigation. Recently, a team of Indo-French astronomers have discovered a planet twice the size of our earth that is largely composed of diamond.[72] Another rocky planet called '55 cancri e' has a fundamentally different chemistry of being rich in carbon and covered in graphite with diamond core. Thus the entire universe becomes the provenance of natural resources for humanity and this reservoir that appears almost limitless and inexhaustible has been drawn into the domain of utilisation and consumption by humankind.

Appropriate technology has been innovated and developed with feasible applications for assured and secure access to space resources. Thus, the viability of harvesting celestial bodies has been proved from many aspects, including docking procedures, extraction capability, *in-situ* processing and facilitation of transportation; while cost-benefit analyses have assured of economic profitability. No wonder, corporate sages of space business community have shown keen interest in space activities and are eager to set up space mining industry to tap mineral treasures from extra-terrestrial natural reserves that offer treasures beyond count and resources beyond imagination. Planetary Resources Inc, a commercial conglomerate, has harnessed sufficient funds for venture, state-of-the-art technology and trained manpower to prospect and harvest celestial resources. The overall risks, as calculated, are surmountable and within safety margins; and the economics of the venture assures rich dividends. Thus their intention is real and this is just the harbinger of what is to follow. The race to competition looks crowded and does not seem far behind.[73]

Defiance of existing legal regimes, perceived to be inadequate to the growing needs of society, more so, in an environment of systemic deficiency of ineffective sanctions, is easy and passé. But treaty commitments have many dimensions and its selective adherence is dangerous. At the same time, no serious breach of the Treaty due to untamed ambitions can be countenanced without protests and demarches. Great nations, perforce, have to assume global leadership with equally great responsibilities. It behoves them not to set a wrong precedent that may be emulated by irresponsible or errant states. Consequences of such contrary behaviour may be catastrophic and survival of humanity at large may be at stake; and this may tantamount to not too great statesmanship with futuristic vision. Blemishes on wisdom remain with posterity.

Surprisingly, international comity, too, is not opinionated or remonstrative enough on this issue while diplomacy is discreetly muted, even though it seems more by default than by design. Lately, however, some whispers have been noticed in the Legal sub-committee of COPUOS but right ears do not seem to have heard.[74] Incidentally, it is written in the book of proverbs, 'Where there is no vision, the people perish'. This may sound sheer pontification but its appeal represents and echoes the inherent spirit and ethos of OST.

Let's also accept a historical fact that the OST is a product of Cold-war geo-politics of the last century that required consensus and it could be obtained on a threshold of minimal law with maximum flexibility; by introducing platitudes with ambiguity for perpetuation of national self-interest. Therefore, the OST carries a historical burden of forced uncertainties and compulsive deficiencies and thus is neither comprehensive nor holistic. There is obvious lack of exactitude and gaps of procedural details, whether advertent or inadvertent. Secondly, OST has been overtaken by fast developing space technology and its expanding applications that could not be visualised at the time of its drafting and negotiations at the Committee on the Peaceful Uses of Outer Space (COPOUS). Thirdly, the breed of present-day entrepreneurs venturing into space activities is rich in finances and innovative in management. Ergo, a genuine need to revisit the OST for updation and adaptation.

Take for example, the clause in the first paragraph of Article I of the OST, 'The exploration and use of outer space...shall be carried out for the benefit and in the interests of all countries...and shall be the province of all mankind'. It is a well-meaning statement but general in nature, nebulous in content and ambiguous in meaning. Of course, space jurists have donned on it lofty interpretations and attempted to find meaningful and binding purpose out of this, yet it seems at best a value-based statement rather than a substantive rule of law. And for another, lack of inclusion of definitions in the Treaty further lends it to varying interpretations and makes *ad idem* understanding difficult.

Moreover, in the present millennium, space activities are no longer the monopoly of governmental agencies nor initiated primarily for military dominance or aggrandizement of national prestige. Outer space has transformed into Neo-Outer Space and reins of activities in this strategically economic domain have been taken over by private enterprise that has technological competence, financial resources, trained manpower, entrepreneurial acumen, futuristic vision, and patience to wait during the gestation period. But private sector may independently pursue its own agenda and inclinations, preferences and motivations that may not always align with the Treaty obligations or match communitarian aspirations or respect espoused values of international law.

Nevertheless, outer space domain has potentially turned into political arena offering attractive commercial opportunities with free play of market forces and economic liberalism. Therefore, the temptation of the treasure troves of mineral resources, observed to be existing and technologically exploitable from the celestial bodies, is hard to resist business proposition with attractive metrics on utilitarian economics. Hence, space commercialisation is about to be actualised. Political encouragement has added the business zest and a lofty consideration of the needs of humanity, apart from those of individual states, imparts altruism to the argument. Hence, just for lack of a legal provision, humanity cannot be denied long-term benefits of space resources. It is for the intelligentsia to find viable solution to get over this legal hump.

With eager entrepreneurial and business decision for seemingly responsible space mining, sufficiency on financial front, and tested technological methods for assured and secure access to space resources, the urgent needs of humanity cannot be made to wait indefinitely for formal legal glitches or non-iteration of modalities in the OST for the then unforeseen potentialities. It must be conceded that global natural resources have nearly exhausted and we cannot be complacent of new finds on celestial bodies. It constitutes a dire necessity of present and future generations of humankind and mineral troves of space cannot be permitted to lie unused and fallow despite feasibility from all aspects. The primacy of common benefit to humanity and global betterment cannot be compromised. Therefore, the challenges of illegality may be tackled and remedied by legal means and measures. If so necessary, we must revisit space law for adapting it to contemporary and future needs of humankind as well as consolidate global public interest in space by defining the modalities for benefits to all states. Transformative change generally needs radical thinking and a change of mind-set towards progress.

SOME SUGGESTED SOLUTIONS

The contention here is not to condone the overtures of the US and others but to provide a perspective that must be considered coolly for its pros and cons. Whatever be our legalistic opposition or juristic objections, humanity cannot be devoid of the exploitable availability or deny itself a fund of vast celestial natural resources so direly required on our planet for sustenance, growth and betterment. Law cannot be an obstructive force nor can remain static in a denial mode without acknowledging its social responsibility. Jurists believe that law is dynamic, sensitive and adaptive to the changing needs, incumbent challenges and foreseeable exigencies of society.[75] Therefore, the solution is not to hermeneutically mutate the existing law but to strive for a positivist change with puritanical faith.

On the contrary, there is a persisting mind-set that the polity tends to transcend the law and bend it to its vested advantage or find favours. This has to change, as belief and in practice, to eschew preference for 'privilegentsia' of corporate lobbies. Else, it may incur heavy political costs of destabilisation in the long run. In totality, space order is becoming much more complex yet fragile in an era of power politics, business influences, strategic manifestations, and technological prowess. As a result the Treaty is coming under tremendous pressure for its inadequacies and may develop uncomfortable fissures.

Sometimes, the intensity of market forces and the lure of commercial considerations tend to transcend communitarian aspirations in utter disregard of the values enshrined in the OST like non-appropriation, freedom of access, and sharing the benefits among all states. However regrettable, the situation where space commercialisation is about to be actualised for private profit has been reached in space activities without concurrent law or regulatory mechanisms being yet in place. Of course, it should be understandable that no institution, whether the state or inter-governmental set-up, howsoever potent or venerable, can prevent indiscretion of whatever magnitude. The real test of sanity lies in the follow up for correction with best cooperation and least abrasion all around.

Therefore, the key-position lies in understanding the current scenario realistically and to contemplate rationally on what we can settle for and in what manner. In this process of cogitation, there should be no hesitation to revisit the space law instruments, even though the solutions can be in diverse forms and with varying compromises yet we should not ignore the rational choice perspective. In this process we need to be all together in pace and unified in mind. It is wisely said that walking with a friend in the dark is better than walking alone in the light.

Incidentally, let not the US smugly believe that it is alone in the race to mining of celestial natural resources and would remain in the lead for long to reap sustained benefits. The scenario of space activities is fast changing and new players are racing past. For example, China, today, openly matches its technological prowess with the US whether in Anti-satellite weapon (ASAT) test or space lab construction or other high-end space activities. Russia is versatile in space technology and competent to undertake any type of activity in outer space and on celestial bodies and it may not take long to adapt and demonstrate suitable techno-capability for this purpose.

Japan is another country that works silently but on diverse fronts of space applications. And potential of business conglomerates has not been assessed here. Therefore, it may not take long for other competitors, individually or jointly, to reach the goal post and then in such a dynamic scenario of increasing variables, the disparate interests may clash to pose a challenge to the US and its space-miners. Unprepared for the incumbent challenge and without having law on its side, the US position may seem tenuous and weak. It will, therefore, be prudent to strengthen its legal standing early in the venture rather than grope for justifications later. This calls for a suitable quick-fix lawful solution so that we do not move forward in the right direction with guilt but with a conviction of righteousness.

LEGAL SOLUTIONS—from Analogous Legal Regimes

Let's first explore the possibility of finding a parallel provision to our instant problem in analogous legal regimes viz. the UN Convention on the Law of the Seas (UNCLOS) and the Antarctic Treaty[76], generally called the Global Commons. The effort seems worthwhile because legal systems governing these regions appear parallel and similar to that of the outer space domain and can provide applicability *mutatis mutandis* on the basis of commonality of geo-physical characteristics and governance models.

Further, the management of common heritage of mankind mandates that the natural resources are not individually excavated to be privately appropriated for personal benefit. It is a generic concept threading these domains and this requires uniform modalities on sharing of benefits. And if an adaptable clause is found, it will offer an advantage of prior acceptance by global community and will need little negotiation or convincing. We, therefore, need to probe on this aspect.

In the regime of Antarctica, commonality relates primarily to denial of sovereignty of global nations on any part of the domain though a few nations have laid such claims over Antarctica territory.[77] The Antarctic Treaty system started taking shape from a basic treaty in 1959 and has added four *specialis* agreements. The most important and relevant for our purpose is the Convention on the Regulation of Antarctic Mineral Resource Activities, 1988 (CRAMRA).[78] Its objective was to regulate development of mineral resources and protect Antarctic environment from pollution as well as safeguard from impending risk of causing un-stability of glaciers.

CRAMRA did not embody any elaborate management code for mining activities, it did, however, provide for a comprehensive institutional system for regulatory controls and collection of fees. The Convention, of course, permits mining of resources but with unanimous agreement of all signatories, which will be almost impossible to achieve. No wonder, this Convention failed when France, Australia and others withdrew support and started playing antics with alternative proposals like declaration of World Wilderness Park.

This was followed by Protocol on Environmental Protection to the Antarctic Treaty, 1991.[79] It has ordained *status quo* and imposed an indefinite moratorium on exploitation of mineral resources, except for scientific research. This ban, in any case, extends to a minimum period of fifty years from the year the Protocol entered into force, i.e. till 2048 AD and cannot be revoked. Overall, this model of moratorium is a negative measure and does not suit the needs, the objectives, and the urgency of commercial exploitation of celestial natural resources. It is also pertinent to mention here that the US does not accept or treat the outer space domain as Global Commons and as such no similarity of geo-physicals or parity in treaty would be relevant or important.[80]

Another domain with possible similarities is that of seas and oceans and its governing law is embodied in the UN Convention on the Law of the Sea. This, though conceptually similar on Common Heritage of Mankind over seabed mineral treasure of manganese nodules yet is not truly congruent on many other aspects. And even on this confluence, there is moribund status with little traction and no rules for controlled or rational harvesting of mineral nodules or equitable or proportional sharing among nations have been framed, despite three decades of its existence and the establishment of an institutional system in International Seabed Authority.

Regrettably, this regime provides only limited congruency and the prime disadvantage is that even Part IX of UNCLOS, 1982 that related to compulsory sharing of benefits and technology with other countries was unacceptable to the developed states as unfair and iniquitous. They had the same stand on mandatory sharing of benefits during negotiations for the MA. Thus, the attitude and approach of the developed world is loud and clear. So the situation here, too, is dismal and tantamount to denial by law on commercial use of existing mineral assets of the Global Commons.

So the global community has been deprived of the benefit of harvesting these rare minerals that lie buried under water on the seabed due to sheer lack of consensus on modalities. The lack of cooperation among signatories to the UNCLOS can hardly be commended for their failure and procrastination. Thus our search here has also failed to cull out a living, beneficial and working management model for adaptation to the common heritage of mankind in outer space which could help resolve the legal bottleneck on commercial mining of celestial natural resources and future potentials that may be offered by outer space.

In conclusion, it may be stated that in spite of comparable finds of natural resources, their utility for human needs, and the congruent umbrella of common heritage of mankind, the legal regimen for each sphere is at nuanced variance and incomplete on modalities to meet the common objectives. Perhaps, each domain is different in human perception and distinct in detail despite apparent similarities and sporadic congruence. Ergo, no solace from this discourse and our hunt for a separate, specific and suitable regimen must continue and fast enough because 'miner-preneurs' are all charged up and celestial resources are direly needed for the global community for it sustenance and betterment. Therefore, we need to look elsewhere for solutions.

LEGAL SOLUTIONS—the Outer Space Treaty

The most obvious and basic solution is to comprehensively revise the OST in a broader effort to update and adapt the Treaty in a holistic manner to make it relevant to contemporary aspirations of international community, making it capable of handling millennial challenges, take account of the developing innovative technologies and their anticipated applications so as to eschew need for repeated amendments. It is a historic opportunity that should be seized by international comity and not dither on political bickering and vested interests. As a caution, it is urged that the revision of OST should be fashioned on its existing tenets and espoused values that consider prosperity of humanity, better standards of living, and common benefits to all countries as primary creed of the global community.

This, of course, is a laudable solution but it is beset with many difficulties, e.g. of consensus in negotiations, dilatory diplomatic processes, and arduously long discussions spanning years, if not decades. Procedurally the Treaty has no in-built mechanism for its amendment which can only be effected by resolution under the UN rules of procedure. "Hence, in the near future, any tweaking of the OST appears unlikely."[81] On the other hand, the US may not have the patience to wait for such an imponderable of a broad spectrum solution which will have miniscule relevance to its immediate predicament. However, hybrids of this solution are also thinkable.

The wise say, past can be a good prologue to change for the future. Accordingly, we find here that the specific rule that needs modification already sits on the Treaty. In a way, the narrative of OST seems fairly complete and highly workable in almost any situation with minor amplification, rationally devised, and ably textualised. At the same time, propagation of motivated interpretation and favourable construction of clauses can lead to detrimental consequences.

To repeat, the OST prohibits national appropriation under Article II and by implication, commercial take-away for private profit. While it permits under Article VI that non-governmental entities can undertake space activities in exploration and use of outer space, including the Moon and other celestial bodies that shall be the province of all mankind and activities shall be carried out for the benefit and in the interest of all countries. So the essential element here is to protect the interests and benefits promised and due to all countries, including the US, from any kind of peaceful use of celestial bodies.

This can be achieved in many ways without adversely affecting the interests and benefits of all 'other' states. In a way, this implies that the OST needs a shift in its narrative from rigid compliance to that of societal justice. But justice can wear different shades of meaning in different perspectives. For example, there is an inherent contradiction in the concept and belief of 'freebies' to all, even non-participating, nations as a result of the efforts of a few. It may be a cherished value of inclusivity and cosmopolitanism yet is not equity nor justice nor good economics. This practice may even snowball into a trend of unconscionable bargaining and 'state-unionism' of non-achievers. International community may be beset with asymmetrical fortunes and fractured futures for the first and the third world countries yet pitfalls of this nature must be avoided studiously and sincerely while working on a sharing formula.

A possible option can be to draft a resolution providing the definition and scope of interests and benefits and laying down the modalities of sharing as conceptualised and presenting such a resolution in the UN General Assembly for voting. Help from COPUOS can be elicited for drafting an appropriate resolution containing suitable provisions for the avowed purpose.

If considered necessary, a dedicated sub-committee can be appointed to achieve the needful and at desired speed. Such amendments to the OST have been made in the past in this manner. For example, the UN Resolution of 2004 that amplified the provision relating to the application of the definition of the launching state or the Resolution of 2007 regarding clarification on registration of space objects. As an alternative, a *specialis* Protocol to the OST can be texted for the purpose and international approval sought in the same manner. However, the protocol may require an enforcement agency for its effective implementation in the form of say, World Space Authority, with adequate management powers and authority for sanctions.

LEGAL SOLUTIONS—the Moon Agreement

The Moon Agreement is more permissive on the matter and perhaps, easier to change, as has been discussed earlier. The MA fully acknowledges the existence of almost limitless treasures of mineral resources on the celestial bodies and envisaged the feasibility of their exploitation in the near future and does not exclude the possibility of commercial appropriation. Despite this professed liberalism, the MA is less acceptable to the space fraternity and has elicited limited ratification. Perhaps, because it declares such celestial natural assets as Common Heritage of Mankind[82] though this profound concept has found acceptance with international comity in other legal regimes, e.g. the Law of the Seas and the Law of Global Commons. The only handicap appears that while granting the *res communis* status to the celestial resources, the MA has yet to evolve rules germane to its legitimate exploitation, commercial use, and private appropriation. At best, it exhorts, "State Parties to this Agreement...[to] undertake to establish an international regime, including appropriate procedures, to govern the exploitation of the natural resources of the Moon as and when such exploitation is about to become feasible".[83] Inspite of clear indications of feasibility of exploitation and eagerness of the private sector to engage in commercial space operations, this has not happened yet. And herein lays an opportunity to purposefully guide and suitably amend the MA to bring it to the mainstream.

The option is that the US can ratify the MA and then persuade members to resolve this issue to its satisfaction. MA is no monster barring an odd inconvenient provision and has at best reiterated the OST of which the US is an adherent. So the hesitation for accession is difficult to comprehend.

Else, it can induct its co-thinkers, who are sheer fence-sitters, to ratify the MA and then get the desired changes in the Agreement or frame modalities for the exploitation regime that can be negotiated and concluded within the member-states. In fact, the MA is already ripe for 'the review' or revision under Article 18 and it accepts the rule of majority concurrence at negotiations rather than astute consensus of COPUOS working procedures. This article of MA makes it further convenient by providing that, 'A review conference shall also consider the question of the implementation of the' principle of Common Heritage of Mankind (CHM) and establish an international regime to govern exploitation of natural resources in view of "any relevant technological developments". Of course, the CHM regime would have to specify and guard the interests of and benefit to all states and this metaphor will have to be quantified on some criteria with a formula of monetized conversion for release of avowed benefits to the states. This is where we stand today with conscious choices and seek traction in the right direction for the best solution. Initiative may emanate from any direction.

LEGAL SOLUTIONS—UN Trusteeship of Celestial Resources

It does not seem prudent that for absence of explicit permissibility in the vintage legal regime, the humanity be denied an advantageous and purposeful access to celestial natural resources so direly needed on Earth for ultimate benefit of humanity. Yet, if individual states or their citizen are allowed to mine, appropriate and commercially dispose such excavated or processed resources, it will rile the postulates of the Treaty and negate the benefits assured to 'all states'. It is also conceivable that legitimate occupation of celestial realty for mining may sooner or later turn into illegitimate ownership bordering on pseudo-sovereignty. History empirically proves that in the past wise rulers have always sent their merchants and traders first before conquering any territory. European conquests of Asia and Africa have mostly followed this pattern. This tactic may work for the outer space too.

Another legal solution may be to place outer space including all celestial bodies, except Earth, under the trusteeship of the UN. United Nations Office for Outer Space Affairs (OOSA) could inherit this task of managing and leasing of real estate of the celestial bodies but its mandate and organisation is not equal to the job profile. Therefore, space resource governance can be entrusted to a new agency, say, World Space Authority (WSA) that can be professional and competent. This will ensure that the space-miner is only a lease holder of the real estate and not an owner with proprietary rights. This system of trusteeship governance under WSA will also ensure that national sovereignty does not prevail in the outer space or on celestial bodies. Further, the lease system can generate lease money from the users of celestial areas based on the quality of the realty and expected returns which can be distributed among beneficiary states according to an agreed formula. This model of 'space resources governance' will thus comply with the principle of inclusivity embedded in the OST.

NORMATIVE SOLUTIONS

With dominance of private sector in commercial space activities, corporate stakeholders' expectations, non-ethical business compulsions and astute profit considerations would tend to gain primacy over textual space law and thus, its chasms may become more prominent and pliable. Man has not exactly covered himself with glory in his commercial and business activities in free economies on the earth. Driven by his unquenchable greed for profit and cut-throat competition for survival, business values, ethical trade practices, and commercial morality have often been sacrificed in the process. This situation in space economy would call for a normative structure of self-governance by private players in outer space. This may be voluntarily negotiated and put in place by the guild of space users as self-binding ethos or initiated by the US government as a code of conduct in the form of subaltern regulatory measures under the relevant legislations as righteous guide to space business, to discharge its vigilance and supervisory obligations and safeguard its international liability.

Further, the US business community will be venturing in to the space activity of mining celestial resources and appropriating these for commercial purposes and for private profit before specific rules of the game have been drafted, approved and enforced. Thus, there is a possibility of liability arising out of such exploitation and a subsequent mandate for shareable compensatory payment. This can arise based on the edict of 'the province of all mankind' and the principle of inclusivity 'for the benefit and in the interest of all countries' enshrined in the Treaty. Sooner or later, necessary modalities will be evolved for equitable or proportionate sharing of monetized benefits based on some kind of consideration or weightage and shares of other stakeholders shall become due and payable. The space business community must pledge to disburse payments, so determined, whenever and wherever payable. This will be a confidence-building measure to the world community about their genuine intention of partaking the *res communis* on an assurance of paying back decreed or agreed amounts. This should be the norm but with an imbued sense of obligation and abiding altruism in the interest of mankind.

PRAGMATIC SOLUTION

With due deference to international treaties and international law, their speed in evolution and consequent enforcement is tortuously slow in relation to technological breakthroughs, developments in innovative applications, and business decisions for financial investments. This scenario does not augur well for space activities where pioneering efforts get the gold. Therefore, pending the lead in this domain for legal solutions to emerge and come into force is not an option due to their elongated timeframe. This prods us to mull on a pragmatic solution that is fast enough in implementation, does not foul with the Treaty provisions, and respects the cardinal tenet of inclusivity for sharing benefits under the OST. This solution could be that the corporate world venturing into mining of celestial resources and commercial appropriation thereof makes a cost analysis of the operations and based on the sale revenues obtainable makes a calculation of net profit out of which a certain percentage, say X or ten percent, can be apportioned aside for the benefit of all states. This share of an agreed portion of accruing profits from such activity can be used in the interest of or to benefit all states or shared in some ratio and weightage as and when decided. However, a word of caution that 'all states' should not start behaving as a 'Space Union' to claim their pound of flesh or collectively bargain for unconscionable benefits.

The quantum of such apportioned profits can be called Space Benefits Fund (SBF) on the lines of CSR. The amounts so determined can be deposited in an escrow account with the UN to be disbursed when modalities for such distribution are finalised and put into practice; or utilised for measures towards sustainability of outer space environment for the common benefit of mankind. It is possible that based on the rules framed for profit-sharing or disbursement methodologies or benefit-monetisation formula, the funds already deposited in escrow accounts may need plus-or-minus adjustment. The space corporate world should promise to honour its commitment and make-up for any such deficiency when so demanded by competent authority. Overall, this should seem an equitable and just deal for all parties and hopefully would put space relations on a definitive basis consistent with the Treaty provisions. Of course, acceptance of such compromises is not easy and requires thorough bureaucratic consideration of pros and cons from respective standpoints. This process, however, demands urgency.

Institutional Support System

In nutshell, it seems risky to permit asymmetrical medians to the OST, as short cuts, even for a desirable space activity, that is discordant with the template of existing legal regimen. Hence, the solution selected should be legal and compatible, else we need to amend or change the prevailing instrument to bring it in consonance with our contemporary needs, compromised values, revised mind-set, and collective wisdom. But whatever be the option chosen, it becomes apparent that we would consequentially need a strong institutional mechanism, particularly in such commercial environment, for regulatory purposes, e.g. leasing of celestial sites for mining, inspection of mined quantum, collection of lease monies as SBF as well as its distribution among beneficiaries, and of course, to settle disputes that could be common in such a business milieu. Existing set-up of OOSA is not geared for this purpose and will not be adequate for the enlarged ends and objectives.

It seems desirable to propose for a new organ of the UN that may be named World Space Organisation (WSO) which may supersede and subsume the existing OOSA. Thus, the new Organisation may be assigned a mandate to entrust it with wider scope of duties on commercialisation of the outer space, commensurate infra-structure, requisite administrative authority, and appropriate funding or self-generating revenue resources. This could turn out to be a unique organisation with composite functions and multiple tasks concerning outer space that may be akin to the International Sea-bed Authority, ICAO, Supervision of Global Commons, UNEP, Space Debris Management and allied concerns.

The proposed Organisation would need legislative powers for the formulation of regulatory procedures and business rules for its functioning; governing powers for domain management in grant of mining leases or control of space flights and collection of charges and levies as revenue; policing powers for law and public order as well as for safety and security; executive powers to effectuate commercial business and enforce rules for disciplined space flying and authorised mining activity; supervisory powers for inspections and verification of compliances attendant with authority to order sanctions for breaches; and lastly, quasi-judicial powers for settlement of disputes in the first instance as well as to order remedial measures and ensure enforcement. This list, however, is neither comprehensive nor complete and can be expanded or amended as deemed necessary or with operational experience.

It is possible to surmise of resistance to the idea of a new organ of the UN as well as visualise diplomatic difficulties, procedural formalities, and need for funding provisions for the establishment of WSO dedicated to space governance. Therefore, for the period till the formation and functioning of such an over-arching organisation, it may be suggested, *in interim*, to form a Celestial Resources Authority (CRA) for regulatory controls, e.g. leasing of astral sites for specified period, licensing for mining, and control of quantum mined. Another important function would be collection of lease fees as revenue; and a share of accrued profit as SBF for distribution as benefit to entitled countries.

CONCLUSION

The OST regimen has served the world community well in governance of outer space for half a century and has successfully weathered challenges through supporting conventions or normative guidelines and declarations to expand the Treaty landscape. Fortunately, the Treaty has been adhered to in letter and spirit and there have hardly been any aberrant behaviour or serious infractions. Lately, a couple of the US space laws, discussed earlier, have gone beyond the specific provisions of the Treaty to promise its citizen certain rights to private appropriation and commercial disposal of excavated celestial mineral resources that the state itself does not possess nor are bestowed by the Treaty.

Nevertheless, in view of depleting terrestrial natural resources, use of celestial mineral reservoir seems vitally necessary for the prolonged sustenance and common benefit of humanity. Here, we may differ due to ideological dogmas or for national interests yet we are together in our inspirational dreams and espoused objective. Present threshold of technology makes it feasible to exploit celestial excavate-able resources in commercial quantities and dispose of profitably. Interests of humanity should take primacy and law adapt to this goal. Therefore, contemporary imperfections of the OST that have come to notice now with advances in technology, sprouting commercial possibilities, and proffered business funding should be corrected and 'futurised' to the best of our ability.

In view of the above objective, a few compromises on the interfering US laws have been evolved and options proffered. It is understandable that making a considered and conscious choice for an optimal solution is difficult for various reasons like cognitive biases in perception, upholding of traditional values, sovereign compulsions, compatibility with international obligations, consonance with germane laws, satisfying business expectations, and actualisation of popular aspirations or sheer urgency in implementation. Yet, the dilemma has to be resolved amicably to the satisfaction of all stakeholders and other concerned parties lest space governance may informally agglomerate into space plutocracy of the global rich and the powerful.

The easiest option seems to acknowledge inclusive principle relating to 'the benefit and in the interest of all countries' as per the Preamble and Article I of the OST and accordingly set aside an X-portion of net profits from astro-realty exploitation for the avowed purpose and deposit the same in an escrow account, for the time being, under the custody and control of UN OOSA. This could be apportioned and disbursed to entitled parties in due course when modalities for sharing are settled. The next best choice appears to steer through the MA to achieve the desired result with tactics for nuanced success, as proposed above, though its conclusion may take some time.

Irrespective of the solution opted for, it becomes incumbent on the US, as a leader in space activities, to strive to make commercial space mining ventures as transparent as possible to win credibility for genuinely spurring its space economy from the private sector. Further, the prevailing world-wide asymmetry in technology threshold of different countries makes them relatively vulnerable in economic exploitation of celestial natural resources and thus puts them to disadvantage which should be neutralised as best as possible. May be, mining leases could be demised after a specified period under lease retirement policy to facilitate new entrants. Therefore, the challenge is to maintain a level playing field amidst uneven economic contest among differently-abled space players. The US and the UN should contribute their mite in this regard so that we use the bounties of the outer space prudently and sustainably and share them magnanimously.

NOTES

1. It is likely that certain countries like China and India may not involve private enterprise in strategic or commercial space activities for a long time.
2. Treaty on Principles Governing the Activities of States in the Exploration and Use of Outer Space, including the Moon and other Celestial Bodies, 1967. 610 UNTS 205 (1967); 18 UST 2410, TIAS No 6347, 6 ILM 386. Often referred to as Outer Space Treaty or the Treaty or OST.
3. HR 2262. The President of the US signed it into law on 25 November, 2015.
4. Agreement Governing the Activities of the States on the Moon and other Celestial Bodies, 1979, available at <https://treaties.un.org/pages/ViewDetails.aspx?src=TREATY&mtdsg_no=XXIV-2&chapter= 24&clang=_en>
   It entered into force on 11 July, 1984. It has received 17 ratifications till February, 2017.
5. Lee Drutman, "How Corporate Lobbyists Conquered American Democracy" in *The Atlantic*, 20 April, 2015. www,theatlantic.com/business/archive/2015/04/how-corporate-lobbyists-conquered-american-democracy/390822/
6. <http://www.govtrack.us/congress/bills/114/hr1508>
7. Summary of Purpose to the proposed Act.
8. Text of the proposed Act.
9. Section 51303 (a) of the proposed Act.
10. Section 51303 (b), ibid.
11. The Committee Report, HR-1508, of 15 June, 2015, p. 6.
12. Ibid, pp. 7-8.
13. Ibid, p. 8.
14. G. Gal, "Acquisition of Property in the Legal Regime of Celestial Bodies" in *Proceedings of the Thirty-Ninth Colloquium on the Law of Outer Space*, (1996), p. 47.
15. M. Smith Matching, "Space-related Intellectual Rights to Industrial Needs" in ISU International Symposium, *Retrospective of the 1996 Symposium* (7 November, 1996). Quoted from Rashi Shahrawat and Ramanpreet Singh Sidhu, "Celestial Body Mining: What is and What Could Be?" An unpublished paper.
16. PA Dasch and ors, "Conference on Space Property Rights: Next Steps", in *Proceedings of the Forty-Second Colloquium on the Law on Outer Space* (2000), p.174.
17. GH Reynolds, "International Space Law: into the Twenty-First Century" in 25 VAND. J. TRANSNAT'L L. (1992), p. 225.
18. Case No 01-0116-CIV-JORDAN in the District. Court of SD Florida. An unpublished case.
19. The Committee Report, HR-1508, of 15 June, 2015, page 8.
20. The Report of Inspector General of NASA on the subject submitted in 2011.
21. HR 1508, p. 8.
22. VCLT, Article 31.
23. HR 1508, p. 8.

24. Ibid, p. 20.
25. Ibid.
26. Proposed Section 51303 (d). Also refer Report ibid, p. 20.
27. In short Space Competitiveness Act or SCA.
28. US Commercial Space Launch Competitiveness Act, 2015, section 51301 (1).
29. Daniel A Porras, "Astro-propriation: Investment Protections for and from Space Mining Operations" in Rajeshwari Pillai Rajagopalan and Narayan Prasad, eds, Space India 2.0 (New Delhi, Observer Research Foundation, 2017), pp.311-334.
30. HR 2262, https://www.congress.gov/bill/114-congress/house-bill/2262/text, section 51303.
31. Space Competitiveness Act, section 51301 (1).
32. Ibid, section 51301 (2) (a) and (b).
33. This clarification was pronounced by Senator Brian Babin in his remarks to 10 Annual Eilene Galloway Symposium on Critical Issues in Space Law, Washington, DC, 9 December, 2015. Quoted from Daniel Porass, n. 29 ante. p. 315.
34. Lotta Viikari, *The Environmental Element in Space Law: Assessing the Present and Charting the Future* (2007), p. 50.
35. For example, Final Environmental Assessment for the Blue Origin commercial launch is available at http://www.patrick.af.mil/shared/media/document/AFD-141107-004.pdf.
36. COSPAR is Committee on Space Research. Planetary Protection Policy prepared by the Committee was adopted on 20 October, 2002 and has been later amended on 24 March, 2005. Refer http://w.astro.berkley.edu/~kalas/ethics/documents/environment/COSPAR%20 Planetary%20Protection%20Policy.pdf
37. Space Competitiveness Act, section 51302 (b).
38. Refer <http://www.govtrack.us/congress/bills/115/hr2809>
39. Ibid.
40. Ibid.
41. Vienna Convention on the Law of Treaties, article 31.
42. Comment by Jeff Graeson, CEO, Agile Aero reported in Space.com, 18 July, 2017.
43. Mukunth Vasudevan, "Fiat Luxembourg: How a Tiny European Nation is Leading the Evolution of Space Law" in *The Wire* dated 15 July, 2017.
44. Ibid.
45. Ibid.
46. Gbenga Oduntan, "Who Owns Space? US Asteroid-Mining Act is Dangerous and Potentially Illegal", in The Conversation (November 25, 2015, 10:34 a.m.). <theconversation.com/who-owns-space-us-asteroid-mining-act-is-dangerous-and-potentially-illegal-51073>
47. John Locke, *Second Treatise of Government* (1690), Chapter V.
48. Words in parentheses added for clarity in understanding.
49. Gerardine Goh, Dispute Settlement in International Space Law, A Multi-door Courthouse for Outer Space (2007) ,161.
50. Fabio Troncheti, *The Exploitation of Natural Resources of the Moon and other Celestial Bodies*, p.223.
51. The OST, Article VI.
52. HR 2262, Title IV
53. The OST, Article I, first paragraph.
54. Agreement Governing the Activities of States on the Moon and Other Celestial Bodies, 1979. UN Resolution 3235 (XXIX), annex. In short, the Moon Agreement or the MA.
55. The Moon Agreement, Article 1 (1).
56. The Moon Agreement, Article 6 (2).

57. HR 2262.
58. Refer Minority views and the opinion of the legal expert, Prof Dianne Gabrynowicz, appended to the Committee Report HR-2262.
59. The Space Treaty, Article IX.
60. The US Constitution, 5th Amendment.
61. Agreement Governing the Activities of States on the Moon and Other Celestial Bodies, 1979. UN Resolution 3235 (XXIX), annex.
62. First paragraph of Preamble to the OST.
63. The Moon Agreement, Article 4 (1).
64. Eric A Posner, Law and Social Norms (Harvard University Press, USA, 2002). He advocates this view in his book.
65. NASA ensures that humans in space do not contaminate other planets and moons and alien matter does not infect the earth. Its rules specify that any space mission must have less than a 1-in-10,000 chance of contaminating an alien world or *vice versa.* For this purpose NASA has an appointed Planetary Protection Officer. *The Times of India* (Chandigarh Edition), August 4, 2017.
66. Ricky Lee, *Creating A Practical Legal Framework for the Commercial Exploitation of Mineral Resources in Outer Space.* (Murdch University, 2009) 341.
67. Thomas Packenham, The Scramble for Africa (Little Brown Books, 1992, New edition).
68. Norry Harn, Commercial Mining of Celestial Bodies: A Legal Roadmap, 27 (4) GEO. INT'L ENVIRONMENTAL L. REV. (2015) 629-644.
69. Martti Koskenniemi, *The Gentle Civilizer of Nations: The Rise and Fall of International Law 1870-1960* (Cambridge University Press, 2002-Reprint) 110-112.
70. Evert C Dolman, *Astropolitik: Classical Geopolitics in the Space Age* (London, Frank Cass, 2002) 52. Also refer James Clay Moltz, "Space and Strategy-From Theory to Policy" in Eligar Sadeh, ed *Space Strategy in the 21st Century: Theory and Policy* (London, Routledge, 2013) 15-38.
71. The Space Treaty, Article IX.
72. Reported by Chris Wickham, *REUTERS,* First Posted: Thursday, October 11, 2012 09:36 AM EDT. The Indo-French team of astronomers comprised Nikku Madhusudan and Olivier Mousis.
73. For a detailed study on the subject refer "Mining of Asteroids: A Legal Analysis for Effective Governance" in G S Sachdeva, Outer Space: Law, Policy and Governance (New Delhi, KW Publishers Pvt. Ltd., 2014), pp. 155-204.
74. 55th Session of Legal Sub-committee of the COPUOS (4-15 April, 2016) at Vienna. Refer http://ww.unoosa.org/oosa/en/ourwork/copuos/lsc/journal.html.
75. For more details on this view point refer W Friedmann, *Law in a Changing Society* (Steven & Sons, 1959).
76. Karan Kamath and Shraddha Dubey, "Celestial Mining by Private Parties" (2016), an unpublished article.
77. John J. Barcelo, "The International Legal Regime for Antarctica: A Foreword" in 19 CORNELL INT'L L. J. (1986), 155-161, p.156.
78. 27 ILM 859 (1988)
79. 30 ILM 1455. (1998). It came into force on 14 January, 1998.
80. Refer US Code, Section 80309 and the American Space Commerce Free Enterprise Act, 2017.
81. Ajey Lele, "Conclusion" in Ajey Lele, ed., *50 Years of the Outer Space Treaty-Tracing the Journey* (New Delhi, Pentagon Press, 2017), p. 200.
82. The Moon Agreement, article 11 (1).
83. The Moon Agreement, Article 11 (5).

CHAPTER TWO

Harvesting of Asteroids

Analysis of Legality for Good Governance*

INTRODUCTION

Humanity has industrialised rather fast in the last couple of centuries to deplete natural resources with indiscriminate usage and consumerist disposal attitude, thus losing on sustainability. This dearth has made humans to desperately look for resources anywhere and everywhere. The economic necessity for new source deposits is obvious and needs no vindication. Alternatives have been sighted on the celestial bodies in the outer space that are so rich in minerals and metals. Thus, the entire universe becomes our provenance of natural resources and this reservoir which appears nearly limitless and inexhaustible has been drawn into the domain of utilisation and consumption by humankind. This fact had been surmised for long but has lately been confirmed by spectrometry studies and remote sensing data analysis.

Further, appropriate technology has been developed only recently and its applications made feasible. The viability of mining celestial bodies has now been proved from many aspects including docking procedures, technical extraction capability, facilitation of transportation, and economic profitability. Therefore, near-exhaustion of mineral resources on the earth and their infinite availability as ore deposits on almost all celestial bodies, particularly near-earth asteroids within the solar system, is soon expected to give birth to a new industry of space mining to tap mineral treasures from extra-terrestrial

* This is revised and enlarged version of a chapter with similar title in G. S. Sachdeva, *Outer Space: Law, Policy and Governance* (New Delhi, KW Publishers, 2014).

natural reserves. The ores from outer space are assessed to be rich in common utility minerals having a high element of currently precious metals like silver, gold and platinum, among others.

Asteroids are natural rock formations that have splintered away from the mother planet or a moon and have adopted their own orbit determined by velocity of separation and interaction of the natural forces of gravity of ambient bigger bodies. A few of the asteroids from the Solar system come in for a very close fly-by with Earth and this phenomenon fascinates astronomers. Lately, remote observations and sample collections of the soil from a couple of asteroids has revealed a rich bounty of metallic ores. This prospecting infuses hope for commercial exploitation of the asteroids for minerals so acutely needed by humanity for its sustenance and welfare.

Fortunately, technology has also almost come of age where it makes 'lasso-ing' or riding on asteroids, with the help of robot forces, technologically feasible and excavation of natural resources economically viable. In this connection, it will be of interest to mention that an asteroid named '1999 KV4' is estimated to be worth $25.7 trillion in mineral resources. And by one estimate the population of asteroids is about 600,000 and this number is increasing with discoveries every day.[1] One only needs to wait for an opportune time of fly-by nearest to Earth and catapult devices for commercial exploitation of asteroidal natural resources.

It is, therefore, natural for corporate sages of business community to show keen interest in this space activity. A commercial conglomerate has harnessed billions of dollars to invest in space mining ventures. This corporation, styled Planetary Resources Incorporated has obtained state-of-art technology and trained manpower to exploit, to begin with, an asteroid close in orbit to the earth. Another is Deep Space Industries (DSI), also operating from Luxembourg. The overall risks as calculated are surmountable and within safety margins; and economics of venture assures rich dividends. The mining corporations have, therefore, made an announcement of its intention to privately prospect and exploit the natural resources available on the surface and inside of the asteroid Eros for commercial purposes. This is the harbinger of what is to follow. The race to competition does not seem far behind.

The practicality and seriousness of this intention leads to the question of legal permissibility of commercial mining activities on the selected asteroid and other celestial bodies. This assumes importance because the legal regime of outer space is at variance from that of the planet earth in many substantive aspects. The activities and relationships in outer space are broadly governed under the international law but superimposed with the principles of Outer Space Treaty.[2] The OST declares that the use of outer space 'shall be the province of all mankind' and national sovereignty in any manner or by any means is prohibited in outer space. By logical inference, appropriation of asteroidal resources by mining corporations for private profit would not be licit and patently illegal. Therefore, let's not create a legal delusion by involuted arguments and twisted interpretations. However, space activities by non-governmental entities, may be from private sector, are permitted, *albeit* under continued supervision and national responsibility.[3]

Another legal instrument that can throw light on this issue is the Moon Agreement.[4] This document in its Preamble recognises that 'benefits...may be derived from the exploitation of the natural resources of the Moon and other celestial bodies'. Scientific observation into outer space and sample investigations have proved the truth of this statement by mapping rich reservoirs of mineral wealth and possibility of actual mining now is a hard reality. On the other hand, global mineral resources have been depleted to an alarmingly low level and future scarcity stares us in the face. New sources, out of dire necessity, needed to be searched anywhere and everywhere. The moon and celestial bodies like asteroids offer an abundant availability and benign opportunity. Man, as yet, believes that he is supreme and the entire universe is at his command and solely for his benefit. It is, therefore, natural that humankind is at the threshold of resorting to exploitation of material resources, renewable as well as non-renewable, of the outer space.

The Moon Treaty (MA) also reiterates, "The exploration and use of the Moon shall be the province of all mankind and shall be carried out for the benefit and in the interest of all countries"[5] *albeit* allows "activities in the exploration and use of the Moon anywhere on or below its surface".[6] This permission to excavate natural resources can be logically extended to other celestial bodies including asteroids, within the solar system, by the applicability clause.[7] This Treaty further mandates, "The Moon and its natural resources are the common heritage of mankind" and "[N]either the surface nor the subsurface of the Moon...or natural resources in place, shall become property of any state...or of any natural person".[8] Hence, benefits of such activities, even by private business entities, must accrue to 'all countries' in an equitable measure to satisfy the avowed objective of benefit to humankind.

In nutshell, the search for alternative provenance has been made practical by Planetary Resources Inc with the proposed project of mining of asteroids and to begin with, it is Eros. Hence, actual mining, in whatever manner, of celestial bodies appears just round the corner. It is sure to become a reality sooner than expected. However, the legality of such activities and that too by private enterprise for commercial purposes remains moot and highly suspect. Only a contrived legal casuistry, and that too with syllogistic fallacies, can support such moves or uphold such motives under the existing legal regime of the OST. It is, therefore, proposed to discuss in this chapter the legal permissibility of such commercial mining activities on asteroids, and incidentally on celestial bodies, in the outer space and evolve policy options and legal solutions.

As the existing legal provisions are inadequate and inhibitive for the specificity of purpose, a fitting and pertinent legal framework, as envisaged and provided for in the Moon Agreement, must be explored, amplified and put in place to release this treasure trove for optimum use by humankind.[9] Scientific progress has made it incumbent that legally permissive amplifications are procedurally evolved and promulgated before competition and chaos seeps in on the celestial bodies to disturb peace and stability in the outer space. Else, it will be too late to introduce a proper economic order of sustainable usage and regulated extraction of resources with equitable sharing of resultant benefits as per the OST stipulations. The urgency is stark and the task laborious. Undue procrastination may be detrimental.

ASTEROID FACTOIDS

Asteroids are in the news and are getting too close to the earth, and too often, thus causing anguishing scare for humanity and at the same time flashing their mineral treasures to charm the business tycoons of the world. These stray passes and random flybys have elicited great interest from scientists in different specialisations to study their orbital perigees, gravity parameters, and material composition as well as risks of their crash into Earth. Warnings have been sounded at times. On the other hand, some space organisations have landed probes on asteroids, like the US landing on Eros, for exploration and investigation and prospecting of their mineral wealth. And now Hayabusa-2 plans to blast the surface of *Ryugu*, create a crater by blast and collect underground samples of the soil around September, 2019.[10]

Discovery and Naming of Asteroids

The earliest discovery of an asteroid was made by an Italian priest and astronomer Giuseppe Piazzi in 1801. He was making a star map when he accidentally discovered the first asteroid orbiting between Mars and Jupiter. This happened to be Ceres and till today remains the largest asteroid ever discovered. Although Ceres has all along been classified as an asteroid, it has lately been deemed as a dwarf planet due its large size. In fact, it alone accounts for a quarter of the total mass of all the thousands of known asteroids in or near the main asteroid belt while the smallest known asteroid is 1991BA.

The diversity of exo-planets is large, more than 800 planets outside the Solar system have been found to date, with thousands more waiting to be confirmed. With advanced detection methods in this field, many more exo-planets will undoubtedly be discovered in the years to come. Therefore, naming of celestial bodies is a serious business for scientific studies that needs tremendous uniformity and must work across different languages and cultures to support collaborative world-wide research and avoid confusion. Towards this intent, the International Astronomical Union (IAU),[11] as an international scientific organisation has, however, framed certain rules that deserve universal acceptance and application. The IAU dissociates itself entirely from the commercial practice of selling names of planets, stars or even 'real estate' on other planets or moons. These practices will not be recognised by the IAU and their alternative naming schemes cannot be adopted.[12]

Despite stern warning from the IAU, companies like 'Uwingu'[13] are promoting their naming initiative and a campaign to sell for nomination of asteroid names. This gimmick is meant more as a fund-raising device though ostensibly for space outreach and research for SETI,[14] exploration and education. A scientific mind would not have confused the astronomer fraternity with such profusion of nomenclature that is more insouciant than scientific. The IAU has asserted that these "open source naming options" have no bearing on the official naming processes and has stressed the importance of a unified procedure[15] based on scientific studies and unimpeachable criteria.

However, the rules are less strict on how asteroids are named when compared to exo-planets and other bigger bodies. There are asteroids named, rather flippantly, after Mr Spock of 'Star Trek' and rock musician Frank Zappa. But frivolous and playful nick-naming of asteroids after pets or for similar reasons or as a joke is no longer allowed.[16] Of course, there are seven asteroids named, in more solemn tribute, to commemorate the sacrifice of the seven members of the crew of the Space Shuttle Columbia, who were killed while returning to Earth in 2003. As an alternative, asteroids can also be designated by a combination of alphabets and numerics or by mere numbers alone instead of according specific and meaningful names. For example, asteroid Apophis has just been allotted number 99942. There are nomenclatures for other bodies also that are known by mere numbers or alpha-numeric lexicon, e.g. Gliese667Cc. Incidentally, the latest exoplanet discovered by an Indian team of Physical Research Laboratory, Ahmedabad is named EPIC211945201b.[17]

Nature of Asteroids

Asteroids are the leftovers from the formation of our solar system about 4.6 billion years ago. It is believed that in early stages, the birth of Jupiter prevented any planetary bodies from forming in the gap between Mars and Jupiter, causing the small objects that were there to collide with each other and fragment into the asteroids as seen today. Thus, asteroids are small, airless, and mostly irregular shaped rocky formations that have since been revolving around the Sun. These are too small in mass to be treated as planets and are, therefore, called planetoids or minor planets; because these are smaller than known and recognised planets but bigger than meteoroids which are just stones of different sizes and shapes.

These asteroids orbit around the Sun, especially in the inner solar system. In total, the mass of all the asteroids put together is less than that of Earth's moon. But despite their smaller size, asteroids can be dangerous. Their orbits have deflected near-Earth and many have hit in the past, and more will crash into our planet in the future. Some craters and pock marks on the surface of Earth are good evidence of this occurrence. That is one reason scientists are keen to study asteroids and are eager to learn more about their numbers, orbits and physical characteristics. It is believed that living species on Earth have gone extinct earlier due to such impacts. It is also conjectured that the dinosaurs vanished as a species due to one such hit.

Most asteroids are primarily located in a 'Main–Belt' forming a ring between the orbits of Mars and Jupiter. This main asteroid belt holds a concentration of more than 200 asteroids larger than 60 miles (100 km) in diameter. Scientists estimate the asteroid belt also contains more than 750,000 asteroids larger than three-fifths of a mile (1 km) in diameter and millions of smaller ones that are too small to count. However, not every celestial body in the main belt is an asteroid; for instance, comets have recently been discovered there, and Ceres, once thought of only as an asteroid, is now observed to be much bigger in size and dimension; and is now considered a dwarf planet.

Despite this concentration, many asteroids lie outside the main belt. For instance, a number of asteroids called Trojans lie along Jupiter's orbital path. There are three groups—Atens, Amors, and Apollos—known as near-Earth asteroids which orbit in the inner solar system and sometimes cross the path of Mars and Earth. At times, some other asteroids also freak out of their regular orbit to become 'near-Earth' objects that swing much closer to our planet, sometimes even within 100,000 miles or nearer. Asteroids "that have been nudged by the gravitational attraction of nearby planets into orbits that allow them to enter the Earth's neighbourhood" are called Near-Earth-Objects (NEO).[18]

Population of Asteroids

It has been believed for long time that asteroids are low density rocks with almost non-existent gravity. Perchance, these broke away from mother landmass and happen to be orbiting around the Sun but at times the orbit comes perilously close to the earth to cause alarm. In a recent instance, an asteroid space rock, designated 2002 AM 31, zoomed past the earth on 22 July 2012 orbiting at 13.7 moon distances. It qualifies as near-earth asteroid (NEA) and is estimated to have been 2000-4500 feet wide, that is equivalent to the size of a city block.[19] In a similar incident asteroid LZ1, NEA, unexpectedly dashed past the earth in mid-June 2012. Such occurrences of tumbling of rotating asteroids from their orbits are not rare though happen with irregular frequency; and many times are scary till actual occurrence.

The known population of asteroids is numerous and still more are being discovered.[20] According to reliable estimates by astronomers approximately 9000 are orbiting in the solar system generally in clusters called belts that have been classified into families. Of these 1500 are considered within relatively easy reach. Some of these have been individually identified and named or designated by numbers or both. Vesta is, as yet considered to be, the second biggest rock formation with origins similar to that of the earth. It materialised from condensation of diffused matter and its mass started to congeal from the same molten material as the earth. Its exploration and investigation can thus reveal many truths about origin and formation of the earth and possibly, of early universe.

Ceres, however, is believed to be the biggest asteroid in size within the solar system and as yet remains an unexplored mystery. It has not so far been approached due to its distance from the earth and other attendant hazards. There are also other asteroids and dead comets that are smaller in size like Rosetta, Mathilde, Eros, Gaspra, Steins, Ida, Ivor, Juno, Pallas, Aten, Amor, Alinda, Amalthea, Apollo and Itokawa, to name just a few. Asteroid Arjuna, however, is more earth-like. It orbits in low inclination of low eccentricity and it has an orbital period comparable to that of Earth's one year. A major concentration of asteroids within the solar system is believed to exist around the planet Jupiter and orbit around Sun.

There are many belts of such celestial bodies which are called families and are classified as such based on their orbits. The major NEA families are Trojan asteroids, Cybele family, Hilda family, and Hungaria family. The specific asteroids of interest to us are those orbiting in near-earth perigees or that are rich in mineral deposits of precious or scarce metals. Asteroid Psyche has been discovered to be a treasure trove of iron and nickel. Another asteroid Nereus has very low gravity, almost zero but is believed to bear abundant deposits of precious ores.

Physical Characteristics of Asteroids

Asteroids come in a variety of shapes and sizes, and irregular forms. Some are solid bodies, while others are smaller piles of rubble bound together by gravity. Nearly all asteroids are irregularly shaped, although a few are nearly spherical, such as Ceres. They are often pitted or cratered on the external surface due to impact of stray rocks crashing into them. For instance, Vesta has a giant crater some 285 miles (460 km) in diameter. The surfaces of most asteroids are thought to be covered in dust. As regards size, asteroids can reach as large as Ceres, which is 940 km (about 583 miles) across. On the other hand, one of the smallest, discovered in 1991 and named 1991BA, is only about 20 feet (6 m) across.

As asteroids revolve around the Sun in elliptical orbits, they also rotate, sometimes tumbling quite erratically to reach near-Earth orbit. Again, more than 150 asteroids are known to have a small companion moon, with some having two moons also. Binary or double asteroids also exist, in which two asteroids of roughly equal size orbit each other; while triple asteroid systems are known as well. Many asteroids, seemingly, have been captured by a planet's gravity and thus have become its moons. For example, likely candidates for such moons are Phobos and Deimos for Mars and most of the distant outer moons of Jupiter, Saturn, Uranus and Neptune. These are weird asteroids and one, which orbits the Sun between Neptune and Uranus, comes with its own set of rings. Another has not one but six tails. Further, the average temperature of the surface of a typical asteroid is minus 100 degree F (minus 73 degree C). Asteroids have stayed mostly unchanged for billions of years — as such, research into them could reveal a great deal about the early solar system and also possibly about the origins of the Earth.[21]

Classification of Asteroids

Asteroids, generally, are bodies of rock, metals and ice range. The classification of asteroids is based on their orbits or composition. But asteroids are often classified according to their spectral type that is according to the light they reflect. Most asteroids fall into three classes based on composition. The C-type or carbonaceous are greyish in colour and are the most common and constitute more than 75 percent of known asteroids. They are of dark material and probably consist of clay and stony silicate rocks e.g. 253 Mathilde. These inhabit the main belt's outer regions. The S-type or silicaceous asteroids are greenish to reddish in colour e.g. Eros. These account for about 17 percent of known asteroids, and dominate the inner asteroid belt. They appear to be made of silicate materials and nickel-iron.

The M-type or metallic asteroids are reddish in colour and constitute most of the rest of the asteroids, and dwell in the middle region of the main belt. They seem to be made up of nickel and/or iron. There are many other rare types based on composition as well, for instance, V-type asteroids typified by Vesta have a basaltic, volcanic crust but this variety does not bear significant presence in the solar system. Another type is X group that includes miscellaneous types of asteroids that are with similar spectra but are likely to have different compositions. And other group of asteroids as the Greeks, Trojans and Hildas hang out in stable points near the orbit of Jupiter.

When an asteroid, or a part of it, crashes into Earth, it's called a meteor or meteorite. These are also called 'shooting stars' that can be seen flashing brightly across the horizon for a brief moment. These are not actually stars at all but bits of matter that travels at the speed of 26 miles per second and burn up in the earth's atmosphere and glow for a few seconds. Objects similar to meteors, also called aerolites, sometimes strike the earth. These may weigh many tons and may not completely burn up in the atmosphere. A meteorite weighing some 70 tons was found in Tanganyika in 1931. Again a meteor crater 570 feet deep was caused by such impact in Arizona, USA. Such examples can be multiplied.[22]

Composition of Asteroids

The typical compositions of meteorites are of two types. One is Iron meteorites with a composition of 91 per cent of iron, 8.5 per cent Nickle and less than 1 per cent Cobalt and copper. The meteorite composition was found to be too harder than iron and led to the development of steel.[23] These meteorites have also provided Platinum and Palladium that are used in electronics, car components and as catalyst in chemical reactions. The other types are stony in character and bear a different composition. These contain 36 per cent Oxygen, 26 per cent Iron, 18 per cent Silicon, 14 per cent Magnesium and smaller quantities of just over 1 per cent of Aluminium, Nickle and Calcium. These burn the brightest while falling through the atmosphere.

Vesta is another special asteroid in many ways. At present a NASA probe on planetary sciences, called DAWN, is orbiting around Vesta to study its spatial characteristics, physical composition, and gravity parameters, among other tasks. The probe team is also mapping its resource deposits and has noticed crystalline structures of HED (Howardite-Eucrite-Diogenite).[24] It is surmised that Vesta has in its history passed through a violent collisional environment and its topography is pock marked with the impact of a bombardment of meteorite rocks. Its surface also shows undulating spatial topography with lines like that of basins. More information may be provided by this project.

However, knowledge gained from observation satellites and robotic visitors so far is promising for exploitation of celestial natural resources rich in rare metals and minerals. Technology and harvest prospecting of quality and quantity of ores have prodded business houses to consider economic viability and take calculated risks in excavation. Planetary Resources Incorporated is one such corporate entity that has mustered enough financial and technical resources to initiate the process and have made known of their intention to mining of asteroids in the near future. Another mining giant is Deep Space Industries (DSi) and a budding corporation with similar goals and objectives is Asteroid Enterprises Pty. Limited. However, Moon Express remains the first private company to secure US governmental approval to fly a spacecraft to the Moon with long-term plans for mining of mineral resources.[25] The proposals appear promising from many angles though it needs billions of dollars in investment and a multi-decadal gestation time to fructify.

That these bodies are rich in many raw materials has been well known to geologists and physicists for long time though only recent probes have established the specifics of minerals and volatiles. Minerals that can be mined or extracted include iron, nickel, and titanium for construction. Precious metals like platinum, palladium, gold and cobalt can also be extracted. The asteroids as source of such metals are important because, at present, majority of rare earth metals are obtained from China and this may turn out to be an uncertain supply source for these vital industrial materials.

Apart from these, the priority mining in space should be for water because sending a 16-ounce water bottle into space costs about $ 2500 and an Olympic size swimming pool would cost a billion dollars.[26] Therefore, water is truly an economic resource in outer space because of its vital requirement for astronauts and as cooling agent for certain systems on ISS. Fortunately, water can be mined from different types of ice found on asteroids and other celestial bodies. And it can be economically broken down into liquid oxygen and liquid hydrogen that can be accumulated for storage. While oxygen can help to sustain the lives of prospector-astronauts on site, hydrogen can be used as rocket fuel and stocked as local tankage in orbiting propellant depots for in-situ utilisation as well as to refuel on-journey vehicles. The ideas, though ambitious on purpose as well as economics, yet appear exciting and viable in the long term.

Incidentally, it would appear of interest to mention that planets have been spotted, observed and discovered which are super-rich earths made of diamond that are still in the process of morphosis. In this connection, it seems equally pertinent to inform that recently a team of Indo-French astronomers[27] has discovered a planet twice the size of our own earth, orbiting a star visible to the naked eye that is largely composed of diamond.[28] The rocky planet called '55 Cancri e' orbits a sun-like star in the constellation of Cancer and is moving so fast that a year there lasts a mere 18 earth-hours. Its radius is twice that of Earth and its mass is eight times greater. It is also incredibly hot, with temperatures on its surface reaching 3,900 degree F (2,148 C). The surface of this planet is having fundamentally different chemistry and is likely to be carbon-rich and covered in graphite. It is estimated that at least a third of the planet's mass, the equivalent of about three Earth masses, could be diamond. The planets, in fact, are much more complex entities and future explorations may strive to prospect and discover such enviable bodies within our own galaxy.

In fact, all the gold, cobalt, iron, manganese, molybdenum, nickel, osmium, palladium, platinum, rhenium, rhodium, ruthenium, antimony, zinc, indium and tungsten mined from the Earth's crust, that are really essential for economic and technological progress, came originally from the rain of asteroids that hit the Earth after its crust cooled and stayed embedded near the surface.[29] This is because earth's massive gravity pulled all such native heavy siderophile (iron-loving) elements into the planet's core during its molten youth more than four billion years ago. This left the crust depleted of such valuable elements and whatever remained has been indiscreetly mined. With globally asymmetrical industrial usage such assets have been nearly exhausted while the present needs of developing nations are escalating. Hence, this constitutes the compulsion to look out for extra-terrestrial mineral sources.

Impact of Asteroids on Earth

Ever since Earth formed about 4.5 billion years ago, asteroids and comets have routinely slammed into the planet. According to NASA, the most dangerous asteroids are extremely rare, though do exist. Generally, an asteroid capable of catastrophic global disaster would have to be more than a quarter-mile wide, because researchers have estimated that only such an impact would raise enough dust into the atmosphere to effectively create a 'nuclear winter', thereby, asphyxiating human life and severely disrupting agriculture around the world. Asteroids that large in size strike Earth only once every 1,000 centuries on average, NASA officials say.

Smaller asteroids that are believed to strike Earth every 1,000 to 10,000 years could destroy a city or cause devastating tsunamis but not total extinction. On such a parameter, dozens of asteroids have been classified as 'potentially hazardous' by the scientists who track them. Some of these, whose orbits come close enough to Earth, could potentially be perturbed in the distant future and could head on a collision course with our planet. Scientists point out that if an asteroid is found to be on a collision course with Earth 30 or 40 years down the road, there would be time to react. Of course, suitable technology would have to be developed and perfected yet viable possibilities include exploding the approaching object at a safe distance or diverting it. Laser technique could offer another viable solution.[30]

A couple of recent instances of this nature are recapitulated here. The largest meteorite crater on the earth is Chubb, located about 60 miles from Hudson Strait. It was discovered in 1950 and measures over two miles wide and its rim rising to 550 feet above the plain. Another incident occurred on 15 February 2013 when an asteroid slammed into the atmosphere over the Russian city of Chelyabinsk. This created a shock wave that injured 1,200 people. The space rock is thought to have measured about 65 feet (20 meters) wide when it entered Earth's atmosphere.[31]

However, for every known asteroid, there are many more that have not been spotted or discovered due to distance, size or the limitations of our observation devices. In fact, there are swarms of meteors that fall towards the earth, are called 'radiants'. These are named after the constellation in which they appear, e.g. Leonids, Perseids, etc. All crashes of asteroids on the earth may not be so innocuous or benign. And it is equally probable that some of these may be highly damaging and may offer shorter reaction times while targeting Earth. This could both ways prove gravely threatening with consequential lethal results.[32] Technology developments are afoot to find more warning and reaction time so the humanity on earth can be saved.

Exploratory Missions to Asteroids

The first spacecraft to take close-up images of asteroids was NASA's Galileo in 1991, which also discovered the first moon to orbit an asteroid in 1994. Again in 2001, after NASA's NEAR spacecraft intensely studied the near-earth asteroid Eros for more than a year from orbit, mission controllers decided to try and land the spacecraft.[33] Although it wasn't planned or designed for landing, yet NEAR spacecraft successfully touched down, setting the record as the first to successfully land on an asteroid.

NASA's Dawn mission was launched in 2007 and it began exploring Vesta in 2011. After a year, it left the asteroid for a trip to Ceres, with a planned arrival time of 2015. Dawn was the first spacecraft to visit Vesta, and will also be the first to explore Ceres. In 2012, a company called Planetary Resources Inc. announced plans to eventually send a mission to a space rock to extract water and mine the asteroid for precious metals. This alerted NASA of the bounteous riches and economic resources on asteroids; and since then, NASA has begun to work consistently and with sustained plans for its own missions to establish hegemony over asteroid treasures.

A serious effort to closely study an asteroid by NASA is OSIRIS-REx (in short for Origins, Spectral Interpretation, Resource Identification, Security-Regolith Explorer) tracker mission that will explore and sample the carbonaceous and rocky near-Earth asteroid Bennu. Although the mission was launched on 8 September 2016, it is not slated to arrive around Bennu until 2018. Over the course of approximately next two years, OSIRIS-REx will orbit and study the physiognomy and composition of the asteroid Bennu in great detail before rendezvousing with the space rock and collecting a soil sample to bring home to Earth by September 2023.

Asteroids are generally leftovers from the formation of planets and thus they carry blueprints of the early solar system. Therefore, samples collected from the rocky body will help astronomers learn more about the evolution of our solar system and how planets formed. If all goes according to plan, OSIRIS-REx will return to Earth in 2023, making it the first U.S. mission to pick sample from an asteroid and return to the earth. The efforts of the European Space Agency (ESA) in this direction constitute Rosetta spacecraft that has spied on an asteroid called, *Lutetia.* This spacecraft has taken vivid photographs and clear filter images of *Lutetia* in 2010 with OSIRIS system. For these images and photographs, copyright vests in ESA.[34]

The promising prospecting and photographs of the topography of asteroids by Japan, ESA and a private corporation, Space Explorations, has tempted NASA to revert to asteroid exploration to establish its continued primacy on asteroids. Therefore, NASA is also planning another space rock mission between 2019 and 2021. The agency is looking into sending a robotic spaceship to lasso a small asteroid and haul it close to the moon, where spacewalking astronauts would explore it.[35] To find a target asteroid for the mission, its robotized spacecraft may travel up to three million miles away from the earth by end- 2020.[36] For this mission a specialised NASA team of astronauts is being trained to tackle new challenges and a different environment. The purpose of this mission would be to explore exact taxonomy and definitive mineralogy of the asteroid. The round trip may take just over a year.

Japan has successfully ventured in asteroid prospecting and its first such mission was Hayabusa-1 to *Hokawa*, a stormy asteroid. It was launched in 2006 and it became the first spacecraft to land on and take-off from an asteroid. This mission made history when it returned with a small sample recovered from the asteroid in June 2010. The samples are still under investigation and scientific study. Japan has launched another spacecraft, Hayabusa-2, on a mission to a near-Earth asteroid, *Ryugu*[37] that is about 900 m in diameter and located at a distance of 280 million km from the earth. The mission has taken photographs of the asteroid from a rather close distance of 570 miles on 13 June 2018. Rough estimates indicate its worth at $82.8 billion with a possible profit margin of nearly $30 billion.[38]

JAXA's Hayabusa-2 mission will also attempt to take samples of the asteroid soil. For this purpose, the mission will blow a crater with the help of a squat cylinder that will detonate above the surface to create a crater. Thereafter, the robotic explorer will make multiple touch-and-go landings to collect under surface samples of its pristine rocky soil from the bottom of the crater or near the crater mouth. The mission is expected to reach back on Earth by late 2020.[39] In fact, *Ryugu* is a different type of asteroid that is shaped like a dumpling and is having carbonaceous surface believed to contain lots of water.[40] Thus, it is surmised that the soil sample may contain organic molecules. Japan is also reportedly planning to launch a humanned mission to "rendezvous with an asteroid up to three million miles from the earth". It is, of course, a risky affair due to non-existent gravity yet the astronauts may stay for a month on the asteroid.

ECONOMICS OF ASTEROID MINING

The economics of mining of asteroids is not simple and requires factoring in of a lot of parameters whether for its spatial characteristics to ensure safety of miners, the velocity of the celestial body, the distance of the target from the earth, possibility of commercial utilisation of resources *in situ,* and costs of transportation of raw or processed material to the earth or to any other stocking depot nearby. State-of-the-art transportation technology is not very promising at present and needs to work on simpler logistics and cost reduction. This is happening with reusable rocket vehicles that have been tried and tested successfully by private space operators.

Such ventures may also have significant impact on environmental conservation of the body mined and sustainability of non-renewable planetary resources. For these very reasons, the pros and cons of mining of Apollo and Amor asteroids have been under consideration and evaluation since 1977. This mining effort was expected to provide human civilisation with potential to overcome mineral resource crunch and supply additional energy sources, earnestly hoping to add millions to the global gross product. The economic conundrum of viability remains unsolved. Regrettably, no tangible results have materialised so far.[41]

Further, some scientists and techno-economic analysts view the celestial mining plans with scepticism and do not find these as attractive and cost-effective in future scenario with paranoia about recent decline in gold and platinum prices consequent to current glut in the market. This may be a temporary phase but every aspect deserves fullest consideration whether for significant reduction in space transportation costs, viability of physical attachment of equipment and installations in gravity-free conditions, sustainability of resources mined in a fragile environment or satisfaction of the ultimate motive of profitability from the total project.[42] Celestial mining sector is going to be with the private corporate business.

Asteroid Selection

Selection of appropriate asteroid for mining operations depends on several techno-commercial factors. The most important factors to consider in target selection are orbital geometry and soil characteristics. These include, in particular, low speed for hazard-free physical activity while higher velocities can facilitate planetary-mode assisted faster trajectories for cost reduction. Soil quality will provide support to attachment of toggles. The second consideration is travel time to and from the target which constitutes a major component of retrieval costs. Third consideration concerns the soil density and shape of the planetary body which facilitate mining operations. Thus, these parameters make asteroids in low-earth orbit attractive propositions for techno-viability and profitability. These are the considerations of asteroid logistics.

Further, ensuing developments of asteroid-orbit manipulation infrastructure could offer an irresistible option assuring promising return on investment by altering the trajectory of bodies to nearby interplanetary space in low-earth orbit or achieve proximity to the moon. Theoretically, some asteroids can be inter-spatially taken down on the Moon with the help of nukes and SOPL (Solar Orbital Power Lines) which can be fired to usefully adjust the orbit of the asteroid.[43] But such antics are endemic of collision risks and in certain eventualities results could be catastrophic. Astrophysicists Carl Sagan and Steven Ostro have raised valid concerns about artificially altering trajectories of asteroids or other planetary bodies as the risks are indeterminate and ominous. They have suggested instituting stringent controls on the misuse of orbit-engineering technology.[44] The point made deserves urgent attention and fullest consideration from all aspects.

The third element in asteroid selection is its native material composition and geometrical shape. Asteroids are generally clumpy and irregular in form with geo-spatial asymmetry. Therefore, relatively small metallic asteroids of up to one mile diameter are the preferred population. For example, the asteroid '16 Psyche'[45] is a siderite and is believed to contain 1.7×10^{19} kg of nickel–iron, which could supply the world production requirement for several million years. A small portion of its native material could even turn out be precious metals. In another study, Planetary Resources Inc has assessed for eventual mining a 30-meter long asteroid which could yield gold and platinum worth US$ 25-50 billion.[46] Indeed, a colossal net worth of the project that would be rather difficult to resist.

Other factors governing selection are the extent of local disposability of mined material or in situ processing or intra-planetary utilisation to reduce the payload of shipment to the earth. It is desirable that most of the extracted material must be expended locally or processed to reduce its bulk and weight.

The latest innovation of 3-D printer could be of help. Therefore, NEAs are considered potential candidates for mining mission because their nearby location makes them greatly reduce the economic cost of propulsion energy requirement for launch into Earth orbit. A suitable target on these parameters could be 4660 Nereus that has very low gravity compared to the Moon and offers other attractions.

Mining Considerations

Mining operations would require robotised excavator equipment with special installations to handle the excavated materials; and furnaces and machinery for processing of mineral ore in outer space. The machinery will need to be anchored onto the body of the asteroid provided it is rigid enough to withstand, but once installed, the ore can be moved about more effortlessly due to lack of gravity. Docking with an asteroid can be by lassoing a robot onto the asteroid or performed by using a harpoon-like process, where a projectile penetrates the surface to serve as an anchor and thereafter an attached cable can winch the vehicle on to the surface.[47] The procedure, however, is rather risky and hazardous yet technically achievable with due regard to the safety of astronauts and miners, if deployed.

Once the process of mining starts there are two options for disposal of extracted ore. First option is to bring the mined asteroidal material in raw form to the earth for refinement and commercial disposal. This is an expensive proposition because haulage to the earth is still not cost-effective. The second option is on site processing so that the bulky waste is trashed on the rocky body itself and the small quantity of precious extracted materials are transported to the earth. The extraction processes and procedures may also release propellants, allied energy sources and other by-products. Incidental environmental pollution of outer space is another imponderable of significance.

On cost-benefit analysis, this option may save on recurring transportation costs but processing machinery and ancillary facilities, as capital investment, would need to be installed on the asteroid which may involve heavy outlays. The infrastructure installations may be automated and robot-friendly or manually operated with human presence. Incidentally, automated systems would be much less expensive to build and deploy but manual systems are easy to operate and provide for in-house trouble-shooting. The comparative cost-effectiveness of alternatives will, of course, have to be evaluated in detail for a preferred solution.

Material Harvesting

Material extraction, also called harvesting, is the substantive part of the project and can be achieved by different methods. First is strip mining in which material is scraped off the surface of the celestial body and repeated in successive runs till exhausted or ore quality is diminished below profitability. There is strong evidence that many asteroids consist of rubble piles that make this approach to excavation possible. The second method is shaft mining. In this method, a mine can be dug into the asteroid and material extracted through the shaft. This, however, requires precise knowledge to engineer accuracy of astro-location under the surface regolith and an effective transportation system to carry the desired ore to the processing facility or to the earth centre.

The third method is specific to excavation of ores with high metallic content that can be pulverised to loose grains that can be segregated by means of magnetic devices and useful powder transported to processing facility. Thus granular trash can be discarded locally. Another material-specific method is heating. This is useful in collection of volatile materials like water and gases. Here heat can be used to melt and vapourise the matrix.[48] Thus useful components are easy to separate and waste bulk gets discarded in situ at no extra cost.

The last method is to establish complex automated factory to produce self-replicating machines. The power of self-replication is compelling and it would consume large quantities of harvested asteroidal material. This has been facilitated by technological progress in miniaturisation, nanotechnology, materials revolution, and additive manufacturing. 3-D printing technology is already in experimental use at ISS though this innovation needs a lot more research. NASA has mooted this concept in seminal form but studies assure of its feasibility in a big way.[49] Whatever be the method of harvesting, asteroids offer treasure beyond count, power beyond measure, and resources beyond imagination. Humanity is only now awakening to the riches of the bounteous celestial bodies.

FRIVOLOUS CLAIMS TO CELESTIAL BODIES

From times immemorial, man has vainly desired to personally possess the heavenly bodies and Moon has been the symbol of the ultimate wish. Eastern civilisations have personified this supreme desire; for example, Indian folklore is replete with stories of 'Chanda Mama', referring to the Moon as maternal uncle. There is a tale from Hindu mythology that Lord Krishna in his childhood, once, stubbornly insisted to possess the Moon. To comply with his desire, the imaginative parents put some water in a flat vessel and showed reflection of the Moon to pacify him. The Moon, nevertheless, remained a mystery, for many millennia, with mythical legends and popular folklore. Today, however, we know a lot about our favourite natural satellite, the Earth's Moon.

Another personification of this unfulfilled wish is evident in the tradition to name children on celestial stars and planets. A common name is Ravi, Suraj, Bhan, Aditya, Surya, Arushi, Eshan, Aftab, Khursheed and so on, which all signify an aspect of the Sun. Similarly names like Chan, Chand, Chandrika, Sasi, Rohnish, Himanshu, Nishant, Badar, Aibek, Qamar, Mehtab, Luna, Jericho, etc. take after the Moon. There are other popular names taken from other planets like Mangal, Budh, Shani, etc. This custom cuts across almost all communities and tribes in India and irrespective of the religion. This practice of naming children of both genders after planets and legends is prevalent in the Western world also.

Claims to celestial bodies on frivolous grounds or as half-serious jokes have been attempted for millennia yet none has stood the test of law with proven ingredients and substantiated evidence or the ravages of time to be recognised in custom by communities. On the other hand, ownership and possession is an innate desire of humans and a part of their instinctive nature. In fact, it is the manifestation of this instinct that has impelled mankind to growth and prosperity. Thus, private ownership or *jus in re,* meaning the right to property provides the correct stimulus for material progress. Socialism, on the contrary, induces sluggish material production and impedes economic development on both personal and community levels, except under state coercion.

Mere claim to an extra-terrestrial body, believed to exist in the cosmos, is not enough proof for ownership. This establishes only intention or animus and is not sufficient for the purpose. For ownership of property, the corpus must be acquired in the first instance and at the same time obtain its actual possession with virtual control over its usufructs as well as absolute right to disposal of the same must vest with the owner. *Jus ad rem* without possession would be inchoate and incomplete right *ipso jure*. Of course, on these parameters a first landing on a celestial body, like asteroid, that is *territorium nullius,* with appropriate intention, even for probe or exploration, may fulfil substantive conditions of an ownership claim on extra-terrestrial land and yield a right to mineral resources. This could be valid in international law of territory acquisition but not under edicts of space law.[50]

The Moon has been sold many times over and buyers are confident of obtaining possession one day, however remote and distant. In recent past, there was a seller of plots on the Moon advertising vigorously in the US and to other gullible buyers. Some Indians have also bought these.[51] *Caveat emptor*. The seller neither has the legal right to the property on offer nor has yet taken possession of the same. Without both, the offer does not stand on contract law or make for legal transfer on laws of property. Sheer payment of consideration for an uncertain and speculative promise in the future does not attract the nobility of a valid contract.

The celestial realty can also not be transferred by a gift deed or acquired by lease deed from private individuals. Such dubious transactions have happened unchecked only under loose laws of a few states in the US and also because the OST at best is confusing and at worst internally inconsistent on space property rights. But the maxim of *qui tacet negat* could be aptly applicable, and this means silence of authorities cannot be treated as acquiescence to the fact nor an adverse inference can be drawn. Therefore, a debate on ownership of space property and realty rights is likely to heat up in not too distant future.[52]

Over the last century, there have been many such cases of claims on extra-terrestrial bodies, some serious and determined, others sheer fiction or legal joke but almost all are based on the trivial argument of unclaimed property. These attempts deserve to be debunked as fictional episodes, invalid on facts and void in law. These instances not only highlight a dire need for regulatory laws that are explicit and unequivocal but also necessitate a mechanism to curb and punish such frauds on gullible people. Proper and wide propagation of rules in public interest may ameliorate the situation considerably.

Let's illustrate with a few examples. First, In 2002 Virgiliu Pop, a researcher at Romanian Space Agency, proclaimed ownership of the Sun with online register and threatened with legal notices to owners of the Moon like Bill Hope and Gregory Nemitz and other extra-terrestrial property owners to bill for charges relating to usage of the sunlight. He has later accepted in his book that a claim is just a claim unless supported by ownership deed and its registration. Even these documents add nothing more than certify the fact of its having been staked. Nevertheless, it was intended as a joke and aimed to publicise hollowness of similar claimants.[53]

Real estate on the Moon has been on sale in the US from as early as 1890. Lunar plots, defined by astral longitude and latitude grid references, and with other attractions have been peddled by unscrupulous sellers to the credulous buyers because it was easy to get a Charter for the purpose in the state of New Jersey. On 15 June 1936 Dean Lindsay, a Georgian, averred before a notary to own 'Lindsay Archipelago' comprising islands of space denoting celestial bodies. He anticipated commercial value for these rocky formations and laid his right over them as unclaimed bodies, but regrettably he did not visualise to own up the void of outer space as easement to reach the claimed celestial islands.[54]

In 1948, James Thomas Mangan claimed the 'Island of Space' to establish the Nation of Celestial Space, in short, 'Celestia' on the professed plea that humankind on earth travels 1,500,000 miles each day through the territory of Celestia. On 29 December 1948, Celestia formally applied for membership of the United Nations. It was rejected under article 4 (1) of the Charter of the UN alleging inability to discharge incumbent obligations of a state. In 1956, Mangan became critical of the UN and blamed it for being 'legally impolitic and scientifically impolite'. Later, he declared that Celestia was the only competent entity to frame laws for Outer Space and ordained all nations on earth to obey and abide by this declaration. He also proclaimed that the entry and presence of artificial man-made satellites in outer space tantamount to trespass violative of its state sovereignty.[55]

In 1952, Berklcy Science Fiction Fan Club filed a legal claim for a triangular lunar area covering three craters—Ritter, Manners and Sabine—

and sent a notice to the UN to issue patent and title. This claim was based on discovery of sylvanite in the region and was publicised in the press media.[56] In September 1954, Planet Mars Development Corporation was formed by three businessmen in Arkansas who offered to convey title to competent persons for suitable remuneration. Following the same modus operandi, in November 1955, Robert Coles constituted Interplanetary Development Corporation to offer celestial plots at one Dollar an acre against "General Quit Claim Deed".[57] Another important assertion was made in 2005 by Hope who operated "the Lunar Embassy" and boasted of having solicited 3.6 million extra-terrestrial property clients in 181 countries during three decades of his 'Unreal' estate business.[58] Thus, fraudulent sale of 'Unreal Estate' has been a near-monopoly of the US because all attempts have originated through the permissive laws of states in the US.

Outside of the US, in 1953, Janeiro Gajardo Vera, a Chilean lawyer, claimed the Moon. He approached local property registration authorities and was directed to make a public proclamation of his right to subject property. As per requirement of the applicable laws, he published his claim three times seeking adverse claimants. Fortunately for him, no objections were received by the authorities and the Moon was registered as his property and mutation endorsed in his name. The true motive of Vera, however, was to obtain membership of a club which was refused for he owned no real estate.[59] One may guess if this ruse helped him achieve his purpose.

There is, however, a specific case of a property claim to an asteroid called Eros. The US space agency NASA had made an automated robotic landing of NEAR-Shoemaker probe on Eros in 2001. Gregory Nemitz, a space activist, operating an online database styled Archimedes Institute, who had already claimed ownership to this property filed a bill on NASA and the US State Department for parking fees relating to the landing of the US satellite on Eros. It was to be expected that the US State Department and NASA would repudiate the claim and reject payment of the bill for parking charges. This is exactly what happened.

Nemitz then filed a law suit for his claim of parking fees in the US 9th Circuit Court of Appeals. Plea taken was that OST prohibits national appropriation to assert sovereignty over celestial bodies but does not specifically and explicitly deny constructive individual rights thereto. The contentious litigation was entertained by the court; but on arguments the suit was dismissed because the petitioner was not able to establish ingredients crucial to prove his case. He could neither produce legal documents of ownership rights purchased from the seller nor substantiate taking over of actual and physical possession for the property named Eros. He also could not validate the exercise of his effective control thereon. Nemitz, thus failed on both counts, germane law as well as possessory evidence.[60]

A LEGAL ANALYSIS

The corpus of space law has evolved over just half a century and is still metamorphosing. The instruments are a composite of treaties, agreements, UN declarations, and guidelines. It is partly *pacta* and partly soft law but it makes general and broad mandates some of which lack in clarity and details. It thus has grey areas of doubt and reveals chinks in law. The legality of mining of celestial bodies including asteroids is one such subject dotted with holes. Interpretations of and constructions placed on the OST almost border on the absurd though the logic apparently is robust and flawless. Sometimes syllogistic fallacies do come to the surface but confusion reigns. Under the circumstances, vested business interests are likely to prevail. The situation is still under control and redeemable. Ambiguities can be identified and cured while inconvenient specifics can be addressed, corrected and promulgated for compliance.

The legality and consequent permissibility of mining celestial bodies including asteroids can be derived from two major instruments, the OST and the MA. It is also pertinent to mention that OST contains the fundamentals and is generally treated as *grundnorm* of space law. The OST has been so widely accepted that it has been exalted to Customary Space Law in such a short span of time and is consequentially universally binding, even on non-parties. The Moon Treaty is more specific to celestial bodies regarding their exploration, use and exploitation of non-renewable resources for the benefit of all mankind. But on the other hand, it is a relatively weak instrument with few votaries and rather limited ratifications. The rest of the space law is not directly germane to the subject except for minor relevance or indirect references like environmental pollution and creation of space debris as well as their incidental consequences. So the template is clear for analysis and verdict.

THE OUTER SPACE TREATY

The OST is extra-ordinary in many respects and unique from the legal point of view. It enunciates the fundamental principles of space law that seem really new, if not truly novel. These are obligatory and binding not only on state-parties but all states internationally because of their customary force. Therefore, the legal provisions of the Treaty are mandatory for compliance whether in permissibility or prohibition of a space activity. This is international law of outer space. There may be some grey areas on which the Treaty is either not specific or is silent. These can be interpreted according to the canons of international jurisprudence or general principles of Vienna Convention on Law of Treaties, keeping the best interest of humankind in the right perspective. Indeed, the focus is now clear and fixed.

The Preamble to the Treaty

Let's begin with the Preamble to the Treaty which lays down its aims and objects. Many may, however, argue that the Preamble is not the legal text and hence merely mentions the statement of intent. This view may be technically correct but the Preamble truly embodies the best narration of human aspiration from space activities that is the welfare of all and a desire to usher in and sustain peace in the universe. The ideas are noble and thoughts sublime. The humane aspect of the Preamble is, thus, truly appealing and overwhelming *vis-à-vis* the text of the law.

The Preamble, at the very outset, implicitly accepts that outer space, though still in major part a mystery yet appears a vast reservoir of non-renewable (mineral and metal) resources apart from water availability and diverse other uses or benefits that can, in due course, accrue to humankind. Fortunately, it has now become possible to explore, prospect and confirm their presence and abundance by remote sensing and on-site visits to celestial bodies and asteroids by robot rovers. And on date, capable technology has been developed that has made it feasible to viably exploit these resources, at least in the near-earth orbit.

In view of this scenario, the Preamble begins by stating that the state-parties are 'Inspired by the great prospects opening up before mankind as a result of man's entry into outer space'. Then it recognises 'the common interest of all mankind in the progress of the exploration and use of outer space for peaceful purposes'. And exhorts the states that "the exploration and use of outer space should be carried on for the benefit of all peoples irrespective of the degree of their economic and scientific development".[61] The principles are laudable and reveal a slant towards socialist culture tempered with ultimate humanitarian purpose. This viewpoint, though not new to law, has been for the first time daringly expressed by international community in unity and with unanimity.[62]

The above clauses, though lofty in purpose, yet are pregnant with acute ambiguities and dire uncertainties. First, it accepts space activities by the states. In fact, at that time it was near impossible to imagine that private companies could muster such vast capital funds to invest in space activities, harness complex technologies, and compete with the budgets of states. Hence, these provisions preclude private enterprise with motivation for individual profit and stakeholders' benefit, unless the dividends are shared equitably among all mankind under some acceptable modality. But this would be hard to achieve because capitalistic economic order is not built on altruism and public interest. The incompatibility of espoused causes with corporate reality becomes evident. Thus there is need for change of mind-set.

The Province of All Mankind

The OST enshrines the principle that the outer space, including the moon and other celestial bodies, are 'the province of all mankind'. This concept is similar, if not congruous, to the doctrine of Common Heritage of Mankind from the Law of the Sea and the Law of Global Commons. Though similarities become apparent yet there are subtle differences of significance. For example, heritage has an implication of legacy as *res communis omnium* and carries an inherent possibility of divisibility and apportionment. And this option, whatever be its legality or illegality, has been exercised by the US in extraction of manganese nodules from the ocean seabed.

The text of the Treaty reads, "The exploration and use of outer space, including Moon and other celestial bodies, shall be carried out for the benefit and in the interest of all countries, irrespective of their degree of economic or scientific development, and shall be the province of all mankind". It becomes explicit that exploration and use of outer space belongs as a right to mankind as a whole. It could be interpreted as *res publica* laced with public trust doctrine or *res communis humanitatis* with endemic indivisibility. A comparable Indian concept of such property rights would be *shamlat* or *panchayati* land which is open to the entire village as free common grazing ground in timeless lease. Here also, the connotation of mankind includes future generations in posterity and their inherent heir-apparent right to 'the Province' of opportunities and resources of the outer space.

Further, the Treaty "recognises the common interest of all mankind" in the Preamble and directs that space activities "...shall be carried out for the benefit and in the interest of all countries...".[63] These provisions clearly point towards the stake holding of all countries in the beneficial accruals of any kind or variety from the outer space. Therefore, shares of profit consequent to commercial activities in the outer space and on celestial bodies must legitimately flow to all countries in reasonable proportion. The population of beneficiaries, thus, does not permit national or private ownership, excludes private profiteering and imposes a social responsibility to genuinely divide the economic benefits in equitable proportion. The modalities and scope of sharing may yet have to be devised amicably among the states; nevertheless, the mandate of sharing the benefits is obligatory and binding; it is not merely notional or promissory. There is, however, a school of thought which considers this sharing as 'unearned profit' and deems it unconscionable. But the merit of this argument will crumble under socialist leanings and the advantage of exploitation to the capitalist pioneers.

Non-Appropriation in Outer Space

As a corollary to the doctrine of outer space as Province of Mankind, there is another provision in the Treaty that supports and reinforces it in tandem. This is the principle of non-appropriation in outer space. The text of the Treaty states, "Outer space, including the Moon and other celestial bodies, is not subject to national appropriation by claims of sovereignty, by means of use or occupation, or by any other means".[64] This means that there shall be no national borders or flags of sovereignty on the Moon and other celestial bodies. Ideally, it secures outer space including celestial bodies as a unified expanse of 'Humankind Commons'.

The concept of non-appropriation is amplified by another clause of the Treaty, "Outer space, including the Moon and other celestial bodies, shall be free for exploration and use by all states without discrimination of any kind, on a basis of equality and in accordance with international law, and there shall be free access to all areas of celestial bodies".[65] The assured freedom of exploration and use and free access to all areas of celestial bodies, guarantees inclusivity and that there would be no boundaries, no trespass, no hindrance or let to this right of activity or to movement in the outer space. It promises an egalitarian regime of space operations in outer space with no rights to appropriate any part or portion of outer space or any celestial body for proprietary or exclusive use.

The abovementioned right is, however, regulated and subject to reasonable conditions. It stipulates that states "shall carry on activities in the exploration and use of outer space, including the Moon and other celestial bodies, in accordance with international law, including the Charter of the United Nations...".[66] The applicability of international law, including the Charter of the United Nations, complicates the scenario and solicits an interpretation. It will be seen that traditional international law on some points comes in conflict with tenets of space law. For example, territorial sovereignty and acquisition of territories by different methods are time honoured concepts of international law but space law outright negates these. In a way, however, space law acknowledges collective sovereignty and universal community ownership of all mankind over the outer space and celestial bodies, with a substratum of common interest, enjoining responsibility for sharing of benefits and towards sustainability of environment. Nevertheless, jurisprudence dictates that *lex specialibus* supersedes *lex generalis* and hence to the extent of inconsistency space law shall over-ride and duly operate.

The basic space law ordains that states cannot carry territorial sovereignty to the outer space and celestial bodies. Further, the Treaty being state-centric considers and recognises only states as participants and their activities in exploration and use of outer space as legit and licit. Therefore, a general inference can be logically drawn that there are no private property rights in outer space and on celestial bodies because states cannot confer rights beyond what they themselves have. There is, thus, no scope to accord any wider or liberal interpretation to this provision at this juncture under existing legal scenario.

Freedom of Access and Investigation

Another cardinal principle of space law contained in OST stresses freedom to all states for scientific investigation and access to all parts of outer space including celestial bodies. The Treaty provision states, "Outer space, including the Moon and other celestial bodies, shall be free for exploration and use by all states without discrimination of any kind, on a basis of equality and in accordance with international law, and there shall be free access to all areas of celestial bodies".[67] The Treaty insures this 'freedom to all states', whether signatory to the Treaty with ratification or nothing at all. 'All states' is thus an inclusive concept to cover all states globally. And this clause, at this stage, makes no authorisation to delegate such freedom to private enterprise or individual 'astro-preneurs'.

There is another similar "...freedom of scientific investigation in outer space, including the moon and other celestial bodies, and states shall facilitate and encourage international cooperation in such investigation".[68] This satisfies the quest of humans for novelty and inquisitiveness. The freedom is assured only to states and for scientific investigation and it gives no license for reckless investigative or experimental activities that may cause wanton damage or harmful destruction. The need for sustainability of pristine environment in outer space is clearly implicit in this Treaty clause.

This freedom also carries a correlative duty to respect the corresponding right of other states and not to disturb or interfere in their legitimate operations. This appears a reasonable restriction to the absoluteness of the freedom espoused in the Treaty. The text guides that, "...states...shall conduct all their activities in outer space, including the moon and other celestial bodies, with due regard to the corresponding interests of all other states parties to the Treaty".[69] From this wording, an implication can be drawn that the interests of the states, not party to the Treaty, can be ignored or violated. But not really so, because that would foul with the spirit, if not the letter, of the Treaty. Equality of states, mutuality of interests, and reciprocity of responsibility secures this freedom for all states under the Treaty and should prevail as such.

The connotation of state, in discourse so far, does not include private commercial organisations or individual entrepreneurs. These categories of business would normally operate under business ethics and will be motivated by profit concerns. Hence, the legitimacy of mining activities on asteroids by Planetary Resources and other racing astro-preneurs, for private appropriation of excavated resources, is in doubt. Further, such relaxations for private sector activities may skew the relationships because the latter may not show the same regard or sensitivity to other states that may be expected of or be voluntarily forthcoming from the space-enterprising states as per established international norms of state practice.

HINTS OF PERMISSIBILITY

Use for Peaceful Purposes

The OST permits in its Preamble '...use of outer space for peaceful purposes'. And again in Article IV of the Treaty, it enjoins, "The Moon and other celestial bodies shall be used by all State Parties to the Treaty exclusively for peaceful purposes".[70] This combination of the intent and letter of the Treaty highlights that the nature of activities in outer space to be solely for peaceful purposes. It thus raises two issues, first, that states are permitted 'the use' of outer space and celestial bodies; and second that it should be exclusively for peaceful purposes.

First, 'use' of outer space and celestial bodies is permitted to the state parties, and their 'use' can take various forms, methods and techniques. For example, the use could be visual, observatory and non-invasive like remote sensing or broadcasting. Or it can be possessory and invasive yet non-destructive like satellite landing and parking, picking of soil samples, or tourist habitations. Or the use could be intrusive, excavatory, non-renewable and destructive with possible harmful consequences like mining of mineral resources and other such experimentation.

The second aspect relates to the nature and scope of 'peaceful purposes'. The Treaty only prohibits 'nuclear weapons or any other kind of weapons of mass destruction' from placement "...in orbit around the earth,...install such weapons on celestial bodies or station such weapons in outer space in any other manner".[71] And the states 'undertake not to place' any such prohibited objects in the mentioned places. So far is loud and clear; but the Treaty nowhere defines peaceful activities by their nature, character or traits, except forbidding "The establishment of military bases, installations and fortifications, the testing of any type of weapons and the conduct of military manoeuvres on celestial bodies...".[72] With the mention of specific prohibitions in the Treaty, it can tempt to a possible interpretation that what is not specifically prohibited is permitted or condoned, hence can be deemed peaceful activity. But the validity of such an assumption is illusory.

Be that as it may, it appears certain and beyond reasonable doubt, that the use of asteroids for mining purposes is sure a peaceful activity of high order. Therefore, if government organisation or supervised agencies undertake this activity in outer space it would attract no illegality or violate ban of any kind. Further, the Treaty permits in that, "[t]he use of any equipment or facility necessary for peaceful exploration of the Moon and other celestial bodies shall also not be prohibited".[73] However, a dilemma remains whether the miner-state can claim property ownership rights to the excavated material with prerogative to its commercial disposal for private profit *in situ* or after transportation to its jurisdiction on the earth. The technology to make it fully viable is also still in incubation.

Public-Private Cooperation

But scenarios change fast. Today technology has progressed tremendously to realise the visions of yesteryears. The reach of science and advancement of technology have stretched beyond human imagination. Moon is no distant destination while Mars and Jupiter appear next-door neighbours. Deep and deeper space probes are being planned and astronauts trained for long duration stays in the outer space. These efforts are now being supplemented and gradually supplanted by non-governmental corporate entities. The shift from governmental monopoly to sharing of missions with private sector is clearly discernible and is a harbinger of public-private cooperation.

Alongside government players, private enterprise has also joined the projects and has grown into its own, financially and technologically. Some of the space activities that have been commercialised like, broadcasting and remote sensing and space tourism are already being progressively monopolised by private corporations and entrepreneurs. Private commercial operators are already here trying to broaden their reach and fervently hope to stay and prosper. It seems they now deserve some legal space for activities in peaceful uses. But law fails them in some of their endeavours and has to be contrived to gain legitimacy and extract permissibility.

An indirect mention to space operations by non-governmental entities under the provision for international responsibility of states for national activities lends some solace. The text of the Treaty reads, "States parties to the Treaty shall bear international responsibility for national activities in outer space, including the Moon and other celestial bodies, whether such activities are carried on by governmental agencies or by non-governmental entities...are carried out in conformity with the provisions set forth in the present Treaty".[74] It implies that the Treaty being state-centric, vests total international responsibility on the state, irrespective of who carries out space activities on their nationality.

This article of the Treaty further amplifies, though in a different context, that "[t]he activities of non-governmental entities in outer space, including the Moon and other celestial bodies, shall require authorisation and continuing supervision by the appropriate state party to the Treaty".[75] This means that private enterprise cannot enter space arena for operations without permission from the national state and the government is obligated to monitor such activities and audit their safety for it bears the burden of *vinculum juris* (legal liability) towards international responsibility for any damage caused by such activities in the outer space, in the airspace and on the earth.

Therefore, the Treaty indirectly admits of the possibility of space activities being undertaken by private corporate sector or even individual nationals as legal entities, but under strict governmental care and control. In a way, it will be progressive approach to reduce scramble for natural resources on the earth and mitigate possible global conflict for scarce materials by providing viable alternative sources. In consequence, this viewpoint may facilitate and contribute to global peace.

This further prods us to an assumption that the consortium of Planetary Resources may have legal umbrage. Therefore, the Corporation would certainly have obtained appropriate clearances and approvals from the US Administration under the domestic space legislation namely National Aeronautics and Space Act, 1958 and other relevant municipal laws for their proposal of intent before initiating activities to ultimately mine asteroid Eros. With the re-election of President Obama for the next term from 2013, NASA's plan for manned missions to asteroid shall remain on cards for execution as scheduled for 2025. However, with election of Trump as President in 2017, the emphasis is shifting back to humans on the Moon.

Not-Prohibited implies Permitted

Some jurists take comfort from an old dictum of law that what is not prohibited is deemed to be permitted as an adverse inference. This is a characteristic of criminal law codes which, in generality, list out and elaborate on prohibited actions and behaviour to be eschewed by the nationals and that in the event of violation or breach it would attract stipulated punishment. This method of enumerating aberrant behaviour generally applies to criminal law because the list of good conduct and acceptable acts would be too long and yet not comprehensive making it a bulky reading. Hence prohibitions are included in the code and what does not find mention therein is considered a lawful activity and hence not punishable. The logic is indeed simplistic and *lato sensu*; it does not find valid application in many other branches of law, more so international law.

This dichotomy may not always be exact and sacrosanct as, at times, it may be difficult to simplistically classify human behaviour on opposite sides. There would be grey areas of doubt and acceptance because contrary of false may not always be true and *vice versa*. Hence, there is an inherent syllogistic fallacy in this form of bifurcatory logic or binary segregation. This line of thinking may not invariably lead us to the right answer which has to be specific and categorical in law. There is a legal maxim, *qui tacet negat,* which also challenges this opinion.[76] The maxim means silence of authority cannot be treated as acquiescence to the fact nor can an adverse inference be drawn. Arguably, in this particular context of an international treaty, inclusion of such a provision regarding prohibition on individual appropriation would have been irrelevant; and contrarily non-inclusion assures no *jus in re* for private ownership.[77]

Let's therefore look for what is permitted and patently legal under the Treaty rather than take shelter under flimsy premises of tenuous validity. It is arguable that there is clear and legit right to private companies to operate in outer space and on celestial bodies for commercial purposes. The permission in OST to non-governmental entities becomes vivid from the responsibility that the Treaty attaches to the governments to regulate and supervise private activities by its juridical nationals. Further, there is not even a suggestion prohibiting commercial or business activities in space.

An interesting example of such understanding of the law can be derived from the policy of the Government of the United States that has given a bold go-ahead to a US conglomerate, Planetary Resources Inc., for mining on an asteroid. This authorisation, it seems, has been given under the 10th Amendment which states, "...all powers not delegated to the Federal Government, nor prohibited by it to the States, are reserved to the states or to the people...". Even US Commercial Space Launch Competitiveness Act, 2015[78] confers and supports similar rights. Thus for the US citizen, right to mine in outer space, by direct inference, devolves on the people, though no private claim or title to the mined property is tenable.

In the alternate mode, accepting that if private enterprise and individuals are not properly authorised to undertake commercial space activities; or private ownership of celestial mineral resources is specifically denied, the solution then is not in placing devious construction on Treaty law but to suitably amend the same to make it beneficent and transparent to be able to lawfully reap incumbent advantages so utterly necessary to continued human progress. Time appears ripe to shed prejudices, thaw frozen mind-sets and strive for another wave of reforms in international space law, preferably proactively, in consonance with technological vision and to satisfy growing needs of humanity. Wisdom lies in this option.

THE MOON AGREEMENT

Another international instrument of significance on the subject is the Moon Agreement. It is, of course, more elaborate and detailed on specifics than the OST yet it is also not comprehensive enough to provide direct and straight answers to all and sundry queries. Nevertheless, the Agreement takes full advantage of the experience of the working of the OST in its drafting and synergises the efficacy of the corpus of space law. This Agreement admits of chinks in law and the need for additional regulatory provisions as and when technology advances and man's reach to celestial bodies becomes a safe routine and capabilities to exploit them assume diverse forms not envisioned so far. That stage has now been reached, almost. Therefore, let's search for lawful permissibility of space mining activities by private sector and enterprising individuals under the legal template of the MA.

Preamble to the Moon Agreement

It is satisfying that the Preamble appreciates "...the achievements of states in the exploration and use of the Moon and other celestial bodies," and acknowledges that multifarious benefits "may be derived from the exploitation of the natural resources of the Moon and other celestial bodies".[79] The foreboding possibility and financial viability of such exploitation could cause a scramble for riches leading to crass competition that may result in chaotic economic order.

The negotiating nations were conscious as well as apprehensive of unregulated, unseemly developments in this sphere and thus desired "to prevent the Moon [and other celestial bodies] from becoming an area of international conflict".[80] To ameliorate the situation of scant and sketchy documents of space law, the state parties realised "the need to define and develop the provisions of these international instruments in relation to the Moon and other celestial bodies, having regard to further progress in the exploration and use of outer space".[81]

The Preamble to the Agreement reveals that it is a visionary document that envisaged myriad benefits from the natural resources of the Moon and celestial bodies and that such development will be in the interest of mankind and for the welfare of humanity. Global resources were no longer sustainable and had nearly exhausted. Therefore, avaricious scramble for scarce minerals and metals, so vital for human progress, could be perilous. This document, therefore, recognised the alternative potential sources from outer space and attempted to supplement the existing corpus of space law by elaborating on details and filling some specific gaps. The Agreement, though, establishes a legal regime to regulate orderly exploitation of space resources yet it is still not comprehensive in rules of governance for curbing violations and sharing of accrued benefits. Nevertheless, it was indeed a wise step though a short one.

Applicability of the Moon Agreement

The MA carries a special provision on its applicability. This clarificatory clause seems pertinent and specific. The text reads, "The provisions of this Agreement relating to the Moon shall also apply to other celestial bodies within the solar system...except insofar as specific legal norms enter into force with respect to any of these celestial bodies".[82] It is thus clear that it, rather realistically, applies to the celestial bodies within the solar system only and not, so ambitiously, to the entire universe. It is also pertinent to note that the MA excludes its applicability to Earth under the same article and leaves governance of Earth through its own existing laws, customs and practices.

Unlike the Outer Space Treaty, the MA makes a sensible exception that its legal regime is not applicable to the earth.[83] This exclusion saves the Agreement from a lot of embarrassment, confusion and misinterpretation of its provisions. An allied clause further clarifies, "This Agreement does not apply to extra-terrestrial materials which reach the surface of the Earth by natural means".[84] This implies that the Agreement does not concern itself with self-executing functions of natural order in the solar system but only pertains to and regulates exploratory investigations and various uses of celestial bodies by activities sponsored or activated by humans.

It has been discussed earlier that asteroids are rock formations orbiting around the Sun and are thus admittedly celestial bodies of our solar system. There is no denying that other solar systems would also be having similar orbiting bodies and then multitude of stars in galaxies and an infinite number of galaxies complicates understanding of the celestial system. Further, the above provisions of the Agreement make it amply clear that by virtue of its applicability to celestial bodies within the solar system it becomes directly relevant to asteroids and in regulating human activities on such bodies. Therefore, the MA is the other fundamental international instrument from where to search for legal permissibility of mining on the asteroids and solutions to other germane issues.

Province of Mankind

The MA reiterates this principle cherished in the OST. In fact, here it is in more elaborate and detailed form. This averment can be vindicated from the text of the Agreement. "The exploration and use of the Moon [and other celestial bodies] shall be the province of all mankind and shall be carried out for the benefit and in the interest of all countries, irrespective of their economic or scientific development. Due regard shall be paid to the interests of present and future generations as well as to the need to promote higher standards of living and conditions of economic and social progress and development in accordance with the Charter of the United Nations".[85] The amplifications are inclusive in approach, explicit in content, and laudable in character.

The concept of Province of Mankind outlined in the Agreement puts emphasis on use of Moon resources for collective welfare of humanity and to equitably improve the standards of living of mankind and all-round development as envisaged in the Charter of the United Nations. The best part is that the Agreement does not, in legal egotism, restrict the benefits to *states-partes* only but pledges 'in the interest of all countries'. The altruism enshrined is commendable and should be emulated in other realms of activity as well. Another aspect of liberalisation of the concept relates to the concern for future generations thereby, implying optimal use and sustainability of non-renewable resources. We only need to sincerely live up to these ideals.

Apropos mining of asteroids, it becomes amply clear that the use or appropriation of these are the province of mankind and cannot be individually or privately appropriated either as a rock body or exploitation of extracted material for private profit. It belongs to mankind collectively and has to be sustainable for future generations. And lastly, the benefits must accrue to and flow towards all countries equitably and without any discrimination. Profits cannot be pocketed entirely by private mining enterprise, if at all such activity is deemed permissible, and shall have to be proportionately shared globally according to modalities to be negotiated and promulgated.

Common Heritage of Mankind

The doctrine of Common Heritage of Mankind (CHM) is rather old. It has been concurrently developed along space law and gained acceptance with Law of the Sea. It has been adapted to cover the Moon and celestial bodies in the outer space. This concept had become relevant because of abundant availability of metals and minerals deposited in the rock formations of celestial bodies and the progressive feasibility of their economical exploitation by technological advances. It also seems certain that governmental public funding may not be devoted to such ventures of commercial interest and private enterprise may enter this arena due to lustre of the lucre. Corporate sector is, therefore, poised for this leap and is ready with requisite wherewithal to make such exploitation a reality sooner than envisaged. However, one obstacle to this race is explicit legality under the Space Treaty and germane space law.

An analysis of the related provision in the MA will clarify the situation. The Agreement states, "The Moon [including other celestial bodies] and its natural resources are the common heritage of mankind...".[86] This clause means and reiterates the OST to aver specifically, "The Moon is not subject to national appropriation by any means of sovereignty, by means of use or occupation, or by any other means".[87] If we allude to applicability clause under Article 1 of the Agreement, the implication is that asteroids cannot be appropriated in any manner, by any claim, or by any means.

To clarify any ambiguity, the Agreement further amplifies, "Neither the surface nor the subsurface of the Moon, nor any part thereof or natural resources in place, shall become property of any state, international intergovernmental or non-governmental organisation, national organisation or non-governmental entity or any natural person". Any remainder doubts are dispelled by subsequent clause that states, "The placement of personnel, space vehicles, equipment, facilities, stations and installations on or below the surface of the Moon, including structures connected with its surface or subsurface, shall not create a right of ownership over the surface or subsurface of the Moon or any areas thereof."[88] Thus, the mineral resources of celestial bodies can under no circumstances be appropriated for state benefit or private purposes. It attracts the applicability of the maxim, '*Jus ex injuria non oritur*' which means that no right arises from a wrongful act and solely applies to the wrongdoer.

CHM is a concept of collective ownership which implies that everybody owns the property and at the same time nobody owns it in the true sense of the meaning to make use of it individually or enjoy its usufructs privately. Thus, a Marxist-Socialist leaning is discernible in the concept. This is not encouraging because of the fact that Socialism has since failed and collapsed as an economic system and now is merely a cliché. This may not be taken to imply that the alternative of Capitalism is bound to succeed. This prospect is equally suspect, for Capitalism on earth has so degenerated that it needs to be revisited, remedied and revitalised in consonance with entrepreneurial domination, contemporary work motivations, and societal aspirations to make it suitable for outer space milieu and exuding hope of success.

In other words, it is *jus publica,* an indivisible right of public as international community. Its collective character is based on the model of trusteeship of property but under the space law regime it lacks appointment of a trustee to take decisions in the best interest of the trust and the beneficiary mankind. Thus, this *jus utendi fruendi,* meaning a right of liferent, enjoyment of sustainable usufructs, lies partly dormant and held in abeyance. Perhaps, United Nations is best suited for this task of instituting a governing mechanism and that it may establish an appropriate organ or organisation or authority competent to discharge the assigned mandate of duty and responsibility. Perhaps, an idea of World Space Authority (WSA) can be mooted for this objective.

The Agreement has envisioned a paradigm of CHM and has incorporated some guidelines within it for the utilisation of natural resources discovered on the Moon and other celestial bodies including asteroids. Under the Agreement, "States...undertake to establish an international regime, including appropriate procedures, to govern the exploitation of the natural resources of the Moon... [when the same] is about to become feasible".[89] Man has pushed the frontier forward everyday with success and the envisaged stage of action has been reached. Time is now ripe for framing of suitable regulations 'compatible with the purposes' for sustained excavation and proper sharing of the proceeds over and above conscionable profits of production and reasonable rewards for cumulative efforts to making such exploitation practical and fruitful.

The purpose and object of the proposed 'regime' to be established shall include:

(a) The orderly and safe development of the natural resources of the Moon;
(b) The rational management of these resources;
(c) The expansion of opportunities in the use of these resources;
(d) An equitable sharing by all state parties in the benefits derived from those resources, whereby the interests and needs of the developing countries, as well as efforts of those countries which have contributed either directly or indirectly to the exploration of the Moon, shall be given special consideration.[90]

The proposed management regime highlights three aspects for attention. First, development and utilisation of natural resources shall be at an optimal level and in a rational manner keeping in view their sustainability. Second, profits from the venture shall be equitably and globally shared by all countries irrespective of their being space-faring country or not. Third, there shall be special consideration for the needs of the economically weaker nations as also for those who have bestowed funds and efforts in the development process and cumulative exploration efforts as a result of which commercial exploitation became a profitable reality.

Notwithstanding the above advantages, the permissibility of exploitation by private enterprise remains a moot issue mired in legal controversy and classic ambiguity. Clarity is lacking and that is a dire disincentive to captains of business. Economics of industry is prodded by profit motive and stimulated by an unencumbered legal environment for production. Both parameters are weak and suspect because profits are besotted with ominous risks of sharing and legality shadowed by a penumbra of controvertible doubts. The mining moguls resent the concept of universal sharing as unearned profits that are reprehensible on economics and unconscionable in law. Therefore, legality of mining of asteroids by private industry remains plagued with uncertainty and apprehensions to become an enigmatic decision.

Freedom of Access

The MA, in a similar vein as the OST, reiterates freedom of access to all parts of the Moon, even below its surface. In a way this freedom is more expansive than that contained in the Treaty as it assents digging to reach the subsurface in the process of exploration and use of the Moon. Thus, the use can involve excavation and the Agreement grants permission to move 'freely over or below the surface of the Moon'. This broader freedom should, by logic of applicability, rightfully extend to other celestial bodies and asteroids. A ray of hope for lawful mining of celestial bodies is sighted.

The above proposition can be supported from specific text of the MA that reads, "States parties may pursue their activities in exploration and use of the Moon anywhere on or below its surface...".[91] These activities are further facilitated by authorising states to:

"(a) Land their space objects on the Moon and launch them from the Moon.

(b) Place their personnel, space vehicles, equipment, facilities, stations and installations anywhere on or below the surface of the Moon" and these "may move or be moved freely over or below the surface of the Moon."[92]

This permission or right appears absolute but *summum jus, summa injuria,* meaning extreme right is extreme injury. Therefore, just as every freedom is circumscribed by reasonable restrictions, so is this one. It also carries a set of curbs to ensure equal enjoyment of freedom to other parties operating in the field. First rider states, "Activities of states...shall not interfere with the activities of other states... [and] where such interference may occur, the...concerned shall undertake consultations...".[93] This aspect assumes importance in respect of asteroids which are relatively much smaller bodies and some of these may not be able to accommodate two sets of facilities and installations by two competing mining firms. Consultations would be mandatory under such circumstances.

"To this end, all space vehicles, equipment, facilities, stations and installations on the Moon shall be open to other state parties...[on] reasonable advance notice of a projected visit...to assure safety and to avoid interference with normal operations in the facility to be visited."[94] Accommodative attitude, reciprocity and transparency are the obvious objectives. Therefore, the Agreement expects states to fulfil the incumbent obligation and provides for a procedure of consultation for resolution of any controversy and for ultimate dispute redressal. Diplomatic channels may be used to good effect in this regard.

The MA further exhorts that to resolve any problem due to any hindrance or interference in the smooth operation of activities, when the other party does not discharge its obligation or breaches the right of the other, cooperative consultation is the best solution. The Agreement thus requires that, "State parties shall be guided by the principle of cooperation and mutual assistance" which "should be as wide as possible and may take place on a multilateral basis, on a bilateral basis or through international intergovernmental organisations".[95] Consultations shall be with "mutual understanding and with due regard to the corresponding interests of all other states parties".[96]

The second restriction relates to ensure that activities 'in the exploration and use of the Moon are compatible' with the Agreement and the latter is emphatic in maintaining that status by asserting, "The Moon shall be used by all states Parties exclusively for peaceful purposes".[97] The directive is clear and explicit with no equivocation whatsoever. Therefore, peaceful, exploratory and scientific activities are recognised and approved. This logically implies that mining of asteroids for mineral resources is a peaceful activity and is permissible and lawful.

Apart from the stipulation for peaceful activities, there are, however, scattered cautions and prohibition on certain activities e.g. military manoeuvres. There is also a prohibition on issuing "Any threat or use of force or any other hostile act or threat of hostile act on the Moon...[and] it is likewise prohibited to use the Moon in order to commit any such act or to engage in any such threat in relation to the Earth, the Moon, spacecraft, the personnel of spacecraft or man-made space objects".[98] The agreement thus ushers an era of amity and concord in outer space domain and secures peaceful environment for peaceful activities.

Lastly, there is another obligation imposed in enjoyment of freedom which relates to dissemination of information about activities on the Moon to ensure safety of orbital movement and non-interference in operations. The Agreement requires that, "States parties shall inform the Secretary General of the United Nations as well as the public and the international scientific community, to the greatest extent feasible and practicable, of their activities concerned with the exploration and use of the Moon. Information on time, location, orbital parameters and duration shall be given in respect of each mission to the Moon, as soon as possible after launching, while information on the results of each mission, including scientific results, shall be furnished upon completion of the mission ...or periodically...".[99]

The above stated provision ordains that information gathered on missions to the Moon and results of scientific investigations on the celestial bodies are to be disclosed and widely propagated which means such information should become part of public domain and assimilate into the knowledge fund of humanity. Thus this requirement is in the interest of scientific fraternity to build and catalogue a 'knowledge-paedia' for the benefit of posterity. Further, by inference, this should also apply to visits, by robots or astronauts, to the asteroids. Understandably, this puts the secrecy and intellectual property rights relating to natural assets discovered on the celestial bodies and advantages of experimentation in jeopardy.[100] The business dilemma in freely sharing such information is apparent and discernible.

HINTS OF PERMISSIBILITY

The MA also throws scattered hints of permissibility for use of celestial bodies, including asteroids, for peaceful purposes which could easily comprise mining activities. The references though are not direct yet inferences can be drawn by logical deduction, legal casuistry, and liberal gloss over the provisions.

Despite all the optimism, many of the conclusions remain shrouded in doubt or can be viewed with scepticism. Some hints of permissibility are discussed in succeeding paragraphs to buttress above contention.

Freedom of Scientific Investigation

A freedom guaranteed under the MA relates to "scientific investigation on the Moon by all state parties without discrimination of any kind, on the basis of equality and in accordance with international law".[101] This further provides that, "the states parties shall have the right to collect on and remove from the Moon samples of its mineral and other substances".[102] Thus digging, quarry and excavation on the Moon, and by analogy on the asteroids, is permitted but only for small quantities as samples. *In situ* resource utilisation (ISRU) on celestial bodies may still be condoned by the Agreement but large quantum of excavated ores for commercial purposes and private appropriation is in doubt.

Regarding custody and ownership, the Agreement allows that, "[s]uch samples shall remain at the disposal of those state parties which caused them to be collected and may be used by them for scientific purposes. States parties shall have regard to the desirability of making a portion of such samples available to other interested states parties and the international scientific community for scientific investigation".[103] This clause, though hints at sharing, virtually entrusts permanent possession of extracted samples to the state that caused the materials to be brought from the Moon or celestial body. However, it is silent on commercial disposal or exchange for consideration. Such instances of impropriety are on record and have been discussed below.

There are, of course, precedents where excavating countries have brought back small quantities of surface crust from the Moon for investigation and experiments. Such samples have loftily been declared as assets of mankind and for scientific benefits to humanity at large. But the reality of possessory treatment of moon-rock has belied such pronouncements as propaganda for goodwill. These altruistic statements have later been recanted to claim virtual ownership to the samples.

For example, the US through its six Apollo landings brought back 842 pounds of lunar material. NASA has strictly controlled use of the material, and less than 10 percent has ever been experimented upon and truly analysed. NASA has further claimed that the lunar samples are 'a limited national resource, a future heritage, and that samples be released only for approved applications in research, education, and public display'. The US government has vigorously prosecuted anyone arraigned to have improperly obtained any such samples.

The Soviet Union has also, through three Luna robotic missions, brought back approximately 300 gm of lunar material for scientific experiments. But a part of it was presumably stolen and has been resold by private individuals to unknown buyers. A small portion of the Russian lunar soil sample was exchanged with NASA in return for a certain quantity of US moon-soil sample. This was a barter transaction with consideration from both sides and thus smacks of property transfer.

Both instances clearly establish a streak of ownership right for their exclusive handling, possession and control; and the power to exchange what was truly their 'trust holding'. Considering these precedents, right or wrong, it can, in a way, be argued that though celestial bodies themselves, as a whole, as they exist in nature, are not subject to appropriation yet detached portions of a celestial body can be made succursal to state or private ownership and considered as exclusive possession, if so removed from the space body and transported to the earth. Interestingly, a new interpretation has been proffered that if an asteroid is removed from its natural orbit by any means and stationed near or docked to another planet, it no longer remains that 'original' celestial body. Its character changes and it thus becomes a captured resource that can be prone to exploitation thereafter.

State Responsibility for National Activities

State responsibility is a well-established principle of traditional international law and based on this doctrine similar provisions, enunciating state responsibility for national activities to be in consonance of law, is contained in the OST and the MA. Both instruments concede of activities on the Moon and other celestial bodies by non-governmental entities which can inferentially include individuals and other juridical persons. The only rider that these treaties impose is that such activities shall be carried out under authorisation of the state and its supervisory control. This mandate seems solely for good governance and linkage to the liability.

The MA articulates that states "shall bear international responsibility for national activities on the Moon [and other celestial bodies], whether such activities are carried on by governmental agencies or by non-governmental entities, and for assuring that national activities are carried out in conformity with the provisions set forth in this Agreement. States parties shall ensure that non-governmental entities under their jurisdiction shall engage in activities on the Moon only under the authority and continuing supervision of the appropriate state party".[104] In fact, responsibility and liability have a symbiotic relationship. Therefore, states are liable *in delictum* of operative norms of activities immaterial whether committed by state agencies, or non-governmental entities or individual entrepreneurs.

Thus this provision affords a good hint that activities on the Moon and celestial bodies including asteroids can be undertaken by non-governmental entities which could comfortably connote private corporate sector and individual entrepreneurs as *persona juris*. There is no doubt that such activities have to be for peaceful purposes which can cover mining of asteroids. But the problem arises whether these entities can remove materials from such bodies in commercial quantities and dispose of such removed material for private consideration and also retain the accrued profits in personal kitty. This, however, is likely to contravene the principle of CHM and its tenets.

AN APPRAISAL

The canvas of present day space activities shows that private sector and industry support to governmental space agencies for cargo and crew transportation services by space carriers like SpaceX and Cygnus Spacecraft is bound to stay and progressively expand. Other competitors may also be tempted to join this fray. Further, public budgets are not the right source for such commercial ventures and outlays for these must flow from private kitty. Similarly, corporate sector contribution to peaceful space activities, like communications, television broadcasting, streaming and remote sensing *et al*, whether from the earth-based infra-structure or in outer space, is of great consequence and set to prosper.

Further, state exchequer cannot be the appropriate financer for such non-strategic, commercial projects and has gradually weaned itself off such activities and rightly so. Capital outlays for these must come from private corporate finances. This trend has since commenced and entrenched itself for its usefulness and appropriateness and cannot be reversed. Hence, more 'astro-preneurs' are joining the space business. However, a clarification is still due on legality and legitimacy of certain actions of private enterprise in outer space. Indeed, our specific query here relates to mining of asteroids, and as a corollary other celestial bodies, by corporate business entities for commercial purposes and for private profit. This is discussed in succeeding paragraphs.

The Existing Legal Provisions

The Outer Space Treaty

The OST has no direct and categorical answer and to wade through the complex provisions to hunt for indirect hints of permissibility through the legal labyrinths seems dubious and suspect. It is an honourable treaty between states and binds them to its contents for adherence. In fact, all international treaties are state-centric and *Pacta sunt servanda* is a grand *mantra* of international law. Thus private legal entities and nationals are not *sui juris* or true subjects of this *specialibus* international law. Therefore, an inferential deduction will not bestow substantive rights on such entities. Their operations will be identified with their nationality and treated as such.

An isolated and ancillary reference in relation to state responsibility and international liability has been liberally glossed to suit vested interest. By object and intent, governmental supervision could allude to certification of space-worthiness of industrial support and products from the earth and documentation of astronauts as nationals and so on. This is, thus, a peripheral provision with no direct mandate or explicit permissibility of commercialisation for private profit. Further, the import and vigour of the dictum that what is not prohibited is permitted is rather slender. Drawal of adverse inferences from the silence of statutes do not make for infallible argument or robust law. Therefore, involuted interpretation of space jurisprudence should be unwelcome; it can be unhealthy precedent, even dangerous trend.

The Moon Agreement

The predicament is no better under the MA except that it admits of possible benefits to humanity from exploitation of material deposits on the Moon and other celestial bodies. In view of the limitations of technology at that point in time and apparent remote possibility of its development, acquisition and exploitation by private sector, the Agreement is reticent and carries few perspicuous clarifications on the subject. It is, of course, a well-accepted generality that law trails technology and this Agreement has followed the trend.

The Agreement has thus not taken a proactive approach of a confident visionary to establish a futuristic legal regime. Hence a precise answer to our hypothesis is lacking and solution must lie elsewhere. Fortunately, the MA carries an inherent provision for review after ten years so as to repurpose and adapt itself based on empirical lessons or to technological advancement or contemporary needs of humanity. This promises a possibility for the intended change in law though international politics and vested interests may foul the due process to introduce suitable amendments rather arduous.

Legality: Re-Orbiting of Asteroids

Doubts have been cast on the belief whether asteroids are immovable property in the universe and hence real estate. The pivot of the argument is that the celestial bodies are all moving in their respective orbits and their operating apogees and perigees are rarely prone to variation. Therefore, the constancy of their orbit, in essence, renders them immovable from their pre-determined position or movement. Given the desiderata of their existence and orbital nature, to term these as immovable property or celestial real estate may be inaccurate or debatable nomenclature. At best, these are floating bodies on predetermined routes which may tend to vary occasionally or at sporadic intervals due to interaction of natural gravitational perturbations in the cosmos.

Another line of thinking, taking a cue from floating bodies, treats these as 'moving rocks'. Of course, the natural movement of these bodies cannot be denied and has to be conceded but other differences must also be acknowledged. Scholars of this school have compared asteroids to icebergs of Antarctica on the criterion of their movement alone. But the analogy is incomplete and incongruent on both spatiality and functionality approaches. The icebergs are random roving bodies and their movement is highly prone to circumstantial influences of flow, blockages and temperature that affect their size and speed. Whereas, celestial bodies, in variance, have fixed orbits, constant speed and invariable body mass. Changes in these parameters, if at all, are occasional and unpredictable.

The prime characteristic of celestial bodies is immovability from their orbit as opposed to 'movability' of terrestrial property from any position or point. The crux of the argument is that asteroids are now susceptible to external control under human intervention with possibility to change its orbit, location and size by human effort and volition. This makes asteroid, as a whole, moveable property. In another way, human activity can now reach the asteroids and carry on with acts of mining and extraction on and below the surface of the celestial body at will and pleasure. Further excavated material can be transported away from the asteroid to deplete the non-renewable mass of the body. This may be considered as its 'movability' in instalments or in tranches. Both criteria can now be satisfied.

There is another aspect to human control on 'movability' of an asteroid as a whole body. Scientific knowledge has made it theoretically feasible and development of technological applications will soon render it possible. It is now easily imaginable to alter the orbit of an asteroid or move it closer to the earth or the Moon or even a designated orbiting industrial platform for commercial exploitation. More so, with costs of transportation of extracted ores continuously diminishing and becoming economical due to re-use of space hardware, harvested asteroid may soon lose its very existence. Thus, human ingenuity has converted asteroids into exploitable, movable properties and put on them realty value of significance, yet their very existence individually will be in danger.

In this context, NASA has plans to lasso and capture an asteroid by Orion spacecraft with robotic technology and drag it to a stable orbit near the Moon by 2021.[105] It is not the feasibility of the project but the legality of tagging, bagging and shoving an asteroid that is in doubt despite encouraging opinion by American scholars. First, Prof Matthew Schaefer considers it a lawful space manoeuvre. Despite the mandate for non-sovereignty under Article II and free access to all areas under Article I of OST, this activity falls within the freedom of exploration and use. The logic does not appear logical.

Schaefer believes that the US is not causing any interference till access to another competitor is denied for the same celestial body at the same time. It is not likely to happen that a competitor targets the same asteroid concurrently, given that there is a large population of NEAs and it would be a highly challenging mission on technology that cannot be accomplished by many space-faring states. The pioneer takes the first right. In fact, it is the late comer that must show 'due regard', else it 'would cause harmful interference' in corresponding interests of other country's continuing activities and the second nation of advent is required to 'undertake appropriate international consultations' under Article IX. Therefore, any obstructive interpretation would negate the guaranteed right of the pioneer nation to explore and use any celestial body. Thus, there are no definitive or significant legal barriers, at this stage of the proposed space mission.

However, the proposed activity has an imponderable risk. In case, the retrieval effort fails to achieve the mission and puts the asteroid in an uncontrolled orbit thereby affecting the space environment and/or threatening damage on Earth. This would attract the Liability Convention,[106] but this convention establishes 'fault-based' standard for damage in space and a variety of factors like that it was not launched from the US territory or an advance global warning would defend and mitigate the liability. Further, liability provisions refer to damage by space objects and an asteroid would not qualify as legit source of damage here. But tenets of International Law may find relevance and concern; and the US would have to bear international responsibility for its national activity in space, irrespective of the agency undertaking this.[107]

Space law and jurisprudence is rather nascent and evolving and has not been able to keep abreast with galloping techno-space-applications. Of course, there is no specific law permitting or denying capture of an asteroid but strong inferences can be drawn from OST, that are not in favour of the proposed activity. There should be little doubt that tagging an asteroid and relocating in another orbit for exploration, excavation or strategic import, for exclusive individualised activities, would tantamount to national appropriation, in defiance of OST. Therefore, if such an adventure goes unprotested, it could set a precedent and create a foundation for an international customary norm in terms of "space property rights".[108]

George Robinson maintains that law on asteroid retrieval initiative is unclear and issues involved are complicated. He further asserts that the venture cannot be vouchsafed for the benefit of all countries and all humankind and hence not a legit experiment in space. In the same breath, he comments that the OST is a paper tiger, a Treaty that has gone old too soon and stands in need of extensive re-evaluation and amendment to meet current challenges and visualised certainties like resource exploitation, space migration, and celestial habitations. However, in *abundanti cautela,* the US could entertain consultations under Art IX of the Treaty because the proposed activity may affect the outer space environment or lead to unforeseen consequences. The suggested cautionary step will set a desirable precedent as this provision has never so far been invoked pre-emptively.[109]

The Common Heritage of Mankind

However, in a way, the Agreement has shown vision to acknowledge the possibility for exploitation of the mineral resources of the Moon and other celestial bodies as and when appropriate technologies are able to render such activities plausible from all angles. It therefore introduced the yet untried and untested, doctrine of CHM for trusteeship control of celestial bodies, to ensure sustainable extraction of mineral resources, governance of mining companies, and distribution of accrued profits among legitimate beneficiaries. It is, as conceptual federalism, intended to foster international solidarity through a common right of humanity to collectively enjoy the benefits from the total celestial realty. However laudable, this doctrine remains controversial, enigmatic and an amorphous notion of contemporary international law.

The Doctrine

The doctrine of CHM constitutes an accumulation of estate of all celestial bodies in the outer space for preservation and shared management towards the benefit of mankind. The peculiarity of this concept is that since it designates CHM as collective and community property it becomes *res communis* with a life-time share and stake of every living human being at all times including all future generations. At the same time, these islands of territory are neither subject to state sovereignty on international plane nor invested in individual as property rights flowing from his ingenuity of action or effort of discovery and exploitability. It is neither divisible nor 'partition-able' to any specific demarcated piece of area for any particular person as shared right of heir-apparent. The concept thus has two dimensions—inter-spatial for realty and inter-temporal for generations. This virtually makes

CHM *res nullius* meaning that it is literally owned by nobody yet collectively owned by all humanity that is entitled to enjoy its usufructs.[110]

The concept of CHM seems congruous to the Hindu Law of Coparcenary relating to joint holding of family property. The meaning of parcener is sharer and its French equivalent is—*arconier* and in Latin *jartitio*. This law is customary in intestate deaths and concerns the descent of lands as ancestral property of inheritance from a common ancestor to two or more co-heirs possessing an equal hereditary title to them. The distinguishing feature of this inheritance is that there is unity of title, interest and possession claimed by descent that restrains co-parceners from demanding partition by the writ of traditional law itself. Thus the concept of coparcenary appears fairly congruous to the CHM where individual shares are not marked with defined limits, accepts the interest of posterity and that there can be no division of the common corpus under any circumstances. Another analogous doctrine is that of *Waqf* among the Muslims.

However, the MA, in nutshell, defines the broad parameters of CHM as envisaged in the concept. These are orderly and safe development of natural resources, their rational management and optimal sustainability for future generations,[111] expansion of opportunities for exploitation of mineral deposits, and lastly, an equitable sharing of benefits by all the states of the world and not to be solely appropriated by the mining magnate or the cartel of space-farers. The benefits are broadly comparable to enjoying of usufructs of the estate and must permeate to all states.

Critical Analysis of the Doctrine

The doctrine of CHM, howsoever laudable, has not found due favour globally. Even signatory states are reluctant to ratify the Agreement resulting in a small number of adherences. The industrialised space-faring states are wary of its socialistic tenets and ingrained obligations. As a result, depositaries have received few accessions[112] despite the UN sponsorship and support to this Agreement.[113] The concept is being re-mulled on reality check with change of mind-set. Therefore, it is mired in doubts and controversies and its original appeal has worn off.

Of course, there are reasons for this disenchantment with the Agreement and the principles of CHM. The latter advocates inclusivity of all states globally and sharing of benefit with non-participants in space efforts and even non-members to the MA. This affirmative action of aid and benefit appears too benevolent. First, the space-faring nations find that inclusive sharing of profits with non-space-faring states that have no contribution in the exploration, prospecting and mining activity; and associated fund utilisation or risk-taking should have no right to or stake in such proceeds.[114] The proposed arrangement of mandatory doles to all states, irrespective of their participation in outer space activities or even membership of the MA, is unwarranted, iniquitous and injudicious. This is deemed as unearned profit and unconscionable in law.

Second, in pursuance to affirmative action for aid and benefit, it is felt that the criteria for disbursals from profit-proceeds should neither be identity-based nor pegged to classifications of non-development or under-development. The action-aid ought to be need based and welfare should hold the primacy of objective. It should be able to stimulate and reinforce a system of empowerment and growth rather than seep in as unproductive subsidy to mask inefficiency and sloth and scandals. Rightfully, inclusivity funds should be invested in drivers of change and development like transfer of technology and training of manpower for sustained benefits with high multiplier effect on the native economy.

Third, the regime of CHM calls for rational governance and effective management of spatial areas and mineral resources because these are not subject to control of any political state. But it remains legally nebulous and an indeterminate governance model. Economics of enterprise seeks a stable environment of legal controls and production parameters but such a regime does not exist to provide surety or security of private right to property or grant of mining leases of reasonable duration to break even to regular profits. In view of the uncertainty of legal permissibility of private mining and lack of management infrastructure, corporate sector is shying away from investment planning thus inhibiting resource development.[115] The dismal scenario has led some scholars like Martin Menter to pronounce that this has caused *de facto* moratorium on mining activities in the outer space.[116]

Fourth, it has ideological implications. The CHM model seems fairly akin to Marxist socialism where total property is under state control while in CHM it could perhaps be under trusteeship of the United Nations. Thus, management of basic production resources would be under bureaucratic supervision and profits of economic activity shall be shared with all the states, by and large, according to their needs and not in proportion to their effort in the process of production. This economic model, with minor variations, has worked in Communist countries in half the world for over half a century.

It was a great populist idea for revolution but it could not provide a growth-oriented economy because you cannot multiply wealth by dividing it. Further, as is wisely said, what one person receives without working for, another person must work for without receiving because the government cannot give to anybody anything it does not first take from somebody else. Disincentive to work and produce is inbuilt in the system that gradually leads to a perception of inequity and injustice. No wonder, in the end the system has failed in its espoused objective and has collapsed. The communist economies are faltering and are striving for an overlay of capitalism. Their economic survival is at stake unless they modify their economic ideology. Thus the changeover to mixed economies is in process in many erstwhile Communist countries including Russia and collapse of communist stance in China is well presaged and leads to empirical despondance.

This discourse holds no brief for Capitalism because that also requires amends and needs to be revisited with a new mind-set. This is only to caution that history does not repeat itself, it is we who do not learn from our mistakes. Following this wisdom and experience, the CHM of the MA must incorporate the drivers of capitalist economy for optimum wealth generation blended with modified and moderated sharing of proceeds in cash and kind and technology that allocate due rewards to human labour and cause visible justice, particularly to developing states. At the same time, the CHM regime must show ample regard to entrepreneurial skills and more than interest, returns on investment for the gestation period and risk-taking.

Lastly, there is an apprehension from procedural angle. The CHM as enunciated in the Agreement is in raw form with mere statement of objectives. It has yet to be developed into a proper regulatory framework with statutory authority for enforcement and compliance. International negotiations are arduous and laborious task beset with tantrums and setbacks that have to be handled with deft diplomacy and pertinacious resilience. This is no easy task, as experienced in generic obstacles encountered in long drawn negotiations over Law of the Sea Treaty[117] and hiccups during conclusion of

Wellington Treaty on Antarctica. Nevertheless, the Agreement shall have to be repurposed and refurbished; and the paradigm of CHM evolved with care and sensitivity and soon enough. Human ingenuity promises to tackle all these challenges.

Need for Review of the Moon Agreement

A farsighted provision contained in the MA relates to its review after a period of ten years from the date it comes into force. It thus vouches for a futuristic and proactive approach although such review is optional and need-based and premised on experience gained on its operation. The relevant clause of the Agreement reads, "Ten years after the entry into force of this Agreement, the question of the review of this Agreement shall be included in the provisional agenda of the General Assembly of the United Nations in order to consider, in the light of the past application of the Agreement, whether it requires revision".[118] Hence, refurbishing of the Agreement is due by stipulated time factor, advances in space technology, the rise of private 'astro-enterprise', and the force of circumstances.

The MA can boast of an inbuilt flexibility rarely found in international treaties and similar instruments. This character is better revealed by the next clause that states, "However, at any time after the Agreement has been in force for five years, the Secretary General of the United Nations, as depositary, shall, at the request of one third of the State Parties to the Agreement and with the concurrence of the majority of the State Parties, convene a conference of the State Parties to review this Agreement".[119] It thus infuses the possibility of upgrading and sustaining its relevance to times based on lessons learnt from experience and effectiveness of its operation. Further, it also provides for an easy and simple procedure to requisition a conference when so deemed necessary. The foresight and simplicity exhibited is indeed overwhelming.

The last clause of this Article is still more radical and forward looking. It mandates a task and purpose for the review conference rather than groping for an objective or merely act on the agenda of the requisitioning states. The text dictates, "A review conference shall also consider the question of the implementation of the provision of the article 11, paragraph 5 [a legal regime to govern the exploitation of the natural resources], on the basis of the principle referred to in paragraph 1 of the article [the Common Heritage of Mankind] and taking in account in particular any relevant technological developments".[120] This is also in pursuance to undertaking given by the states "to establish an international regime...to govern the exploitation of the natural resources of the Moon...This provision shall be implemented in accordance with article 18 [for review of the Agreement] of this Agreement".[121]

Another germane clause, that provides ample support in tandem to the above provision and elaborates on the procedural formalities to facilitate and formulate an international regime in deference to their undertaking to do so, urges states that, "[i]n order to facilitate the establishment of the international regime referred to in paragraph 5 of this article, state parties shall inform the Secretary-General of the United Nations as well as the public and the international scientific community, to the greatest extent feasible and practicable, of any natural resources they may discover on the Moon".[122] This declaration of discovery assumes significance because all exploitable assets on the celestial bodies merge into the property pool of CHM while exercise of national sovereignty and private property rights in the outer space are strictly prohibited.

These provisions are a great solace and leave sufficient room for specifically devising a governing modality for regulating use and appropriation of locked-up mineral deposits on the celestial bodies. These also provide guidelines and principles to work on a purposed and updated regime responsive to contemporary human needs on the earth, in concordance with state-of-the-art technology and infusing camaraderie of public-private partnership because states may not venture into mining projects with funds from public exchequer. A ray of hope is visible from here and this path can be trodden with confidence to reach legality of mining the asteroids by private corporate sector. The legal regime, yet to be devised, can be adapted to grant of leasing rights for mining to private ventures for a reasonable period to be sufficiently profitable for sharing dividends to benefit all countries.[123]

Need to Establish a Strong Governing Authority

Assuming that desired changes in Treaty law can be brought about by international cooperation to enable private enterprise to undertake mining of asteroids and other celestial bodies with express legitimacy, another perplexity accosts us. This relates to the need for a regulatory authority because the relatively low key setup of OOSA does not appear equal to the task.

Perhaps, WSA can be suggested as an alternative to the existing dispensation. The Authority could thus be entrusted with enlarged job structure of executive, regulatory, and quasi-judicial effectuations.

This organisation in the form and style of WSA, under the aegis of the United Nations would implement the legal and regulatory framework for the management of human activity within the outer space and on the celestial bodies. The Authority so proposed would, therefore, need proper mandate, commensurate structure, judicial jurisdiction, requisite teeth, standard procedures, and administrative funding. It could work on the lines of International Civil Aviation Organisation (ICAO), improve thereupon and exercise authority commensurate to the tasks assigned, including grant and management of commercial leases for regulated mining on celestial bodies. It may also have to discharge duties for inspection and verification to stem over-exploitation and encroachments. Some of the functions can be outsourced or delegated to commissions or committees.

An additional task of this Authority would be to govern the CHM as total aggregate of estate of humanity on a trusteeship basis and ensure optimal and sustainable use of celestial deposits and regulate their exploitation through allocation of leases on rent. This system can be likened to the custom of Co-parcenary under the Hindu Law for management of joint family estates or to a comparable system of *Waqf* properties under the Muslim Law. The functions of the Authority would also entail finalisation of lease agreements at best terms, monitoring of the operation of commercial leases on celestial bodies, ensuring collection of rent from the lessees, a mechanism for conflict resolution and modalities for distribution of proceeds to the stipulated beneficiaries as per formulated proportions. An additional task would be to control and regulate excavation to allay environmental concerns. This task would demand high standards of probity, impartiality par excellence, and stewardship ethics of the highest order.

It is pertinent to mention in connection with grant of mining leases that no company or commercial entity has a fundamental right to a particular lease on specific terms. In a suit on the matter, the Supreme Court of India has judicially decided on merits that no private company has an unalienable right to gain mining lease or prospecting license of a designated area. In such cases discretion exercised may not suffer from any legal infirmity or impairment of obligation.[124] Similarly, certain areas on the celestial bodies may, conjecturally, be reserved in public interest for infra-structural needs or for environmental conservation or scientific exploration. WSA as leasing authority should have adequate powers for such compulsive reservations in the larger interest of mankind.

There is, however, a rebellious view that attempts to demolish above arguments. It maintains that the very idea that everything in the universe is somehow collectively owned by the mankind, which is governed by governments, then it should be up to them to grant 'permission'. The idea of a super authority to supervise and authorise is obnoxious and pernicious. Their view is that UN control is an utterly corrupt and inverted view of property rights. The germane laws of the earth uphold that this rights flow from individuals and the first right even for unclaimed territories[125] or sighting of new lands goes initially to the individual and then only gets transferred to the state by the nexus of nationality.

In the same vein, those pioneer corporations investing in R&D and working to gain access to an asteroid and mining its natural resources should be able to, by all logic, own and appropriate this property. It is well known that mining of an asteroid is an extremely complex, difficult, life-risky, and expensive endeavour and fruits of their labour cannot be denied and they should, under all arguments, own the accruals of their entrepreneurial risk-taking. The state can legitimately tax the income or the gains but cannot snatch away their fundamental economic right to property and profits. Further, the sole rational purpose of a government is to uphold and protect the rights of its nationals including their property and assets, irrespective of its location. That is a duty of the state that it cannot abdicate. In the worst eventuality, if the asteroid miners are sensible and capable, they may shift to space settlements and ultimately form their own extra-terrestrial governments in order to safeguard their inherent right to property. The scenario seems imaginary and too fictional, at least for the present, albeit probable.

CONCLUSION

The appraisal compels us to conclude that the existing space law affords no scope for legitimately deducing that mining of asteroids by private enterprise for commercial disposal of material so extracted and be sole retainer of profits. No provision of OST or the MA permits large scale excavation of ores from celestial bodies for processing or sale *in-situ* or on the earth because they have neither mining lease rights to the mineral deposits nor property rights to the extracts under the CHM regime. Further, profits from such ventures, if permitted to operate, are to be apportioned equitably with developing states and a reasonable share also paid to the space-faring nations who helped to make such exploitation technically feasible and economically viable. However, the modalities and proportions for division of proceeds among the beneficiaries are yet to be devised.

Anyway, such a vast reservoir of mineral deposits so useful to humanity for its sustenance and betterment cannot be allowed to lie dormant and unutilised indefinitely. Therefore, rational considerations urge us towards liberal but termed grant of property rights on celestial bodies because these can be useful drivers and effective stimuli for development and growth beneficial to mankind for the avowed purpose. Thus, the tussle and choice is between grant of individual property rights or resigning to a slow rate of progress in the realm of outer space and delayed exploitation of resources so vitally required on earth for global uplift. The only rider should be judicious regulation of such rights, effectuation of mining leases for sustainable exploitation of natural resources and honest compliance by stakeholders. This needs an 'advanced' rule of law for celestial governance to escape chaos and the easiest route to evolve and implement this would be through revision of the MA.

Wisdom prods us and exigency commands to put this proposed order in place, soonest. So, all stakeholders may sincerely strive to achieve this paradigm with open mindset and by putting values above populist politics or parochial interests. Acceptance, rather than expectation, should be the *mantra* towards this goal. And, we should not waste time on sheer symbolism and vague promises but work for effective regulations to yield tangible results.

In the end, it must be accepted that a new legal regime with stricter regulatory mechanism for commercial exploitation of extra-terrestrial resources would need better governance of the bounteous celestial treasure deemed to be held in responsible trusteeship. It would also need to provide for equitable sharing of allocated profits for common benefit of all countries. These are contentious and sensitive issues and would need a high benchmark of accountability and transparency. An organisation in the form of WSA, to begin with, may efficaciously acquit itself of incumbent duties successfully, professionally and diplomatically. It is, of course, a proposal in raw, skeletal form that can be widely debated and suitably refined.

NOTES

1. Refer website <asterank.com>
2. *Treaty on Principles Governing the Activities of States in the Exploration and Use of Outer Space, including the Moon and Other Celestial Bodies, 1967.* (In short OST or Outer Space Treaty).
3. Ibid, Article VI.
4. *Agreement Governing the Activities of States on the Moon and other Celestial Bodies, 1979.* Popularly called the Moon Treaty or the Moon Agreement.
5. Ibid, Article 4 (1).
6. Ibid, Article 8 (1).
7. Ibid, Article 1 (1).
8. Ibid, Article 11 (1) and (3).
9. Ibid, Article 11 (5) and Article 18.
10. AP report from Tokyo, "Japan probe arrives at asteroid after 4-year space odyssey" in *The Times of India* (Chandigarh Edition), June 28, 2018, p. 14.
11. IAU was founded in 1919 and it officially demoted Pluto to a dwarf planet status in 2006.
12. Megan Gannon, "Can You Buy Exoplanet Naming Rights? No, Astronomy Group says", in Share, April 12, 2013.
13. It is a word from Swihili language that means "sky".
14. SETI is Search for Extra-Terrestrial Intelligence.
15. Megan Gannon, "Can You Buy Exoplanet Naming Rights? No, Astronomy Group says", in Share, April 12, 2013.
16. Chales Q. Choi, "Asteroids: Fun Facts and Information about Asteroids" in Space.com, November 21, 2014.
17. *The Times of India* (Chandigarh Edition), June 19, 2018, Times Special page.
18. http://zeenews.india.com/news/space/young-delhi-boys-discover-asteroids_791993.html. Accessed on 8 August, 2012.
19. The Daily Mail, London, 21 July, 2012. http://www.business-standard.com/generalnews/news/asteroid-as-big-ascity-block-to-hurtle-past-earth/35012/. Accessed on 21 July, 2012.
20. Two "Mainbelt" asteroids have been provisionally discovered in August, 2012 by four schoolboys from Delhi (India) which have been confirmed by further observations. The team used a complex procedure called "Astrometrica" using exclusive data to look at specific part of the sky for moving objects over a period of time. It is a rare feat deserving of commendation.http://zeenews.india.com/news/space/young-delhi-boys-discover-asteroids_791993.html. Accessed on 28 August, 2012.
21. Chales Q. Choi, "Asteroids: Fun Facts and Information about Asteroids" in Space.com, November 21, 2014.
22. The Book of Knowledge, vol. 5, pp. 210-11 (London, The Waverley Book Company Limited, Year not shown, possibly 1958).
23. Ibid.
24. L. Wilson, K. Keil, S. J. Love (1999). "The Internal Structures and Densities of Asteroids". *Meteoritics & Planetary Science* **34** (3): 479–483.
25. Calla Cofield's report from Space Commerce Conference, 2016, "Extra-Terrestrial Gold Rush: What's Next for Space Mining Industry" in Space.com, November 21, 2016.
26. Ibid.

27. The team comprised Nikku Madhusudhan and Olivier Mousis.
28. Reported by Chris Wickham, *REUTERS,* First posted: Thursday, October 11, 2012 09:36 AM EDT.
29. For additional information see John S. Lewis, *Mining the Sky: Untold Riches from the Asteroids, Comets, and Planets.* (Perseus, 1997).
30. Chales Q. Choi, "Asteroids: Fun Facts and Information about Asteroids" in Space.com, November 21, 2014.
31. The Book of Knowledge, vol. 5, pp. 210-11 (London, The Waverley Book Company Limited, Year not shown, possibly 1958).
32. Chales Q. Choi, "Asteroids: Fun Facts and Information about Asteroids" in Space.com, November 21, 2014.
33. Interestingly though, this unplanned landing on EROS became a matter of claim for spacecraft's landing and parking charges by G. Nemitz, who asserted ownership of this asteroid. On refusal of payment, he sued NASA and the US government in a US court. Nemitz, eventually lost the legal suit.
34. ESA 2010 MPS OSIRIS Team.
35. The Associated Press report, "Space info—Asteroids" published by FoxNews.com, January 21, 2014.
36. Reported in *The Telegraph* (USA). Details not officially announced.
37. Ryugu is named after an undersea palace from a Japanese folklore.
38. Refer website <asterank.com>. Also refer Times of India (Chandigarh edition), September 6, 2018, Chandigarh Supplement, p. 7.
39. AP report from Tokyo, "Japan probe arrives at asteroid after 4-year space odyssey" in *The Times of India* (Chandigarh Edition), June 28, 2018, p. 14.
40. Mike Wall, "Japanese Spacecraft approaches a dumpling-shaped Asteroid" in Space.com, June 15, 2018.
41. Brian T O'Leary, Mining the Apollo and Amor Asteroids, 197 *Science* (1977): 363. Also see Tom Gehrel, ed., Asteroids, 1979.
42. For more details refer Mark Sonter, "Mining Economics and Risk-Control in the Development of Near-Earth-Asteroid Resources" in *Space Future.* Accessed on 8 June, 2006.
43. SOPL is a constellation of reflectors, deployed onto orbits, to channel power from the Sun to a chosen point in the Space.
44. "Cosmic collisions and the longevity of non-space faring galactic civilizations" in *Interplanetary Collision Hazards*, Pasadena, California, USA: Jet Propulsion Laboratory - NASA, 1998. Accessed on 1 July, 2012.
45. Psyche is an asteroid of M-type with a diameter of 1 km.
46. "Tech Billionaires bankroll gold rush to mine Asteroids". *Reuters* News report 24 April, 2012.
47. John Brophy, Fred Culick, Louis Friedman *et al* (April, 2012). "Asteroid Retrieval Feasibility Study". Keck Institute for Space Studies, California Institute of Technology.
48. David L. Kuck, "Exploitation of Space Oases", Proceedings of the Twelfth SSI-Princeton Conference, 1995.
49. Robert Freitas, William P. Gilbreath, ed. (1982). Advanced Automation for Space Missions, NASA Conference Publication CP-2255 (N83-15348).
50. Reasons discussed later in the Chapter. Under international legal requirements for establishing claim to Territory or property, the discoverer must touch or step on the land body.
51. It was reported in Newspapers in 2011 that Ms. Mayawati, the then Chief Minister of UP (India), was gifted one such plot on the Moon.
52. Natalie Wolchover, *Life's Little Mysteries*, Space.com, 24 April, 2012.

53. Virgiliu Pop, *Who Owns the Moon? Extra Terrestrial Aspects of Land and Mineral Resources Ownership*, Springer, 2009.
54. Ibid, p. 2.
55. Ibid, p. 3.
56. Ibid, p. 4.
57. Ibid, p. 6.
58. Ibid, p. 2.
59. Ibid, p. 5.
60. Nemitz v/s the US (2004), US District Court, Nevada.
61. The Preamble to the Outer Space Treaty.
62. Declaration of Legal Principles Governing the Activities of States in the Exploration and Use of Outer Space, UN General Assembly resolution 1962 (XVIII), adopted on 13 December, 1963.
63. Treaty on Principles Governing the Activities of States in the Exploration and Use of Outer Space, including the Moon and Other Celestial Bodies, 1967. Article I.
64. Treaty on Principles Governing the Activities of States in the Exploration and Use of Outer Space, including the Moon and Other Celestial Bodies, 1967. Article II.
65. Ibid. Article I, paragraph 2.
66. Ibid. Article III.
67. Ibid. Article I, paragraph 2.
68. Ibid. Article I, paragraph 3.
69. Ibid, Article IX.
70. Ibid. Article IV, paragraph 2.
71. Ibid. Article IV, paragraph 1
72. Ibid, Article IV, paragraph 2.
73. Ibid. Article IV, paragraph 2.
74. Treaty on Principles Governing the Activities of States in the Exploration and Use of Outer Space, including the Moon and Other Celestial Bodies, 1967. Article VI.
75. Ibid.
76. G. S. Sachdeva, *Outer Space: Law, Policy and Governance* (New Delhi, KW Publishers, 2014), p. 166.
77. For a detailed discussion on the subject, refer G. S. Sachdeva, ibid, pp. 165-204.
78. HR 2262. The President of the US signed it into law on 25 November, 2015.
79. *Agreement Governing the Activities of States on the Moon and other Celestial Bodies, 1979.* Popularly called the Moon Treaty or the Moon Agreement. Refer the Preamble.
80. Ibid, the Preamble. Words in parentheses are added.
81. Ibid, the Preamble.
82. *Agreement Governing the Activities of States on the Moon and other Celestial Bodies, 1979.* In short, the Moon Agreement or MA. Article 1.
83. Ibid.
84. Ibid. Article 1, paragraph 3.
85. Ibid. Article 4, paragraph 1. Words in parentheses are added.
86. Ibid. Article 11, paragraph 1. Words in parentheses added based applicability under article 1.
87. Ibid. Article 11, paragraph 2.
88. Ibid. Article 11, paragraph 3.
89. Ibid. Article 11, paragraph 5.
90. Ibid. Article 11, paragraph 7.
91. Ibid. Article 8, paragraph 1.
92. Ibid. Article 8, paragraph 2.

93. Ibid. Article 8, paragraph 3.
94. Ibid, Article 15, paragraph 1.
95. Ibid, Article 4 (2).
96. Ibid, Article 2.
97. Ibid, Article 3, paragraph 1.
98. Ibid, Article 3, paragraph 2.
99. Ibid, Article 5, paragraph 1.
100. Ibid. Also refer Article 11, paragraph 6.
101. Ibid. Article 6, paragraph 1.
102. Ibid. Article 6, paragraph 2.
103. Ibid.
104. Ibid, Article 14, paragraph 1. Words in parenthesis are added.
105. Leonard David, "Is NASA's Plans to Lasso an Asteroid Really Legal" in *Space.com,* August 30, 2013.
106. Convention on International Liability for Damage Caused by Space Objects, 1972.
107. Leonard David, "Is NASA's Plans to Lasso an Asteroid Really Legal" in *Space.com,* August 30, 2013.
108. Michael Listner in Ibid.
109. Article IX of the OST has been once invoked post facto after Japan and China executed Anti-Satellite Test in 2007. Refer Leonard David, "Is NASA's Plans to Lasso an Asteroid Really Legal" in *Space.com,* August 30, 2013.
110. For more details, refer Kemal Baslar, *The Concept of Common Heritage of Mankind,* Martinus Nijhoff Publishers, 1998, p. 80ff.
111. Ibid.
112. Only 17 ratifications till end of 2017.
113. As on December, 2017 only 17 states are parties to this Agreement. Most space-faring countries have neither signed nor ratified the Agreement. India, though a signatory, has not ratified yet.
114. Ricky J. Lee, *Law and Regulation of Commercial Mining of Minerals in Outer Space*, Space Regulations Library, Springer, 2012, p. 203.
115. Ibid, p. 204.
116. Refer Martin Menter, *Astronautical Law*, US Industrial College of Armed Forces, 1959. Digitised in September, 2010.
117. UN Convention on Law of the Sea, 1982.
118. *Agreement Governing the Activities of States on the Moon and other Celestial Bodies, 1979.* Article 18.
119. Ibid.
120. Ibid. Words in parentheses added for clarity.
121. Ibid. Article 11, paragraph 5. Words in parentheses added for clarity.
122. Ibid. Article 11, paragraph 6.
123. Ricky J. Lee, *Law and Regulation of Commercial Mining of Minerals in Outer Space,* Space Regulations Library. Springer. He has suggested "to create a new regulatory regime."
124. *Monnet Ispat and Energy Ltd, vs. Jharkhand and Central Governments.* Supreme Court Cases, July, 2012. A gist of the verdict was published in Times of India, 28 July, 2012.
125. Such a case has recently happened on African continent where an Indian has staked claim to the unclaimed geographical territory. He traced this vast tract of land from Google maps and verified from boundary demarcations of adjacent countries. He has applied to the UN for separate recognition because law maintains that occupancy creates a right *in rem* on unclaimed properties or territories.

CHAPTER THREE

Commercialisation of Astro-Estate

Legal Implications of Celestial Habitations

INTRODUCTION

Humanity became a space-faring species on 12 April 1961 when cosmonaut Yuri Gagarin was rocketed into orbit high above the earth on a 108 minute space flight. He was thus the first human being to enter space. Within weeks of this record, an American astronaut, Allan Sheppard, was blasted into space on 5 May 1961, reached an altitude of 115 miles (185 km) and splashed down in the Atlantic barely 30 miles (48 km) away from the launch site. This flight lasted 15 minutes and is recorded as the shortest flight till date. Since then, cosmonauts from many nations have flown into outer space, orbited the earth, and achieved many more firsts.

The first persons to set foot on a land other than the earth were astronauts Neil Armstrong and Buzz Aldrin. They made the first Moon-landing aboard Apollo 11 and the Eagle Lunar Module landed on the Moon on 20 July 1969. Armstrong stepped outside the Lunar Module first, followed by Aldrin. Theirs were the first human feet stepping on the surface of the Moon and it was commented, 'A small step for man and a giant leap for mankind'. Their moon-walk lasted two hours and thirty one minutes. It was a historic moment though a few astronauts from different countries have visited the Moon on later opportunities. The longest stay on the Moon has been by astronauts Harrison Schmidt and Eugene Cernan in December 1972. They spent 75 hours on the Moon and performed moon-walks for a total period of 22 hours. The astronauts say that the moon dust smells like gunpowder and is extremely soft.

These iconic achievements by the astronauts have excited many young and old adventurous brave hearts to travel to the outer space, visit the Moon or Mars, and to even stay there as permanent resident, regardless of the consequences. This popular upsurge of interest in space erupted in the last decade of the last century, when advertisements appeared for 'Honeymooning in Zero Gravity'[1] and affordable space rides at US $ 98,000.[2] Another forecast promised, "First Tourists to blast off to Space in 2001".[3] Well, this did not materialise but it did not fail either because efforts in the direction are propelled by many and are still persistent and concerted.

Humanity is witnessing the third travel revolution; the first being invention of the wheel and the second being petrol-driven vehicles. And now, we are on the cusp of a third great travel revolution of space travel on rockets. Parodying aviation, it may be called 'Spaciation'. In this context, Blue Origin of Jeff Bezos now urges to plan a holiday in space for the year 2018.[4] This seems probable because Blue Origin has successfully test fired a reusable sub-orbital rocket called New Sheppard for the seventh time and that is a tremendous success. This vehicle is expected to fly a tourist capsule with a capacity for six passengers to an altitude of more than 100 km above the Earth.[5] This estimation now seems realistic and can be relied upon.

At the same time, Richard Branson's Virgin Galactic is selling tickets for commercial flight on its 'six-passenger, two-crew' SpaceShipTwo for US$ 250,000. And then, there are other private corporations also in the fray and competition in commercial space travel segment is heating up. The latest offer for the super-rich with adventuresome spirit wanting to escape this planet for eight days in luxury environs is pegged at $ 55 million per passenger. This is from Axiom Space; and Hollywood celebrities Brad Pitt, Leonardo Di Caprio, Angelina Jolie, Kate Winslet[6] and Katy Perry, among others, have reportedly opted for it. The tourist spacecraft will be "a mash-up of boutique hotel, adult space camp and NASA-grade research facility. It is designed to hover approximately 402 km above Earth".[7] The tariff includes 15 weeks of training and acclimatisation also. The service is expected to start in 2022.[8]

It is hotly promised considering that the successful development of reusable vehicles for commercial space travel will eventually reduce the cost of an orbital trip to $ 100,000. This would be a common man's dream. Therefore, the public response to offers of space travel is encouraging and promising, particularly, from the US, Japan and Germany. In fact, currently there is a sort of competition among the populations of New York and Washington DC to travel or migrate to a space habitat like the Moon Village or the Mars Colony.[9] This may reflect an ominous trend of the millennium.

Safe and successful space transportation will eventually take humans to space-floating spaceships, like the ISS, that may actually be hotels or motels offering exciting holiday packages for exclusive experience of near-Zero gravity, celestial sights in *lumiere* splendour, unexplored cosmic perspective, and a thrilling enjoyment of a new genre which may be well worth the risk and expense. Other destinations could be resorts on the Moon where one could stay on a short trip; or a sojourn, or may be, even for permanent residence patronizing a one-way ticket to the Mars; or as member-citizen of ASGARDIA.[10]

In view of the evolving safe and competitive space travel opportunities and gradually reducing tariffs, the ensuing trend of space tourism and migration may strengthen. Therefore, among the multifarious commercially exploitative uses of the celestial bodies, one such use could be for human habitations, whether for a short visit or for permanent residence or to escape annihilation on Earth. Various opinion polls on this intention and sale of even one-way ticket to the Mars[11] show that the human race seems prepared and ready for migration to other celestial bodies in the outer space regardless whether it is a one-way ticket or a return ticket. This implies that humans are willing to go to space jaunts and celestial habitations as tourists, holiday seekers, and temporary visitors or even for permanent living forsaking their affection to and affiliations with the mother Earth. This change of mind, stirred feelings, and overwhelming desire to migrate portend a different sentiment and disenchantment with present habitat. The trend is ominous and disconcerting.

Whatever be the reasons for such an intention to migrate, it puts a certain commercial value on astro-estate on habitable celestial bodies like the Moon or Mars, among other possibilities. This means that a consideration for such realty is imaginable and can be negotiated by the state or corporate enterprises or even desirous individual tycoons. This modus operandi operates on terra Earth and the same transaction procedure can be transported to the celestial bodies in the outer space. But for the present, who owns the Moon or the Mars and has a right to offer a tenancy or transact sale of the realty in individually usable parts? The seeds of commercialisation of astro-estate are here and we just wait for them to sprout and blossom, and, to our surprise, it may happen pretty soon.

HABITABLE DESTINATIONS IN SPACE

This proposition presupposes that safe and regular transportation service to the habited celestial body is available at scheduled frequency or unscheduled charters to fare paying passengers. This is becoming feasible and public service space transport operations may commence within a few years. Towards this end, competitive efforts are being made by SpaceX, Virgin Galactic, Blue Origin, and other aerospace giants to start 'offerable' public service operations. Promising indication emanates from successful experiment of Blue Origin to test-fire a reusable rocket vehicle for sub-orbital services.[12] This will carry tourists to an altitude of more than 100 km in a capsule of six luxury seats and a crew of two astronauts. It constitutes the flight of the next generation and further progress will continue step by step.

Besides Blue Origin, SpaceX, and Virgin Galactic, there are other private corporations also in competition that are equally engaged in quick-pace activity to reach the goal post earlier. Other runners in this race for space business are Bigelow Aerospace and Axiom Space, who intend to offer similar services and sooner too. Among these, Axiom Space plans to cater for luxury segment at premium tariffs. It is believed that China as well is racing fast in this direction to pip the American giants at the finish line. Its plans and execution for commercial space travel appear at advanced stage.

A luxury space hotel is in the same league. A start-up, Orion Span, has plans to launch Aurora Station in 2021 and accommodate guests in this hotel from 2022. Frank Bunger, Founder and CEO of this enterprise unveiled his idea at Space2.0 summit in San Jose on 5 April, 2018.[13] Aurora module architecture and interiors are simple and can house two crew and four guests. It will orbit at 200 miles above Earth and initially offers no extra-vehicular activities (EVA) like spacewalk. If the demand grows, it can add more modules and get bigger. It is ultimately planned to convert this station into "Space Condo" as a sustainable human habitation where cubicles will be individually sold for reasonable consideration.[14]

Another important parameter of habitability turns to availability of life-support systems on the celestial body. Among others, the two most vital ones are the presence of water for human survival and for creating splitable hydrogen as fuel; and some sort of locally available material like Helium that can be used or converted to meet power and energy needs. It is pertinent to mention here that there is a global movement spearheading to declare water and its variants like ice, available on celestial bodies, as an economic resource of value. Further, the locale must provide pliable regolith or material that can be used without much processing for *in situ* construction and other civil engineering needs. It is understood that the Moon surface is soft and dusty. Besides, there are other ancillary considerations while selecting a habitat location like nearness and reachability from the landing site and proximity advantages to other logistic functions. Local cultivation is another attractive parameter. Based on these availability criteria, possible habitation destinations can be discussed.

Most of the celestial colonies are advertised to be self-sufficient settlements. This is because replenishment logistics of daily needs to be imported from the earth for tourism business and permanent settlers is neither feasible nor an economical proposition. Therefore, the locals will have to grow adaptable breeds of agriculture, horticulture and kitchen garden crops. For other items also, they will have to explore and find substitutes of processed and recycled products. Towards this end, astronauts at ISS have, for over two decades, indulged in astro-bio-culture experiments to grow greens and their efforts have yielded good results.

Zinnias were the first flowers to bloom and then sunflowers blossomed in 2012. The crew has tasted fresh lettuce leaves, Zucchini and an occasional helping of fresh vegetable to alleviate their food blues. In the Russian Chamber of ISS, wheat, pepper and rice have been grown. Dwarf wheat was grown earlier on Mir space station. And now, six broccoli seeds have hitched a hike to the ISS for experiments. Three of these seeds are embedded with probiotic bacteria to help plants grow without water, fertilizer or gravity. So has algae and other plants been sent for experimentation. Agro-scientists are hopeful of positive results from the contribution of such microbes in vegetation growth.[15] It should, therefore, be possible to carry agro-harvesting techniques like Hydro-ponics and Aero-ponics to the Moon and Mars.

It is believed that astronauts had taken advantage of a personal planter box to tend by this 'Do-it-Yourself' (DIY) therapy and have reaped psychological benefits of gardening in their isolated environment and sterile interiors. Scholars like Charles Guy have studied plant-human interactions and have experimentally established that man has an instinctive affinity with other life-forms, called 'bio-phillia', and can get peace of mind and tranquillity in return. Peggy Whitson grew six soybean plants in a box at ISS in 2002 and confirmed it has psychological perspective for relaxation and a soothing feeling. Another advantage of greenery could be to purify air through photo-synthesis. NASA is also pondering over the possibility of farming on Mars to make available food supply for the mission planned for 2030 and to achieve this, has created a veggie chamber at ISS in January 2016. The experiment seems successful.

Early Visualisations of Space Habitats

Space colonisation is neither a new idea nor a novel concept. It has been doing the rounds among astro-physics academics, surreal artists, and Scientific-Fiction thinkers for almost a century, when even technology for space travel had not developed. The earliest recorded design of space habitat in the early twentieth century can be credited to an Austro-Hungarian rocket pioneer, Herman Potocnik. Described in his book,[16] his structure is a 100 foot ring-shaped station that would rotate to generate artificial gravity. He also provided a large parabolic mirror that would focus sunlight on water pipes to heat them and generate steam power.

In an another visualisation, Gerard K O'Neil designed a space habitat in the form of two rotating 20 mile long cylinders that are provided windows with reflecting mirrors for sunlight. An O'Neil type colony would have 500 sq. miles of living space that could accommodate and support up to several million populations.[17] It was indeed an ambitious project that proposed construction with local lunar materials but did not cater to the energy needs of the colony or its inhabitants. Again in 1929, JD Barnal proposed a spherical habitat 9.9 miles in diameter that could house up to 30,000 people.[18] But such theoretical concepts never took practical shape.

The idea, however, got impetus in 1970s' with NASA's focus after lunar landing by Apollo and gained currency as technology advanced to make space transportation feasible and economical. In 1975, a Stanford University Group designed a 10,000 person space habitat in the form of torus. The station would rotate once per minute to generate gravity. Lunar regolith and rubble could be used to coat the outer surface of the ring to provide radiation shielding. Space elevators would carry visitors from a docking hub at the centre to the outer habitat ring in commutation of distances.[19]

Gradually, however, the interest so generated started taking different imaginative shapes and novel visualisations to solve global challenges ahead, to transform our world by unlocking hidden market opportunities, and put us on path to space society. Precise avowed purposes of such distant-habitats were three, the first being, to create new habitable lands for fast expanding global population. The trend of population explosion had, in fact, become apparent early in the last century and this thinking had slowly started taking shape.[20] The present predictions, however, from Bezos to Musk and their business peers, promise safe, regular and economical space travel rather soon and that will not only help orbital trips or visiting the space domain but also afford opportunity to colonise the habitable celestial bodies for relatively longer stays or permanent residence.[21] Humans may thus soon become a multi-planet species.

The second purpose is to ensure survival of humanity in case of a global holocaust resulting in total annihilation of mankind on earth. This thought is prompted by Hawking's sentiment that future of earth and humans is not safe and that it could migrate somewhere in the universe to save the Homo sapiens from total extinction. Stephen Hawking warns that humanity is vulnerable to extinction and may have just less than 600 years to leave the earth and settle elsewhere as hedge against catastrophic destruction and to be able to re-propagate there so as to escape cataclysmic wipe out.[22] Else, it may face extinction and revival only by the fortuitous will of God.

Elon Musk expresses the same paranoia for different reasons. Humanity's brutal and bellicose past provides ample justification for prospecting and pursuing human settlements on the Moon and Mars. He believes human civilisation faces threat from asteroid strike, climate change, global nuclear holocaust, or the genie of artificial intelligence. Our planet, thus, can be crowded, polluted and a crazy place for healthy, sensible living. Instinctive human pugnacity and risks from competitive and irresponsible politics can be other frightening factors towards catastrophes beyond human imagination and control. Thus planet earth may plunge into dark ages if human breed and seed is not preserved elsewhere, so that it may one day return to its mother planet to rejuvenate and resuscitate it from Dark Age.[23] The vindication for establishing celestial habitations sure seems unimpeachable.

The third purpose of space habitats is to create wealth by exploiting natural resources so abundant on celestial bodies and so depleted on the earth. In fact, humankind has nearly exhausted its natural resources which it still needs so direly for its betterment and welfare. Remote sensing and contact observations have assured of limitless resources of minerals and other energy materials that can be excavated, processed in situ and final product transported to the earth. Technology is in sync with such assumptions and projects are being propped up by private enterprise for commercial exploitation. Space habitations would make such an exercise feasible and easy.[24]

The above human yearning or survival necessity or business proposal would all need space logistics in abundant measure and supporting technologies are expanding to cater to such demands. Orbital OTK is pioneering critical space logistics innovations like on-orbit satellite servicing, cislunar explorations, supplies replenishment couriers including human space support flights. However, the company's largest and most important programme is NASA's Commercial Resupply Services (CRS) Initiative. There are plans to expand business into human transportation also. Space logistics is coming of age to support space tourism and permanent habitations in space when the need arises.

The Moon Village

The most promising destination in space seems to be our very own Moon because it offers several advantages. First benefit is its proximity to Earth from where the tourists and immigrants will proceed to the habitat and most of them will eventually return. This relatively shorter distance will make visits economical and affordable with comparatively lower tariff than other destinations. Further, suitable material from the lunar regolith for construction of the habitat edifice can be sourced and excavated from the land and terrain of the Moon itself rather than importing and transporting from Earth. Scientific observations have proved that there was volcanic activity on the Moon in the past that has created lava tubes and underground caves. On the Moon, these tunnels could be a kilometer or more across in width and height and many hundreds of kilometers in length.[25] These natural formations seem safe from cosmic radiation and environmental intemperance so as to serve as human habitat. Necessary modifications, alterations and fixtures would be relatively easy to install.

And, of course, water requirements and energy needs can also be met by local availability. It is now conclusively established that there is presence of water on the Moon though its total quantum of availability is yet to be estimated.[26] This local existence of water will be helpful in two ways, e.g. for life support and sustenance and for creating hydrogen and oxygen through electrolysis that can in combination serve as fuel for space vehicles. And this constitutes a paramount advantage over other celestial bodies without water in any form. Thirdly, the Moon crust has been analysed and found to be a rich concentrate of Helium-3. Thus, this abundantly existent material would be easy to excavate from the near surface and it is known to be a great source of energy and power. This discovery affords tremendous advantage and the material can be processed *in situ* to generate power and energy for the diverse needs of the tourists and migrants.

Convinced of the viability of such a proposition, engineer-artists have conceptualised designs of such human habitats like Woerner's Moon Village[27] (WMV) for comfort and conviviality. Scientists have also visualised the facilities, personal amenities, and services that need to be catered for in view of the externalities of and vulnerabilities from the lunar eco-system like near-zero-gravity, lack of atmospheric air, rotational thermal variations, and other travails of the unaccustomed environment. This plan may have certain defects and deficiencies yet, the design can be a useful blueprint for further developments and refinements.

Thought has been devoted to other details of the support infrastructure required in terms of electric power supply for various purposes, e.g. lighting requirements, thermal temperance, cooking needs, commuting vehicles, usage of electrical devices, and so on. Further, Vodafone Germany and Nokia Bell are teaming up to establish 4G network on the Moon by 2019,[28] exactly half a century after astronaut Armstrong set foot on the Moon in 'a giant leap for mankind'. This will support the operations of rovers collecting scientific data and reporting back from astral body's surface. The collaborators have commented, 'This is a crucial first step for sustainable exploration of the solar system. In order for humanity to leave the cradle of earth, we need to develop infrastructures beyond our home planet'. And "This project involves a radically innovative approach to the development of mobile network infrastructure" so as to save energy from data transmission and devote it to do science.[29]

As a prequel to the Moon settlement of WMV, United Launch Alliance (ULA) and Bigelow Aerospace are collaborating in a plan to place a space station in orbit around the Moon by 2018. This move has also been prompted by the US desire to return to the Moon and the possibility of outsourcing certain activities to commercial private sector. The collaboration is expected to be successful because, ULA can take pride in having developed three families of rockets, namely, Atlas-V, Delta-II and Delta-IV, and have launched more than 1300 missions. Bigelow in its own right can boast of having attached and activated Bigelow Expandable Activity Module (BEAM) to the ISS in 2016 which is considered the precursor of inflatable space station.[30] This expandable habitat is thus lighter and collapsible than traditional rigid capsules and can fit in more living space into a given rocket. It also affords flexibility in joining together additional modules to cater to the escalating demand or expansion programmes.

Future space stations would hardly be state-funded, though governmentally regulated, and its logical to expect that these would operate commercially under corporate control and driven by business motivations. The latest offer in private-sector products is BEAM type space station. It is new B-330 that is a stand-alone station yet has capability for connective modular attachment and expansion of facilities as desired. It can dock to ISS or own models and provides versatility in use as multi-module space solution.[31] Thus B-330 could serve as an independent orbiting outpost or an intermediate way-station to the Moon or as a lunar depot for stocks and supplies for habitations there or act as a complementary midway refuelling and transit halt to facilitate other plans for settlements and diversified commercial activities on Mars.

The Mars Colony

The next best celestial destination for human habitation, approved by the present exploration status and remote sensing observations, appears to be the famed Mars Colony. Considering that humans on this planet would require physical environment and living conditions almost similar to those naturally habituated to on the mother Earth, it becomes imperative to source water and energy-giving material because the logistics of carrying these from the planet Earth reserves is not feasible due to shortage on earth, unviable in economic costs, and safety in transportation. Scientists have proposed mini nuclear reactors as an alternative proposition for a power source to make liquid oxygen and propellants as well as for reliable power supply for living needs.[32]

Prospects of water availability seem promising because at higher altitudes on the Mars, hydrogen has been detected which is indicative of the existence of subsoil water or ice. Previous observations from Mars Odyssey probe have also indicated towards possibility of ice hiding around the equator of Mars and a particular type of ice around the polar sections. Latest observations by scientists have discovered a lake on Mars that is about 12 miles across and hidden below a mile thick sheet of ice on its South Pole. This find is a bonanza and has positive implications for habitation on Mars though the characteristics of sub-glacial water are still to be ascertained.[33] But its utilisation has its own viability negatives from various angles like carriage of reactors and recurring need for specific fuel, creating infrastructure, ensuring environmental safety parameters, and adapting the output to space applications. The proposition is inherent with imponderable risks and low probability of expected success.

Solar energy is another possible source for this critical pre-requisite to facilitate living on the Mars. This natural emission as received can be suitably harnessed but sunlight will not be available uninterrupted all the time for consistent generation and regular output though it may provide a supplemental alternative or in emergencies of disrupted supply. Fortunately, presence of water in some form has been discovered on the Mars and volcanic veins on its terrain are believed to contain ice. It is also surmised through remote observation that the Red planet has sources of running liquid water albeit with high salinity and tastes similar to ocean water. Yet, if this is available in abundant quantity, it can sufficiently meet many other vital needs.

Construction of habitat structures is another challenge. Our unfamiliarity with the Mars regolith, difficulties in its excavation, and processing pliability for building purposes remain imponderables. Apart from this, the task of building habitats with local materials may pose difficulty in mustering labour force or robotized workers. A ready-made solution to this can be the existence of lava tubes or natural underground caves created by volcanic activity.[34]

Space missions have observed chains of collapsed pits and 'skylights' which scientists, based on high-resolution digital terrain models, believe could be transformed into human colonies. Due to lower-gravity environment of the Mars, evidence shows that lava tubes so formed are even up to 250 m in width and can be suitably converted into protected habitats large enough for streets or even towns. These habitats are considered environmentally shielded and safe from cosmic radiation and micrometeorite dust.[35] These tubes when sealed into dwelling units would also provide insulation against the pervading smell of the outer space that has been tested with naked olfactory sense as something like blasted gunpowder.

Interest in human settlement on Mars has resurged many times through different moves. In September 1954, Planet Mars Development Corporation was formed by three businessmen in Arkansas who offered to convey the title to competent persons for suitable remuneration. Later, MarsOne Human Settlement was announced as an attractive and fully habitable colony for humans and the response was enthusing. Again, Mars Society made it known that beer gets bubblier on the surface of the Mars and thus becomes more enjoyable. This news made beer-lovers ecstatic and drool over the idea; and seduced the affluent among them to, at least, long for a trip to the Mars to taste this promise of bubbliness.

But Budweiser, American beer making company, has reservations because Mar's atmospheric pressure is about 100 times less than the earth and as such bubbles do not rise while gases and liquids tend not to separate. This would turn beer into foamy slop. Nevertheless, Budweiser is experimenting to brew a special beer for the connoisseurs on Mars. Incidentally, Government of India informed in Lok Sabha that TeamIndus of Bangalore is also working on cracking a recipe for beer on the Moon as part of its project to test survivability of yeast in space and how it performs under low gravity of the Moon.

In another revival of interest, Dennis Tito, the first commercial space traveller and week-long resident at the ISS, has now proposed for a private 501-day round-trip to fly by Mars for a breath-taking view of the Red Planet. This was planned for January 2018 but has not materialised so far.[36] It may, however, happen soon though no exact plan for the sojourn has been announced. Another great awakener has been a recent statement by NASA that it plans sending astronauts to the Mars in a 'humanned' capsule. Training of astronauts for this project has already started in right earnest and the proposal appears optimistic yet realistic.[37]

SpaceX is racing ahead to achieve spaceflight to Mars and its debut launch of Falcon Heavy Long-range Rocket on 6 February 2018 has been a great success and highly reassuring of the purpose. Elon Musk commented on the occasion that this is a changing moment in spaceflight and 'It seems surreal to me'. He has promised humanity to take it to the Mars very soon.[38] This vehicle has carried a playful load. It uplifted Musk's red Roadster, an electric sports car built by his other company, Tesla. Strapped inside the car is a mannequin wearing a SpaceX's branded spacesuit outfit. This payload is expected to orbit the Sun for hundreds of millions of years. "It's kind of silly and fun," reflected Musk and added, "but silly and fun things are important."[39]

This launch is indeed a great quantum leap from the earlier Falcon 9 of the SpaceX and becomes a powerful transformational vehicle that can lift a payload of 64 metric tonnes, the heaviest so far. This is so because of two lateral booster rocket attachments those have changed the lift capacity aerodynamics, accoustics and vibration parameters. It is also a monumental milestone for commercial space industry because it is touted to be cheap at mere US $ 90 million. And it is cost-effective because its three boosters return to the earth and can be recovered for re-use. This vehicle is to be used to send astronauts and equipment to the Moon and Mars.

On a positive note from these developments, Musk has delineated a Mars Colonization Plan which he pompously revealed at Adelaide, Australia.[40] He hopes to establish a million-person city on Mars within next 50-100 years. However, in the near future, he expects his reusable combo-ship called Interplanetary Transport System and its improved version with codename BFR[41] that is capable of lofting 150 tons to LEO. He is confident of flying the first cargo mission by 2022 and promises to transport 100 passengers in each trip to the Red Planet by 2024; and thereby establish significant human presence on Mars.

The Mars City will progressively grow as more settlers and supplies come in on regular basis with landing reliability at par with commercial airliners.[42] Astro-culture of plants and seeds will be promoted to begin the cycle of sprouting to edible mellow. This will build the foundation for a permanent and sustainable city on the Red Planet. Despite such iconic achievements and 'road mapped' promises, the sceptics remark that SpaceX has a long history of over-rated positivity and repeated over-promising though eventually achieving the assurance. Therefore, hyped optimism may not be realistic but possibility definitely becomes positive and certainly a step closer.[43]

Lockheed Martin, an aerospace corporation, has announced a bold plan of humans in Mar's orbit by 2020 and a Red Planet Base Camp for human landings by 2028.[44] Efforts seem afoot to actualise this promise. On another occasion, even one-way tickets to Mars were openly offered to the public, evoked great interest, and were booked in plenty. And now, development of solar backpack for survival on the Mars makes an inter-planetary visit more 'tourister' simpler, lighter and cheaper. Another novel development relates to space parachutes for the future. This is to facilitate as astronaut space taxis and are presently under testing by SpaceX and Boeing.[45] Use of space parachutes is also being considered for NASA commercial crew program. Such progressively new gadgets will also promote desire for migration to other planets, which should be disconcerting.[46]

New Celestial Destinations

Liveable human habitats, permanent and self-sustaining, are not yet made functional on the Moon or the Mars and search for new destinations has already started. A new French telescope, Trio, installed at *la Silla* observatory will scan the sky for earth-like planets. This exo-planet hunter telescope provides a new tool to search for light signals from distant worlds, particularly in the Orion and the Pleiades cluster. Such remote finders are becoming popular to identify habitable planets by size, mass and porosity to explore availability of water. Another such search instrument, called ESPESSO, has been placed at European Southern Laboratory in Brazil. It makes search much easier because it exploits light gathering power to make distant objects more clear.[47]

Another proposal from China that seems conceptually feasible is called 'Heaven and Earth'. It is a plan devised by a Chinese architect, Wei Zhao, that proposes for a complete city floating in the sky on 'maglev' i.e., magnetic levitation. It is supposed to be a massive doughnut shaped structure platform with magnets on its underside. These huge magnets at its bottom would repulse earth's magnetic field and counter its gravity to keep the city afloat as an island. The floating platform could rotate and as it spins it would generate energy for itself, making it, theoretically, a completely self-sustaining society for its power needs. The levitated platform could be dotted with lush green forests, bluish mountains and urban centres for human habitation. This conceptualisation has its grey areas, such as the life of magnets, control for landing back safely, or the problem of replenishment logistics. These can be sorted out with time and necessity. For another design, MIT team has won Mars City Design Contest for its Redwood Forest idea.

Ideas are being mooted for floating hotels, like ISS, with leisure and pleasure facilities. It would be easy to construct such structures because countries like the US, Russia, China and others have experience in setting up such facilities. While such visualisations for new entities are doing the rounds, in the US, a proposal has been floated that the ISS, or at least the quarters under US occupation, be privatized because the scientific results returned from there are no more commensurate even with the recurring expenditure incurred annually as also astronaut experience gained so far is adequate and varied enough. So this white elephant may be disposed off to any private enterprise at the market value. Sceptics believe that the idea is a non-starter while Michael J. Listner treats it as a Trump gimmick.[48] Anyway, such floating hotels, if the idea turns into an actuality, may adversely affect the realty lease values on the Moon.

In the meanwhile, defunding of the ISS has gained momentum and the Federal Budget for 2019, in respect of NASA, proposes to eliminate direct public funding of the station by 2025.[49] From now till then is a period of transition to commercial model of control management and governance. NASA, therefore, must consider proposals to use ISS as a future commercial platform. In fact, under the existing understanding between the nations participating in the ISS experiments and astronaut training, 'activities purely for profit like advertising, marketing or fly trinkets are prohibited'. NASA may thus have to develop commercial use policy for the orbiting laboratory and coordinate with other partner nations for a shift from scientific and investigative orientation to commercial and profit-oriented operations in the future.

This would require policy, legal, contractual and programmatic changes and a lot of convincing at the UN and global level. Yet, possibilities and potential for commercial exploitation of the ISS are varied and lucrative like advertisements in the form video interviews of astronauts or their wearing apparel to have logos of Nike, Toyota, etc. or for adventure sports. Actually, pseudo-commercial activities are already taking place in parts of the ISS. For example, an inflatable module built by Bigelow aerospace has been attached to ISS since April 2016 that is being used for commercial research and rented to other governmental entities and academia. This segment is managed by a non-profit organisation called, Center for the Advancement of Science in Space (CASIS).[50]

Permanent Settlements beyond the Earth

Be that as it may, for the present our attention is drawn to the adventurous humans desirous of taking up permanent residence beyond the mother Earth and have, in all seriousness, applied for one-way ticket to the Mars. It seems plausible that they wish to set up an independent, self-sufficient, self-supporting, self-sustaining habitation that may, one day, become a separate nation qualitatively, demographically and politically. Following this approach some believe that the Universe is a plenary extension of human consciousness and it is in the spatio-temporal expanse where the universal mind of humanity pervades. Therefore, space settlements of the future would seem logical extension of this 'alief'.[51]

This may sound fiction today but will be a stark reality of tomorrow. And any epistemological scepticism by idealists and purists would stand unfounded. A new future beckons us loud and clear, towards a vibrant NewSpace ecosystem. Yet, we must reckon with unknown eventualities and be prepared to handle the impending challenges and be equally ready to deal with the ensuing consequences. One such imaginable move by the 'celestians' could be to claim back their real-estate from intruding earthlings to establish their own empire of yore. A couple of examples are discussed in succeeding paragraphs.

The Church of Scientology claims that they are the inheritors of Xenu, who once ruled 'the Galactic Confederacy", an ancient state of 76 planets. It is believed that having existed for twenty million years; the planets were eventually brimming with extreme over-population and suffering its consequences that resulted in unrest for survival. Fearing impending revolt, Xenu literally froze billions of his subjects, captured their souls (*thetans*) and transported them to the earth for elimination. Later, Xenu himself was dethroned, imprisoned and sent to the earth that was condemned as 'prison planet' of Galactic Confederacy. It is for this reason that clergy Scientologists clean the devoted human souls by auditing of their past till obtaining a 'clear state of spiritual awareness' before baptizing them into their secret order.[52]

The cleansing process 'releases' inherent and natural-born powers to control themselves and their environment and ushers in them the 'Serenity of Beingness' with modulated emotional responses. Scientology is built on love and acceptance and employs homophobic doctrine. This mystic religion founded by L Ron Hubbard,[53] like other religions, is steeped in unquestionable myths and beliefs. Thus, it is not wholly based on science or grounded in logic or stand test of reason. It, however, believes that souls are eternal, but humans evolved from clams through a process of mitosis. Regardless of the esoteric philosophy, their claims of paramountcy in galactic space will possibly find few takers to confuse the law or berate the scientific observations.

In 1948, James Thomas Mangan claimed 'Island of Space' to establish the Nation of Celestial Space, in short 'Celestia', on the specious plea that humankind on earth travels 1,500,000 miles each day through the territory of Celestia. In the same year, on this basis, he formally applied, as an agent of Celestia, for membership of the United Nations. The request was rejected under Article 4(1) of the Charter of the United Nations on the ground of inability to discharge incumbent obligations of a state. In 1956, Mangan criticized the UN for being 'legally impolitic and scientifically impolite'. Later, he declared that Celestia was the only competent authority to frame laws for outer space and ordained all nations on Earth to abide by this declaration. He also proclaimed that the entry and presence of artificial man-made satellites in outer space tantamount to trespass in infringement of its state sovereignty.[54]

Another movement that is influencing the like-minded intellectuals and the rich, concerns the evolution of ASGARDIA that claims to be 'the Space Nation'. It is believed that its concept originated in 2016; it is headquartered at Vienna and its present head is Lena De Winne. It has a motto of 'One Humanity-One Unity' with quintessential philosophy of peace in space and prevention of earth's conflicts being transferred into space. It aims to serve entire humanity and look after the welfare of each and every one regardless of personal riches or national prosperity and creating a mirror-image of humanity in space sans states, religion or other earthly divisions. In space we are all just Earthlings.[55]

Asgardia, in Norse mythology, was a city in the skies that was abode of the gods and this state is the realisation of mans' eternal dream to leave his cradle on Earth and expand into the universe where they can live on their own terms, own laws, and own rules. Asgardians are the members of this unique nation-state that one day hopes to join the UN and attain sovereign status and acquire its incidental attributes e.g. a government, embassies, a flag, a national anthem, an insignia and so on.[56] Surprisingly, it is gathering momentum and has launched, Asgardia-1, a nano-satellite into space on 11 October 2017 that is orbiting overhead. Lena De Winne is the current CEO of Asgardia and most of the funding comes from Igor Ashurbeyli, a Russian national.

This state is inviting earthlings to be its citizens and someday hopes to govern itself independent of the comity of earthly nations and may maintain sovereign relations on egality and with compassion. It is imaginable that with passage of time, Asgardians may evolve generationally native, environmentally more adjusted, and behaviourally more convivial on their planet. There is another similar organisation called 'All for Moonkind'. Michelle LD Hanlon is its co-founder. This organisation is so conscious and enlightened that it has obtained observer status at the Committee on Peaceful Uses of Outer Space (COPUOS).[57]

Therefore, these evolved organisations and their intellectual members when permanently migrate to reside in celestial habitations, they may resent international law imposed on them; and may like to shape their own world according to their notion of life ideals, social mores, living relations, concept of human convenience, and societal mind-set. Thus, they may wish to enact their own laws and evolve their own norms suitable and conducive to their living conditions, habitation styles, and inter-active relations.

The 'nativised asgardians' with firmly established roots in their new planet of residence would, perhaps, also want to establish their primal right on their celestial territory, attempt to redeem it and may treat earthly astronauts, industrialists, businessmen and workers as foreign outsiders. With no earthly sovereignty operating there due non-appropriation principle, there may be no collective protective agency and there may be threats to the safety of earthly-humans and to the security of their economic interests. The scenario is a rough visualisation but to our chagrin, may actualise one day. We should thus be prepared and indoctrinated for such an exigency and appreciate the need for global response to be ready for collective protection of global interests in outer space.

This trend to locate new habitable celestial lands and aspire to establish human presence scattered in the entire cosmos, in a not too distant future, is a new phenomenon, an emerging mind-set that portends of ominous consequences. We need to be careful and cautious, whatever be the advantages or disadvantages of these migrations. And with growing possibility of scattered habitations it seems pertinent to consider the quality of societal inter-relations of earth-bound humans with these inhabitants of extra-terrestrial planets. These can impact economics, politics, peace and security, among other aspects.

APPRAISAL OF RIGHTS IN ASTRO-ESTATE

In view of the discussion in the foregoing section, another use of astro-realty has emerged for habitations and hotels. Thus, apart from mining of natural resources on celestial bodies, the next best commercial option of such lands is for travel and tourism. Therefore, there is going to be a competing demand for and pressures on available astro-lands for creating tourism infrastructure. More so, this requirement may prompt prospecting and to bid for prime lands that are closer to perennial water sources and in proximity to aerospace landing sites. As a result, the value of astro-estate may appreciate considerably for tourism and habitations and thus compete with accruals from mining.

Now a question arises as to where do ownership rights regarding the astro-lands vest and reside. It is quite clear in International Space Law (ISL) that "Outer space, including the Moon and other celestial bodies, is not subject to national appropriation by claim of sovereignty, by means of use or occupation, or by any other means".[58] This Article is restrictive and prohibitive in content and scope. Thus, understandably, no state can claim authority, deem to occupy a part of or complete celestial body to exercise sovereignty over it. The denial is clear and complete with no ambiguity whatsoever. Similar meaning should be clear to the private corporate entities that derive their status and rights through the nexus of nationality. There should be no doubt that OST is state-centric instrument that casts international responsibility on the state alone for its space activities regardless of who undertakes or operates these.[59]

This mandate is further reinforced and buttressed by another clause that "Outer space, including the Moon and other celestial bodies, shall be free for exploration and use by all states without discrimination of any kind, on a basis of equality and in accordance with international law, and there shall be free access to all areas of celestial bodies".[60] Embodied here is a positive assurance of a right of access, exploration and use without any let or hindrance. Freedom to all states, and not merely restricted to state-parties to the Treaty, is inherently embedded in this provision. Thus, both clauses (Articles I and II) are complementary and should be considered together for a correct perspective or juridical interpretation.

There is, however, a rider to the above assured freedom to conduct activities in outer space and on the celestial bodies. This restriction relates to respective rights on the basis of reciprocity and mutuality. It cautions that, "...States Parties to the Treaty shall be guided by the principle of cooperation and mutual assistance and shall conduct all their activities in outer space, including the Moon and other celestial bodies, with due regard to the corresponding interests of all other State Parties to the Treaty".[61] Whatever the intent or import of this provision, taking into consideration the entire text in totality, it can broadly be dubbed as a mere procedural Article.

This provision, nevertheless, highlights a cardinal principle of non-interference, well-established in international law also, and assures of no disturbance in 'active' space activities. It, thus, defines mutual correlation of rights and responsibilities constituting an affirmative duty that casts a responsible obligation. Yet, in actual scenario, if a state agency or even a corporate entity occupies certain land area for its bonafide and peaceful activities on a celestial body, then its actual possession cannot be vacated nor activities thereon meddled with in any manner. International law applies, *mutatis mutandis,* to space activities and is binding in its effect. Therefore, it is in this manner that legitimate possession turns into illegitimate ownership.

No wonder, celestial occupation seems so close to virtual ownership without a conveyance deed. Hence the race among the competing aerospace giants to reach the prospective celestial body first to gain the crucial advantage of selecting and occupying the best location and site for their business purposes, whether for mining of natural resources or location of a human habitat or any other commercial purpose. This choice of early acquisition can afford many benefits to the entity in terms of richness of mineral resources, nearness to water source, proximity to landing port, and advantages in logistic support among others. It is wisely said that the early bird catches the worm and, in this case, it could be control over premium astro-estate for better business opportunity and higher profitability.

Analysis of Property Rights on Celestial Bodies

The appraisal, so far, establishes a legal tenet that there is no national sovereignty in outer space including the celestial bodies and the principle of Non-Appropriation in outer space stands vindicated. Many scholars have accepted Outer Space Treaty as customary law of space and have put the weight of their *opinio juris* behind this view.[62] Therefore, the OST does not brook any special preference or specific right in outer space either to any state or entity on any justification. This is empirically borne out by the fact that Bogotá Declaration of 1976, by the equatorial states asserting their superior right over geo-synchronous slots, was deemed untenable and was universally rejected.

Nevertheless, the protagonists of property rights in space vindicate their contention by eliciting support from the non-appropriation principle enshrined in the OST that prohibits claims of national sovereignty in any manner or by any means over celestial bodies but does not expressly prevent individual appropriation.[63] And since land on these astral bodies is unoccupied, uncontrolled and unowned; and as no nation lays any sovereign claim on them, then these territories tend to become *territorium nullius* and, therefore, it should be possible to lay individual claim to ownership. But the concept of CHM under Article 11 of the MA negates this view. Ironically, the fallacy in the argument is overlooked and legal sophistry of the derivative not pricked at all. A legal maxim, *qui tacet negat,* which means silence of authority cannot be treated as acquiescence to the fact nor can an adverse inference be drawn, equally challenges this opinion.[64] Arguably, in this particular context, inclusion of a provision regarding prohibition on individual appropriation would have been irrelevant in an international treaty and non-inclusion assures no *jus in re* for private ownership.[65]

Many have tried this route and sold discrete plots on the Moon and other celestial bodies to individual buyers.[66] It is believed that the Moon has been sold many times over. Bill (Dennis) Hope is a well known name in this business of dealing with astro real estate sales.[67] A boastful claim was made by Hope, in 2005, of having solicited 3.6 million clients in 181 countries during three decades of his 'unreal-estate' business for sale of lunar realty.[68] Of course, the legal dictum of *caveat emptor*, implying that the buyer beware of the transaction, applies in full measure. And it may be further clarified that *jus ad rem* without possession would be inchoate and incomplete right *ipso jure*. But, true reality and non-legality of these dubious transactions will unfold only when buyers claim physical possession and demand a registered transfer of the plot on their name through conveyance deed. This Day of Judgment may not be very far.

Viewed from another angle, it has been asserted that individual private rights in property can exist independent of the overarching sovereignty of a state over the territory.[69] This argument was raised in a court in the US in Nemitz case and was adjudicated on merits.[70] In his plea Gregory Nemitz laid claim of ownership on an asteroid named Eros that he proclaimed on the Archimedes Institute website. To buttress his claim, Nemitz had also pledged this asteroid-Eros property as collateral in a security interest in California. In the meanwhile, the US space agency, NASA, made an automated robotic landing on Eros in 2001. Nemitz asserted that this landing of the satellite without his specific permission tantamount to a trespass by the US agency NASA and that his property rights over Eros have been infringed. He, therefore, was entitled for claiming parking fees relating to the landing on the asteroid Eros and accordingly billed NASA and the State Department for parking charges at the rate of 20 cents per annum recurring till vacation. It was to be expected that such a claim would be refuted and rejected by the concerned authorities.

Nemitz then filed a law suit on the plea that the OST prohibits national appropriation but not constructive individual rights thereto. The contentious litigation was entertained by the court but on arguments the suit was dismissed. It was held that the petitioner could not establish his ownership in that he could neither produce legal documents of the realty rights purchased from the seller nor substantiate actual taking over of physical possession of the named property nor prove exercise of his effective control thereon. Nemitz failed on both counts; to justify his claim of ownership under germane law as well as to produce sufficient possessory evidence for the claimed corpus.[71] Anyway, there has been no appeal against this court ruling.

In 2002, Virgiliu Pop proclaimed ownership of the Sun with an online register and threatened owners of the Moon and other claimed celestial bodies with legal notices for charges relating to the use of sunlight. Later, in his book, Pop accepted that it was a joke to publicise that such claims are hollow and merely certify the fact of it having been staked.[72] In another case, Sylvio Langevin staked a claim of property ownership on several celestial bodies. This assertion was contested in the court and was held legally untenable.[73] It may, however, be alluded here that under customary international law also, there are established principles of acquisition of property and one of the legal requirement for establishing unimpeachable claim to territory or property is that the discoverer or the owner must physically touch, or step on, the land body.

There is, of course, another dimension to the problem of realty of celestial estate, though futuristic in vision yet highly probable. It relates to the possibility that migrants to the Moon or Mars who intend and set up residence in perpetuity there may assert their natural right to the assets of their planet and claim ownership by virtue of being permanent residents of the locale *qua* the outside intruders and exploiters. They may even form their political organisation and administrative government and assert sovereignty over their planet and usurp all property rights of outsiders from Earth in favour of celestial nationals. The situation has been philosophized but such celestial nationalisation can be a real prospect.

Be that as it may, it becomes pertinent again to assert that compromise of non-appropriation principle to permit private rights to celestial estate could usher in a precarious situation fraught with ominous risks. This would open the route to the well-tried method of colonisation under the doctrine of discovery and usurp un-owned property as has happened on Earth. Thus the prime celestial lands would be occupied by the pioneers in business under the legal maxim and well-established rule of property law that supports "First in Time is First in Right".[74] Further, they may take possession of vast tracts of land even though the same is not required for their business or industry. And since occupancy creates a right *in rem* on unclaimed property, their possession of first instance cannot be interfered with in any manner.

Inequity and injustice thus stares the follower space-farers in sharing the left-over or discarded land that may be uneconomical to harvest or unattractive to inhabit or may be even insufficient for their purpose. This would also be highly prejudicial to the principle of "...for the benefit and in the interest of all countries...". The use of astral-estate would no longer remain 'the province of all mankind' or collective *res communis omnium.* The land corpus of celestial bodies will be occupied by the entities technologically capable of doing so, in individual instalments. In this manner, the common benefit to humanity or 'global public interest in outer space'[75] would be negated or even virtually denied.

Simplistically speaking, concept of sovereignty and notion of property rights belong to different streams of studies and law, the former to public international law and political science while the latter falls under the purview of domestic laws and private rights. Again, sovereignty is permanent and perennial while property rights are ephemeral and transferable, yet both can originate, co-exist and survive in consort or independent of each other. Nevertheless, both are inter-twined. Therefore, to extract and develop one from the other would be fallacious logic motivated by partisan considerations and equally detrimental to the established tenets of ISL.

It now seems pertinent to discuss the fundamentals of property rights that can be derived and sustained under the two systems of law viz. common law and the civil law.[76] Under the former system, state owns its entire territory and private property rights are sold to individuals for consideration or conferred on nobles and loyal subjects as rewards or gifts. Such practice has always happened in most monarchies. This system of obtaining property rights in space is inapplicable because states are barred from claiming sovereignty over celestial bodies and hence no property rights on celestial realty can vest in state; and over what it does not have suzerainty or exercise control, cannot be promised or passed on to its nationals or protected by the state.

In the civil law system, property rights are acquired through human toil and labour where individuals hunt for, occupy and develop land areas that are *res nullius* and do not belong to anyone e.g. living in forest areas or clearance of swamps. In this system, the state confers property rights in recognition of their efforts or out of beneficence on the resident landless.

This system works in most democracies and is a civilized way of empowerment of the poor. But this procedure of establishing property rights cannot extend to celestial bodies because their 'use' is a province of mankind as collective corpus; and the celestial realty cannot be legitimately partitioned or 'discretised' for holding in permanent individual ownership.[77]

It may be highlighted that it is not only theoretically possible to conceive of individual property rights without the umbrella of sovereignty of the state but a search into world history may throw up analogous eras as visualised above. For example, in the 9th and 10th century Europe when Roman Empire collapsed, independent sovereign states did not come into being for quite some time. And history is witness to the fact that during this period without a sovereign, trade still flourished and property rights were honoured. It was a reign of *"lex mercatoria"* where rights were self-enforced and mutually respected making the system self-regulatory, self-balancing and self-stabilising.[78]

In such economic relationships, reputational effect was prominent; the rules were fair, players impartial, and disputants willing to abide by the norms. Perhaps, the system continued to work effectively for a while by the sheer momentum of the market forces that were already in motion. Therefore, the historical existence of a working economic era where security protection of the paternal state was legally absent and politically uncertain may not be reassuring enough by itself. Differences are endemic in human relationships due to divergent individual perceptions leading to simmering unresolved disputes and consequent apprehensions of personal safety. Promise of mutual help in need, however genuine, may not materialise in eventuality despite best intentions. Therefore, this empirical understanding may not be a good enough alternative because history as well confirms that humans have also tended to be foes, even in their neighbourhood. And self-resolution of differences by discussion and negotiation appears a utopian situation and may, in actual practice, be neither easy nor always possible. One of the results could be that a situation of law of the jungle and survival of the fittest may prevail. Hence to best enjoy the property and its usufructs, a superintending authority to resolve disputes is deemed imperative.

Thus, this paradigm of idyllic economic environment and idealist human behaviour, in a vacuum without sovereignty, may not prevail in space economy or space habitations because here stakes are too ambitious and motivations could be divergent, even conflictive. So to analyse such incumbent problems or find solution to contemporary commercial challenges on a template of public ISL would be unrewarding or futile. And to deviously interpret OST or to impart it a vested construction would negate its intent and molest its spirit. It must also be equally recognised that space treaties govern the activities of states in outer space; while nationals and corporate entities are permitted to undertake space ventures, but only under continued state supervision.

These corporate entities, as natural citizens of the state have no independent *locus standi* in the space treaties. Applicability of international law to outer space[79] also yields no direct solution as it is based on *pacta* between states and individuals are not its true subjects. Therefore, the predicament points towards a necessity to evolve a separate and specific regimen of Private International Space Law to tackle problems of commercial exploitation of celestial natural resources and the surging possibilities of celestial migration with concomitant property rights, pseudo or legal, among other emerging issues.

Broadly speaking, in a domain of co-existence where there is 'freedom of access and use' for all countries, situations of dispute and conflict cannot be ruled out and without the security protection of the mother state, peaceful living and economic activity may not flourish and even be disrupted by outsiders. At times, survival can also be under threat. Therefore, practically, safe and secure environment is essential for habitations on the celestial bodies and hence the need for good governance to ensure upkeep of law and public order. This can be assured and effectively maintained by a competent authority that may be called World Space Authority (WSA), under the aegis of United Nations.

GOVERNANCE OF ASTRO-ESTATE AND CELESTIAL HABITATIONS

From the foregoing discussion it becomes clear that humanity is ready to venture into outer space to experience the thrill of zero-gravity, enjoy the distinctive pleasures of stay in celestial resorts or even permanently settle down in Moon Village or Mars Colony or other celestial settlements. Dennis Tito's flyby the Mars trip, due in 2018, is path-breaking and interest-rousing. In fact, space travel and transportation facilities exist even today, though not for scheduled and regular journeys. Such offers are just in the wings. Requisite developments to achieve reliable and safe human travel are in the offing and the industry is surging ahead in self-belief. Therefore, the year 2018 is sure going to grab headlines for space travel.

Jeff Bezos' Blue Origin hopes to take its first space tourist into orbit in its Crew Capsule 2.0 aboard its New Shepherd heavy-lift reusable rocket in 2018.[80] In fact, a trend towards re-usable rockets and re-use of earlier used rockets has just started and proved successful. This may reduce cost of travel to space. Equally frantically, Richard Branson's Virgin Galactic is on a countdown to the first commercial trip into orbit just above the atmosphere for six passengers paying US $250,000 each on its VSS Unity spacecraft in 2018.[81] Elon Musk's SpaceX has successfully tested Falcon Heavy vehicle that is able to lift 54 metric tonnes into orbit, the heaviest so far and it promises outings into space. Boeing has bagged a NASA contract for six crewed flights to Space Station (ISS).[82]

Apart from the US 'astro-preneurs', other countries are also contributing efforts in this direction. China is warming up for a manned lunar mission in 2018 on the far side of the Moon. China has also joined the heavy-lift vehicle race with its Long March 5 (CZ-5 rocket) and plans to send a rover to Mars by 2020.[83] India was also to send its rover to the Moon on Chandrayaan-II mission around April 2018, now rescheduled to October 2018. More details have since become available from ISRO. It is stated to be a challenging and critical mission because the payload weighs 3290 kg and will be rocketed on a GSLV Mk-II vehicle. Also that India will, for the first time, carry an orbiter, a lander, and a rover to the Moon. The lander is expected to make a soft landing near south pole of the Moon and Rover will have power to spend one lunar day, that is equal to 14 earth days, and walk up to 150-200 km. It will then go in sleep-mode and will get activated whenever the Sun rays will fall on it.[84]

Prospects are thus promising for longer space travel, too, whereas creating hotels, motels and habitats on the celestial bodies may take some time. In the meanwhile experiments in such living are under way in the US and other countries. India is working on a structure of igloo for future outposts on the Moon and has been successful on a working model under laboratory conditions of lunar terrain. For actual construction of the lunar habitat, scientists plan to send robots and 3-D printers that will use lunar soil and local materials.[85] As for water availability, joint investigation with NASA has confirmed, through diviner instruments, that it is distributed across the lunar surface and not confined to specific areas.[86] These possibilities are sure to become a reality in the near future. Therefore, the crucial problem is not planning and construction of infrastructure and facilities but legal issue preceding this phase of development.

Human activities in outer space and on celestial bodies are primarily governed by the OST and allied international instruments. In basics, the OST mandates free access to outer space and all areas of celestial bodies for exploration and use by all states without discrimination of any kind, on a basis of equality and in accordance with international law. However, this guarantee is subject to the rider of non-interference in others' activities. But the Treaty does not permit states to appropriate the celestial bodies and exercise sovereignty by any method or in any manner though the Treaty allows activities by non-governmental and private entities under state supervision and nodal responsibility, for use and exploration. The snag lies in the fact that commercial use and exploitation of these extra-terrestrial bodies and their natural resources was not envisioned at the time of its drafting and approval. Hence, commercial appropriation of astro-estate for long-term usage as hotel or habitation tantamount to indefinite occupation and virtual ownership that is not-permitted under the Treaty.

Another aspect of such commercial appropriation which fouls with the Treaty stipulates that the exploration and use of outer space and celestial bodies 'shall be the province of all mankind' and 'shall be carried out for the benefit and in the interest of all countries'. The implications of this Article are that the celestial bodies are *res communis* and cannot be partitioned in real estate. So is the mandate of the MA under 'CHM'. As such, under the existing space law individual permanent ownership for commercial purposes is not permissible and cannot be acquired; and, secondly, that the benefits, or in commercial context, profits derived in any manner of their use, should be diverted to or utilised for the benefit of all countries. This seems analogous to the obligation of CSR.

This principle of customary space law is non-negotiable whereas its faithful implementation is beset with problems that solicit solution. It is to be appreciated that temporary landing or parking of a spacecraft on a planet is different in kind, purpose and legality than use of celestial real-estate for tourism industry or residential habitation. Yet, the march of human progress and advancement should not be halted. To overcome this hurdle, it can be suggested that if individualised ownership cannot be self-acquired or obtained out of 'the province of mankind' then, at least, specified and demarcated spatial estate can be leased out with reference to period demise for development as commercial ventures with rent payable to any designated space authority.

This approach would involve establishing a custodial authority or revive the trusteeship concept over the province of all mankind that would approve of allotment and execution of leases pertaining to celestial properties. This, of course, would be a specialised function of estate management and the present OOSA is neither vested with this authority nor would be competent to handle and discharge this duty under its existing format. Therefore, the UN, with consensus of the members, may need to create a suitable authority or organisation vested with custodial and trusteeship powers for devising rules, executing lease deeds for commercial allotment of sites on celestial bodies, ensuring compliance of lease terms, and collection of lease money as per the agreement.

Another area of contention is to ensure that benefit of use reach all states as assured in the Treaty. This again seems a difficult task because neither modalities for benefit distribution or for any levy and its collection have been formalised nor proportionate share of each country has been defined or any formula of sharing approved for apportionment of the realised lease rental corpus. This problem area needs urgent attention. But *ad interim,* a provisional lease fee may be fixed and collected from leaseholders and this amount be kept in an escrow account in favour of the UN for disbursal later in due shares to the beneficiaries and through any suitable mechanism and designated institution.

PROBLEM MANAGEMENT AND IMPLEMENTATION MECHANISM

It is axiomatic that laws should not be an obstacle to human development and progress of mankind. The OST was never intended to be restrictive or obstructionist. In fact, its character is just the opposite. It assures freedom of access to all states, irrespective of their accession to the Treaty or not, and to every area of outer space without any reservation or discrimination. The Treaty generously grants benefits of exploration and use to all states for inclusivity and empowerment. And it treats exploration and use of outer space including celestial bodies as a province of all mankind in terms of global collectivity and all celestial bodies as *res communis* of humanity. So, it is just that at the time of crafting of the OST, the enhanced competence of private enterprise, commercial opportunities in outer space, and growing technological viabilities for exploitation could not be fully visualised and legally provided for. It is no failure of drafters or an original deficiency of the Treaty; it is sheer irony of circumstances and rapid techno- progress.

Frankly speaking, the universal appeal of the OST has worked admirably for over half a century and has thus become sacrosanct deserving of reverential abidance. Hence, flouting the Treaty by mauling its spirit in a hegemonic or authoritarian attitude for national or business interests will be blasphemy. The principles enshrined in the OST are fundamental and regulatory; and least prohibitive in character. Only with the passage of time and galloping scientific and technological progress, certain gaps have now become apparent that need to be filled responsibly and smoothened constructively to guide the Treaty in the desired direction to foster global commercial progress and enable voluntary demographic migration to extra-terrestrial settlements. Solutions to these visible gaps and a suitable mechanism to implement the proposals are suggested in succeeding paragraphs.

Problem Management

It is understandable that all the suggestions proffered and implementation mechanism cannot be effectuated immediately, yet the world comity and stakeholders and 'techno-juris' fraternity can strive to arrive at a broad understanding of the hiccups and a way to remedy this. It is a wise refrain that clarity about the problem is a first step in the right direction and much more important than the subsequent process of problem solving. Therefore, let us honestly accept that the OST is a non-negotiable rule book, a *Grundnorm,* and we may be identifying and groping for wrong solutions if we abdicate our trust in the Treaty.

Indeed, a laudable alternative would be to patiently work for a holistic improvement in the Treaty to cover its revealed shortcomings as well as envisioned exigencies so that the Treaty in its new *'avatar'* can live long to serve the humanity. All stakeholders may pledge to support the Treaty in peaceful and orderly, egalitarian and equitable commercial use of celestial bodies and agreed sharing of the usufructs of human labour in outer space.

The UN is, thus, bound to succeed in its endeavour of good governance of outer space and assuring the global community of the cherished principles of freedom for all, access to all areas, province of all mankind, and common benefit of all countries.

The OST regimen is not equipped with an independent enforcement agency for facilitating its implementation and ensuring verification of compliance. It merely depends upon states to discharge the stipulated responsibility under the customary international law. Thus, the authorisation and regulation of space activities of the private actors is entrusted to the states, but regrettably some states are not acquitting this duty responsibly and are offering a long rope to the space corporate sector. This seems least desirable and let us clearly understand that good governance under international treaties cannot be outsourced to private enterprise, instead it has to be resolutely delivered by the pact parties as customary responsibility of the states or by an organisation like the UN (under whose aegis the Treaty was formalized) or it's duly constituted representative entity.

The proposals made here may not easily find favour for immediate negotiations and prompt implementation. Therefore, certain transitory and easily workable adjustments are suggested in procedural methods and institutional enforcement for consideration and *ad interim* implementation. Firstly, let's convert the perceived obstacle of non-appropriation into an opportunity by treating all astro-property of celestial bodies as trusteeship of mankind and that trust be reposed and vested into the UN. This proposition will also satisfy the mandate of 'the province of all mankind'. And the UN, in turn, may create a competent custodial authority in, say World Space Authority (WSA), to optimally and sustainably regulate its diverse uses for commercial exploitation on terms equitable and beneficial to all stakeholders.

The management of custodial property for commercial exploitation may be organised through lease of land areas to prospective users with a rider of time period of its demise that is reasonable to break-even the costs of outlay followed by a term of profit making, say perhaps for 33 years.[87] The propriety of leasehold of property will ensure freedom of access over areas unencumbered by lease and elicit regard for the principle of non-interference. It will consequently reduce disputes and obviate the necessity for the leaseholder to seek protection from its national sovereign. Thus, control and compliance will rest in WSA.

Further, the concept of lease has an inherent notion of levy of rental that can be fixed for annual payment and revised every eleven years based on amortisation of investment, recurring operative costs, and resultant escalation of profits. This task can be entrusted to specialists in the respective field for calculation. The lease rental can be realised by the WSA and utilised as permitted under the rules and *pro-rata* apportioned among the beneficiary states as per the modalities of sharing so determined. This will safeguard the Treaty clause 'for benefit and in the interest of all countries'.

There can, however, be another shortcut solution that syncretises the Treaty stipulations, and can enable commencement of commercial operations for excavation of natural resources and establishment of habitations and tourism infrastructure on the celestial bodies without any impeachable infringement of the OST. In this action plan, the astro-preneurs can occupy land of their preferred choice for their respective business and inform UN/OOSA of their activities on the chosen planet or asteroid as per the existing law. This is legal under the doctrine of 'first in time, first in right' over unoccupied lands. This customary norm is supported in legality by precedents of previous space landings and rover movements and digging of soil samples.

The desired activity can, thus, commence straightaway under the liability provisions in accordance with germane space law. After the commercial activity is complete, the corporation undertaking it can compute its profit yield and deposit a percentage, say 10%, of the profit, *ad interim,* in an escrow account with the UN/IMF for distribution "for the benefit and in the interest of all countries" as and when proportional share is determined and disbursement modalities are formulated and promulgated for implementation.[88] This instant solution satisfies the basic legalities for immediate activation of business plans while formal negotiations can get under way in due course.

Interim or short-term measures, howsoever, expedient and convenient are mere palliatives and are seldom either in the best interest of the system or the stakeholders. Therefore, it is prudent that appropriate remedial measures for the long term and actions for incumbent challenges are maturely discussed, expeditiously negotiated, consensually agreed, and properly implemented.

This wisdom highlights the need to revise and update and 'futurise' the OST and allied international instruments in the light of technological progress in the space domain, private funding and management capabilities, new found feasibilities for newer non-traditional applications, visualisation of future avenues presently in the wings, and harmonising the interests of all stakeholders. We must break silos and change our mindset to upgrade the OST to make it holistic, equitous and futuristic so that it will remain workable, valid and relevant for a long time to meet the aspirations of the new millennials and ensuing generations.

There are, thus, gaps in the OST, despite allied clarificatory international instruments and guideline norms; and almost non-existence of subaltern rules and procedures to implement certain provisions discussed earlier. It is, therefore, for consideration if a committee of government bureaucrats, legal scholars, financial experts, experienced estate managers, and business stakeholders can be constituted to delve into these and other incidental issues to devise working rules of procedure, lease formats for different purposes, determine methodology for calculation of lease rentals, evolve modalities for sharing of the benefits or utilisation of lease proceeds towards global development, and the structure for an incumbent administrative machinery.

Implementation Mechanism

The efficacy of any system depends upon its implementation and quality of implementation depends upon enforcement and the efficiency of enforcement depends upon the sincerity of the mechanism or institution to effectively enforce it. Therefore, whatever solution is elected; short-cut, long term or futuristic; its results on-the-ground effectuation can be traced to the personality of the institution governing the system. As on today, the UN entity handling space affairs is OOSA. It mostly acts as information receiving agency and information dissemination office with a moderate co-ordination role. It, thus, has little executive authority to properly govern the outer space domain, questioning the veracity of information submitted by the states, and verification of compliances, to say the least. This is definitely inadequate for the expansion envisaged.

The solutions discussed above throw up numerous tasks of governance of domain, management of astro-estate, execution of lease deeds, maintenance of records, decision making in conflicting claims, realisation of lease rentals and their apportionment, periodic revision of lease rentals, inter-stellar immigration documents, record of human movement, and compliance verification of uses, among others. This list is not comprehensive and many other functions will spring up in practical working. OOSA with its existing charter, organisational format, and manning posture can hardly undertake and discharge such specialised and sensitive tasks satisfactorily. Ergo, the need to form a new, competent and professional, entity to effectively undertake entrusted responsibilities seems imperative and urgent.

For the overall maintenance of public order in outer space and for the management of commercial exploitation of all types of celestial resources, mined or real estate, creation of an interim entity called, World Space Authority (WSA) has been mooted. This would act as trusteeship body and custodial authority to discharge abovementioned executive responsibilities and regulatory duties. It could thus, at best, work as mentor and regulator. This would require a mandate for the purpose entrusted, an authentic policy to be implemented, commensurate organisational structure, professional manpower for staffing, and adequate budgetary provisions.

The formation of WSA, at best, may be an in-transition arrangement because assignments will expand with progress of time and technological development. There is, of course, scope for progressive enlargement of functions like governance of celestial settlements, dispute resolution of leases, and verification of compliances, as and when necessity arises. Therefore, additional duties may have to be entrusted and its scope of control may have to be broadened with human migration and settlements on celestial bodies, increasing inter-stellar deep-space probes and other non-traditional operations in space. Thus, recognising these bulges of additional responsibilities, it seems logical that WSA could, at a later date, when deemed appropriate, graduate to World Space Organisation (WSO).

In permanent arrangement, WSO will be a well-suited enforcement agency for broad spectrum coverage of domain governance, policy deliberations, regulatory management, supervisory functions, compliance inspections, and coercive corrective actions. Hence, it deduces a coveted slot for WSO as a full-fledged organ of the UN with exalted status, superior authority, higher competence, additional staffing, and broader functions for eximious performance. After all, outer space and its celestial bodies constituting a domain so big and vast, so scientifically investigable, technologically useful, and commercially exploitable, environmentally vulnerable, intruded for multifarious activities by a multitude of actors, would sure need a higher pedestal organisation equal to the task of governance, trusteeship and management with due authority to arrest aberrations and award sanctions. And, it is with this rationale and consideration that, in the ultimate, creation of WSO is highly commended and strongly recommended.

LEGAL IMPLICATIONS OF COMMERCIALISATION

Commercialisation of outer space and celestial bodies is round the corner and this is happening on many fronts e.g. space-mining, space travel, space-manufacturing, space-tourism, space settlements and so on. Further, these commercial activities are being prospected, promoted and established by private enterprise on purely business lines and for profit motivation. Such impulses may not always be congruous to the welfare and in best interests of other stakeholders like space-travellers, space-workers, space-settlers, and space-use-competitors. Therefore, there may be *inter se* conflict of interest or socio-economic or contractual disputes. These may have legal implications and may require law and order enforcement and dispute resolution mechanism in celestial colonies as well as back on Earth for relevant jurisdiction. A few selected such exigencies are discussed below.

Governance and Public Order

In any social gathering like space hotels or societal inter-action as in celestial settlements, social discipline and civilised behaviour is of utmost importance for friendly atmosphere and convivial living. This may be disturbed by variations of perspective, rigid mindset, habituated norms, behavioural disorder or even criminal acts with *mens rea*. To restrain delinquents from unsocial behaviour or norm aberrations and to deter crimes in the interest of safety of life as well as security of materials and property, there is need for an established authority to ensure good governance, proper policing, maintain public order, enforce rule of law, dispense justice, determine sanctions and execute them. This is a socio-legal requirement in any peace-loving society. However, under certain exigencies, commands of justice may ordain sanctions that may deem palpably evident and circumstantially prudent. Hence, pooling of all functions in a single centre of authority may not be a good idea. It would need division of executive and judicial powers and a rational segregation of functional authority.

Space tourists and celestial settlers are not astronauts and do not attract the special provision 'as envoys of mankind' in outer space under Article V of the OST. They are also not eligible for the protections guaranteed under the Astronauts Rescue and Return Agreement (ARRA).[89] Therefore, this category of persons, as tourist or celestial resident, would temporarily lose their nexus with national affiliation and state jurisdiction; and would be governed under a common template of rules for all residents in space, in transportation or in orbital resorts, irrespective of their nationality. The complexion of such an authority and the strength of its arms is a debatable issue; yet its necessity is vindicated and cannot be denied. Therefore, a governance set-up must be conceded in some form and structure. Such an institution is certainly indispensable to any good polity. And it cannot be effectively controlled from Earth and should better be positioned *in situ*.

Apropos, if a proposal may be ventured, it could be a Sheriff or a resident Mayor on the pattern of British tradition of governance, appointed by the UN, and mandated to hold peace in a settlement area with touristic interests or for each celestial colony. It could be an institution vested with comprehensive powers like policing, magisterial, administrative, judicial and executive all rolled into one but with a caveat for due sensitivity and compassion, restrained discretion, and moral responsibility for ones acts, ordinances and judgements. This necessitates a secular administrative dispensation that is rigorously neutral, strictly objective, and transparently non-partisan. For a similar purpose in spacecraft or orbital hotels or floating pleasure resorts, the Captain of the craft or module could be designated and vested with appropriate powers on the lines of Rights of the Commander of an Aircraft as contained in the Tokyo Convention, 1963.[90]

Another pertinent consideration in this regard relate to terrorism that is rife and rampant on the globe. Social values have deteriorated and individual perception has been blurred with biases. Racial groups and ethnic denominations often take to violence for perceived grievances and illusory wrongs believed to be perpetrated on them. These outfits usually select soft targets to avenge themselves and for spectacular media blitz. So, a disruption by terrorist is a distinct possibility, however, remote. Under a similar situation earlier, aircraft and aviation facilities appeared just the opportunities to succeed. And it is logical to surmise that now space infra-structure, space travel, space tourism, and space settlements could be in target. Thus, security of space activities comes in for prime importance and protection by whatever methods or devices whether through human, mechanical, electronic, optical or even futuristic gadgets becomes imperative. We need to pre-empt such eventuality intelligently and obviate impending risk.

It would be rather simplistic to recommend drafting of analogous treaties as for hijacking etc. due to peculiar and claustral conditions of space travel, uncomfortable low gravity and un-ergonomic cramped environment of orbital resorts and celestial settlements, and security of corporate properties. This may need different and innovative solutions, security techniques, and counter tactics. Anyway, good governance and high vigilance cannot be under-rated. At the same time, it would be natural for the tourist to expect a reasonable assurance of peaceful enjoyment of the trip with commensurate freedom and desired privacy. Therefore, adequate legal adjuncts to the regimen and enforcement machinery should be in place before the tourism industry can increase its footfall and flourish as a service provider.

Standard Contracts for Space Travel

Mankind has well-nigh reached the threshold of technology where the era of hyper-speed travel, inter-planetary tourism, celestial habitations, and commercial space travel appear just round the corner and may actualise sooner than expected. For achievement of this purpose the requirement is for space-capsules, space-liners, and space-ports. The hybrid space shuttle has since undertaken scores of successful missions and its technical competence, safety standards, and effective re-usability has been proved beyond doubt. Developments by private enterprises, like Lockheed Martin or SpaceX or Virgin Galactic or Blue Origin or Bigelow, have all been encouraging and have borne fruit of experience. It now appears that safe, affordable and regular orbital trips round the Earth would soon commence and eventually be extended for space tourism and to habited planets. Space commerce has come to stay and proliferate benignly.

Concurrently, enterprising organisations have carried out extensive market research in the US, Japan and Germany and have thrown up spectacular results. A sizeable population in the US is willing to spend $100,000 for an orbit to view the sublime beauty of our planet from heavenly heights. The Japanese have shown a keen desire to spend even their life-time savings for such a dream trip. In Germany also people have expressed similar longings and willingness to invest in a thrilling experience. The response appears stupendously exploitable and commercially lucrative. The overwhelming enthusiasm is endorsed by the fact that nearly two scores of private fare-paying space tourists have already orbited Earth and stayed at the ISS; and their safe return has boosted public confidence in this commercial service. Thus, there is optimism about the imminence of a splurging space travel industry despite endemic risks and health hazards of such an adventurous transport mode.

Experience tells that any new mode of transportation, when commercialised and offered to the public as a service, carries with it contractual obligations and liability commitments for the carrier *vis-à-vis* rights assured to the user. Safety of travel is the principal imperative. Apart from privity of contract and the liability syndrome, certain duties attach to the carriers under the domestic Tort law also. Despite the reciprocity of rights and obligations between the service provider and the passenger, the condition of safe transportation remains binding and uncompromisable; and demands 'due diligence' in space travel in *quid pro quo* for the consideration paid as ticket fare.

Concomitant regulatory responsibilities devolve on the state to enact domestic laws and the world community as a whole to negotiate international treaties analogous to air travel. The existing legal regime of outer space comprises a few international conventions and agreements, scant statutory law by the states, and a few nascent concepts of space jurisprudence. This law though obliquely permits private enterprise to undertake space activities yet, their commercial character and business motivations in some respects come under the umbra of doubt that needs to be cleared by suitable amendment or a *specialis* protocol to the OST or a justifiably separate and independent Private ISL instrument.

For safe, regular and scheduled service of space travel, this mutual obligation and assurance syndrome is peculiar in many ways and beset with myriad juristic obstacles and legal implications as well as dilemmas of entrepreneurial decisions in the future. The present concerns relate to standardisation of ticketing formats, terms of the contract, and conditions of liability for likely accidents in space travel that constitute a problem that has not yet been considered and addressed. This reveals that the private international law of space is woefully inadequate, in fact almost non-existent, for commercial tidings and to regulate commercial travel service activities of corporate entities in outer space. Analogous rules and procedures exist for air travel that can be applied *mutatis mutandis.* It rings a timely clarion call for radical ideation on the subject.

Past experience reminds that when air travel came on the scene, each air carrier had enforced his own individual format for the ticket and contractual conditions attendant thereto. The ticketing procedure was cumbersome and contracts rarely just or equipoised. Initially, the air carriers contracted out most of their liability on specious grounds like *volenti non fit injuria* meaning voluntary acts (of hazardous nature) need no compensation or the *force majeure* clause implying act of God or doctrine of *lex non cogit ad impossibilia* meaning that law does not compel the impossible or the defence of *abundanti cautela* implying that abundant caution and care was exercised or other arbitrary exonerating reasons. The fine print in the contract was generally neither prominently displayed nor carefully read; thus these negative clauses were least understood as these hardly became apparent to the passenger anxious about his impending journey or enthusiastic about his anticipated experience.

The traveller also often failed to appreciate international dimension of legal implications in respect of the documents signed by him. It was after a lot of personal travails and public uproar that governments intervened for corrective and regulatory purposes and ultimately the Warsaw Convention, 1929 was formalised at the international level. Though the Convention had its weak points and delinquencies, yet it was fairly protective of passenger interests and assured reasonably equitable liability under pre-known conditions. The vested imbalance in mutual interests espoused under company contracts had been fairly rectified. The Warsaw Convention has since operated very well and has now been updated and improved by the Montreal Convention, 1999.

This predicament is bound to be confronted again with the rush for space travel. The era of billionaires who could engage a battery of lawyers to vet or customise their contracts is almost over. Today, it will be the middle class that will scramble for the affordable orbital delights in outer space as a life-time memory in return for lifetime savings. They will be too excited about the promised experience and neither would have legal acumen for a critical examination of documents by themselves nor be able to afford legal scrutiny by professionals. Thus, the passengers may inadvertently overlook their legitimate concerns. That the balance would tilt in favour of operators' cartel is natural and obvious because competition would be scant thus allowing monopolistic and restrictive practices to rule the roost. This likely inequity and coercive paradigm need to be checked by appropriate action by the states and the world community at the global level. The obligation appears *pro bono* binding as well as a mandate of good governance in public interest.

It now seems pertinent to highlight some probable areas of discord that would require harmonisation of mutual interests. The conflict issues would relate to arbitrariness in selection criteria for travel permission, incongruous standards of health fitness prevalent world-wide, disputes on rejection after zero-gravity training[91] and assessment of capacity to withstand G-stress, *prima facie* absolute liability of the carrier in eventuality of accidents, uniform jurisprudential philosophy of the courts on award of damages, compensation in *restitutio in integrum* and other cognate matters. This list is, however, random and not comprehensive.

Space-worthiness of the vehicle, competence of the crew, and negligence of ground crew at blast-off or recovery are other issues for which there is no international agency for certification or independent monitoring or accident investigation. Disputes may also arise on pleas in defence set up by the carriers, like *force majeure,* contributory negligence of the passenger, lack of *abundanti cautela* (abundant caution), limitation of time to bar suits, jurisdiction of court, divergent connotation of wilful misconduct, etc. Of course, this list is only suggestive and not complete on all aspects. But the need for standard commercial documents for universal application in space travel stands vindicated. It is wisely said, uniformity never discriminates.

The remedy, for such aberrations in carriers' behaviour or unilateral contractual provisions, lies in formulating a Convention on Private ISL that would ensure judicious equilibrium of the interests of the passengers, certainty in liabilities, insurance of endemic risks, and economics of the enterprise. The purpose here is to caution the future space travellers to be conscious and vigilant so that they do not forfeit their enforceable rights and actionable interests due to sheer ignorance or languorous attitude or angst of risks or due to the excitement of impending thrill of experience.

It is also proposed as an agenda for the UN to hold an International Convention where states are urged for greater understanding on unregulated issues and are impelled by a normative compulsion to cooperate for the public good. A voluntary standardisation in ticketing and liability concepts by an association of the carriers' themselves would definitely be a laudable step in the right direction. The insurance industry must also contribute its mite to facilitate determination of conscionable premium and quantum of liability based on anticipated risks and actuaries; and data on accidents and consequent damages.

Standards of Safety in Space Travel

Certain acceptable standard of safety is a prime desideratum in space travel. Current statistics of failures in blast-off or accidents in space are no real indicators of actuaries or the threshold of safety in travel. In real life, technology may provide a quantum jump in service applications of its delivery systems but it cannot foster or improve public trust without convincing with proven facts or a connect with accountability. International space law embodies this concept of safety vis-à-vis liability in the OST under article VII. The scope of international liability seems broad and comprehensive yet has been amplified by Liability Convention[92] and further clarified by a UN General Assembly resolution of 2004. Incidentally, Liability Convention has been, generally dubbed and described as victim-oriented document for an entailed casualty. The germane provisions are thus loud and clear but these international instruments are state-centric and make the aggrieved party dependent upon state instrumentalities and their diplomatic compulsions for the success of its claim of damages, reparation or compensation. Thus, *locus standi* of an individual as space traveller to litigate and obtain legitimate dues at an international forum is missing. However, privity of contract through ticket as contract document may help the situation to some extent.

This gap in adjudication for compensation in accident injuries or death or for other reasons can be partly made up through Tort Law, at least for domestic passengers travelling on national space-lines. Tort Law is a fairly developed branch of traditional laws, and in fact, enjoins a duty on the carrier to ensure safe and comfortable travel, granting the technological limitations of the liner as also peculiarities and hazards of the domain. Even the existing laws require that a provider of carrier service, on commercial basis and for consideration, has a duty towards the passenger for the safety in transit. Such a provision applies universally to carriage by road, rail, and air and its analogous applicability and mandate to space travel is automatically vindicated and strongly recommended.

Past experience with other modes of travel puts us wise that any new mode of transportation after trial-testing, when commercialised and offered to the public as a regular and scheduled service, carries with its contractual obligations certain duties towards the passenger *vis-à-vis* rights assured to the user. Safety of travel is prime among them. Apart from privity of contract and the liability syndrome, certain duties attach to the carriers under the domestic Tort law also. Despite the reciprocity of rights and obligations between the service provider and the passenger, the condition of safe transportation remains binding and uncompromisable.

Thus, the service provider is encumbered with two types of liability, the first is the risk liability and the second is default liability. The former is connected with endemic and ambient risks in operations of the service. Many of these are not under the control of the carrier, for example, the weather conditions in upper atmosphere or space situational compulsions due to the floating space debris or the impact of natural disasters like sun-flares or other spatial disturbances. Many, though not all, of these risky occurrences are literally *force majeure* and thus are defensible and condonable. For additional controls, technology and operations would require fail-safe systems and standby or sleep modules wherever necessary or possible. In fact, technology is far more developed as shown by a comparison that the amount of RAM in Apollo Guidance Computer in NASA's first moon mission was 4KB only while many Android phones today have a million times more RAM, i.e., 4 GB. Hence, technology cannot be an omnibus excuse to the carriers to contract out liability.

The other aspect is default liability where there is human involvement. The essence of fault is reliant on the conduct or behaviour of the party imbued with discipline and propriety in action. This mandate of safety commands 'due diligence' in actions in operation of commercial space travel in *quid pro quo* for the consideration paid as ticket fare. This also includes carrier's space situational awareness and access to data, whether free or paid, to ensure safety from the angle of space intrusions by debris and space traffic control. Thus, the law enjoins on the carrier a duty of due diligence and a duty of utmost care by all the involved employees. In such causes, negligent conduct of the party assumes importance and their faltering intention or lack of *abundanti cautela* is vital for ascribing fault to the operator and for claim of damages, so as not to jeopardize the rights and interests of the passenger.

It also seems pertinent to allude here that the passenger, most often, is unable to adduce facts in support of complaint, except his own experience or the factum of death during travel. All other evidence, including the crashed-craft and personnel responsible for the accident, remain within the control of the operator and may indulge in *suppresio veri* and, thus, may not share incriminating evidence or crucial information. Therefore, the complainant needs to be conferred with the advantage of the doctrine of *res ipsa loquitur* (meaning facts speak for themselves, thus implying need no proof) that shifts the responsibility from the complainant to prove its case of damage or loss to a burden on the defendant to justify its innocence or actions or condonability in defence of the claim. However, application of this doctrine has to be carefully modulated in cases of damage suffered by both parties in satellite crashes.

Let us accept that safety is not a single act of an individual or a binary situation confronting the crew in a given predicament but comprises a system of safety management and a culture of operations shared by all concerned in the space travel industry. It may be conceded that standardised safety management system acts like a glue that binds all disparate activities. It is effective only if integrated from the beginning and not foisted later; else it acts as filler for cracks as opposed to adhesion infused in the system. As on today, all space-worthiness certifications are in-house with the national space agency or the object-launcher organisation. This leaves a lot to be desired for space travel safety and sharply points towards an urgent need for standardisation of best practices for safety and their strict compliance, even on voluntary basis.

It is believed that sub-orbital flights are neither certified for air-worthiness nor on the parameters of crash-worthiness. The manufacturers and travel operators insist that this requirement be waived because the industry cannot afford flight test criteria mandated for aerospace design and manufacture. It is argued that under such rules, the development of fail-safe systems and test attrition costs would escalate and perforce would have to be borne by the passenger through raised tariff, thus making such travel economically less attractive leading to loss of business. Therefore, unless a strong message goes to all concerned, the levels of safety will tend to get compromised and will not easily get standardized, thereby jeopardizing passenger safety and undermining passenger confidence. This will be a dampener for space travel industry.

Personal Identification Document for Inter-Planetary Travel

It is always desirable, and sometimes mandatory, that every traveller should carry a personal identification document during journey for facilitation. This could be any national, state-issued public document or a passport for international travel and immigration purposes. But with space travel and space tourism becoming popular and convenient and comfortable, the carriers and service providers may offer multiple destinations to turn it into inter-planetary experience and eventually may extend to deep space visits on inter-stellar travel. Thus a space tourist will have a choice of movement and option to select the destination. Well, whatever may be its timeframe, the beginning is going to be soon.

It becomes pertinent at this stage to consider whether space tourists would continue to be identified by their global nationality and national passports; or may be issued a new inter-stellar document that could be more descriptive of current residence and futuristic in format and content, even for contact with aliens if so encountered. It could be a document called as Space Pass for Inhabitant of the Planet Earth (IPE) on the lines of national pass. It could be used for immigration of tourists on departure and return and as emigration record of permanent settlers on celestial bodies. This process could be analogous to global procedures for the purpose. It is further suggested that it be issued by the UN, OOSA for the present till superseded by a higher Authority or Organisation so designated.

In this digitized world, there can be another alternative that instead of Space Pass hard copy, space travellers may be issued an identification chip of specific size with standardized personal and planetary details which could be embedded under the skin on the same part of the human body. This option of Space Pass will offer several advantages. First, it will be on the person at all times, all places, and all occasions. Secondly, it will be tamper-proof with no risk of loss or defacement or mutation. And, the best advantage could be automated clearance for entry or exit from anywhere and would dispense the need for physical production of hard copy and its part-manual verification.

VULNERABILITIES IN SPACE

Humans are, today, genetically adjusted and generationally accustomed to the physical environment and living conditions on Earth, whether in terms of availability of oxygen in the air to breathe, pull of its gravity, pressure of atmospheric gases, the rotation of Earth on its axis and resultant day-and-night regularity or the revolution around the Sun, and consequential exposure to the seasons on Earth. Thus, all earth-borne living beings are acclimatised to such an environment and can live here in believably good health and for the full expectation of their lives in municipally provided utilities, societal conveniences, and individually procured comforts.

Space travel, it must be accepted, is definitely exciting and adventurous to the mind and body but at the same time difficult, rigorous, hazardous and even dangerous; it constitutes an unnatural experience for the humans of Earth. It, for sure, would not be as comfortable as air travel of today because of its high velocity, multi-mach speed, spin-effect of centrifugal forces, G-effect on blood circulation and spatial orientation, vibration-feel, weightlessness, cosmic and solar radiation exposure, congested and vestibular space, and un-ergonomic posture during travel, among others. Cumulatively, these effects may induce vertigo, nausea, giddiness, headache and vomiting, changes in blood circulation, disorientation and even a black-out condition, generically summed up as symptoms of space sickness. The resultant symptoms can be highly challenging and serious to endure in a continuous journey, with no instant medical support.

After all, space travel and celestial journey is no carnival ride of ease and pleasure; and as such not all prospective aspirants, despite their financially paying capacity, will be medically fit enough in health to be able to fly to the edge of space. Many will not meet the health standards and many more will be weeded out in aptitude tests or after failure in rigorous training in simulated claustrophobic environment and other rigours of space flight. In fact many of these hardships of space travel and travails of the astronauts have remained private experience and have not been shared in public, for whatever reason.

For example, micro-gravity sets our fluids wandering in the body and weakens muscles, the cosmic radiation tears through the DNA, and harsh vacuum outside is an ever-present threat. In general, microgravity impacts metabolism, heat regulation, heart rhythm, muscle tone, bone density, eyesight, and the respiration system. In 2017, the Russian scientists found microgravity causes alarming changes to the immune system that astronauts would struggle to shake off even a minor virus like the common cold. Another research in 2016 found that astronauts who travelled into deep space on lunar missions were five times more likely to have died from cardiovascular disease than those who went in low orbit or on Earth.[93]

Having become aware of the stress and sufferings of space travel, many, except the really determined and brave, will give up their musings at this not too pleasant prospect. Therefore, some of the desirous may withdraw their option with this knowledge and some others may not be able to take the onerous toll for health reasons and retire midway in the exacting training. In fact, a paid tourist goes for fun and pleasure while for an astronaut it is a duty. Thus, the final selectees will not be a large number. And sometimes, even a selectee may be ousted of the mission at the last minute as happened to astronaut Jeanette Epps from the assignment of flight engineer on ISS. She was to take off as replacement crew with other astronauts in Soyuz mission in June, 2018.[94]

It is to be expected that space travel will be full of woes, or at least accompanied with great discomfort, unless one is healthy in body and mind; as well as physiologically well-trained and psychologically thoroughly indoctrinated for this risky and unique, yet a thrilling, travel experience. Despite all the strict selection procedures, long acclimatization and rigorous training, there have been cases of astronauts vomiting in flight, which apart from creating a smelly mess, can lead to a dangerous situation and a fatal risk because in many cases no external medical help can be provided for amelioration.

Space sickness is termed as Space Adaptation Syndrome (SAS) by NASA and astronaut trainers believe that this condition is natural and gets adapted over time and with experience. Jake Garn of Astronaut's Corps has made a mark in SAS severity and represents the maximum level of space sickness in humans. SAS, generally, hits both sexes alike, males and females almost equally and it does not matter if one has flown earlier and has space travel experience. In view of this common occurrence, NASA's training aircraft where astronauts are trained to experience weightlessness is colloquially known as the 'vomit comet'.

The Apollo-8 crew was the first to report space sickness in 1968 and the Apollo-9 crew was feeling so bad that their scheduled spacewalk had to be postponed for this reason. Astronaut Anna Fisher, who became the first mother in space, was said to be sick for first two days of her mission on the Discovery space shuttle in 1984.[95] Wubbo Ockel, the first Dutch astronaut, suffered sickness in space in 1986. A Russian astronaut also puked while in space.[96] And in 2017, astronauts suffered from "space fever" which has serious implications for longer duration deep-space probes.[97]

Again the conditions and externalities on various destinations on different astral bodies in outer space are going to be drastically different for availability of breathing oxygen gas, in ground gravity, atmospheric pressures, temperature variations, and other usual survival parameters. Therefore, even indirect exposure to such conditions may not be conducive to human living, whether for short trips or long sojourns or for permanent living. So there would be need for making human capsules with greater comforts and cabin conditions more akin to those in air travel. Similarly, there will be necessity for construction of structurally suitable habitats and artificially creating liveable internal conditions within such enclosures that are fit for human living provided with daily conveniences and enjoying personal comforts.

These are, as yet, only imaginary blue-prints and sketched visualisations. Woerner's Moon Village is still on the drawing board though touted as ESA's next destination in its journey for exploration of space. But due to its billion-Euro project size, no European country is willing to fund it singly and enthusiasm for a collaborative joint mission is weak. In fact, the idea is yet to catch fire and scientific interest in the Moon is waning. However, the US has lately shown interest in this project and its favourable reaction may ignite other minds to recognize merit in this proposal.[98] NASA has plans to establish a lunar outpost called Lunar Orbital Platform Gateway Project that will be smaller than ISS and its construction will begin in 2022. India has also designed and tested an igloo model of domed habitat unit that has been successful in laboratory lunar terrain. More specific tests are in the offing.

Again Mars Colony, too, is as yet in imagination though its mysteries are fascinating and the US rovers on Mars have travelled long trails in dense atmosphere.[99] Curiosity rover's *in situ* discovery of rain-like dense methane atmosphere is indeed promising information and points towards possible existence of life. The scientists, however, differ in their views and consider rapid changes in atmosphere due to geological processes like 'deliquescence' meaning salt-absorbing water in the atmosphere. Another opinion posits that what was encountered by Curiosity was a random outburst of methane gas and not a methane rain leading to flowing aquifers.[100]

Therefore, in practical implementation, these fantasised visions for human habitat, whether for short stay or permanent settlement, may face many challenges comprising concept faults, design defects, construction material availability, labour limitations in work (due to handicap in complementarities between human capital and machine utilisation), adverse environmental configuration, and assorted technical glitches. It would be, thus, obvious to expect unknown imponderables confronting projects on a strange terrain, with untried materials, in a new external environment and under utterly different working conditions. The dilemmas thus appear genuine for the specialists to reconfigure solutions and may take considerable time to resolve.

Despite the popular belief that human migration to celestial destinations is a snowballing idea whose time has come, there are some dismal prophets with pessimistic perceptions, like Tronchetti,[101] who believe that in space commerce segment, at present, fictional competitive conditions prevail in an almost non-existent market.[102] The euphoria generated may not turn into reality for quite some years. Thus the visualized celestial habitations may take a while before their actuality. Even if it be so, this available time can be converted into a useful opportunity to set things right beforehand, legally, functionally, regulatory and operationally, so that no glitches occur when operations commence. The momentum must be incentivized.

Be that as it may, let's now consider the known and possible impact of continuous living in outer space for whatever period and the possible changes on return to Earth. *Achtung!* The caution is real and necessary. Some effects like high speeds, living in non-gravity environment, low oxygen density, anti-G space suits have been scientifically studied and analysed and found to be reversible, while many others are only surmised on possibilities and inadequate subject observations. These are likely to unfold with time and experience and may even turn out to be irreversible changes. These are briefly alluded to in succeeding paragraphs.

Physiological Effects

Despite the euphoria and excitement about space travel, it must be accepted that outer space and celestial bodies do not offer a very hospitable environment to humans acclimatized to the comforts of Earth. The handicaps are: extremely low or nil gravity, no atmosphere with external pressure, no breathing oxygen in the air, the smell of the soil and outer space, and vagaries of planetary terrain, to list only some of the discomforts. Therefore, due to this altered environment, adverse physiological effects are bound to be telling on the human body and these will be more pronounced and severe for longer travel time in deep space or prolonged stays or permanent residence. Many of the effects may become pronounced only on return to Earth or be irreversible in impact.

Some of the effects are well known with documented evidence collected over decades of human space travel and stay at the ISS, yet there may be many unknown risks to human body and psyche. These are linked with nutrient displacement, oxygen deprivation, and body inflammation. These causes can relate to bone loss leading to weakening and deformity in joints, feeling of fatigue and backaches, weakening and atrophy of muscles, shift in fluids inside the body, reduced immunity condition, and recordable changes in eye vision. Impairment in the faculty of taste also occurs due to mild swelling of the tongue, but under micro-gravity condition though the astronauts can digest most foods yet find difficulty with carbonation and tend to get 'wet burps' due to bubbles wanting to rise and come back up.

Astronauts on lengthy space missions also risk suffering from "Space Fever" because low gravity and weightlessness in space induces an increase in body temperature of about 1 degree C.[103] Such changes appear in about three months' time and debilitate physical and impair mental performance. Thus space fever, in particular, has potential health implications for 'humanned missions' to Mars and other longer deep-space flights. Astronauts actually suffered this condition and its debilitating effects in 2017.[104] Another risk of radiation from space has lately been detected with an unusual isotopic molecular gas, possibly an isotope of Aluminium. This radiation is believed to have emanated from an ancient stellar explosion[105] and constitutes a potential imperilment to humans in space as well as from the radiation absorbed by space objects that return to Earth. We may need serious efforts for protection from this risk.

Therefore, human vulnerabilities in space are being investigated more thoroughly for long-period flights and prolonged stays in space environment. More than 200 researchers are studying the world's only twin astronauts, Scott, who lived in ISS for 340 days and Mark Kelly who remained on Earth as control subject. Their physical and mental health was monitored and mapped at several determining stages for comparison and now both are under scrutiny for their physiology, immune system, eyesight, bone formation, DNA, gut bacteria and other systems and parameters.[106]

Physical changes recorded periodically include 2-inch height gain by Scott due to low gravity and low-oxygen ambient conditions in space. But this has proved to be a temporary change and reversible on return to the *terra firma*. Other changes induced in space include that his body mass had decreased and that the nature and quality of gut bacteria were completely different. Certain changes in faculties have also been observed, in particular, a decrease in his cognitive speed after return to the Earth.[107]

However, some irreversible changes that remained transformed relate to genes involved in bone formation, oxygen deprivation, immune system responses, and DNA repair. Yet another unpleasant aspect of space travel or stay is that it can start off changes in cell's biological pathways that can ultimately trigger cell degradation and mutate cell function. Referring to the DNA code, it has been reported that living in space caused chromosomes to grow longer but altered genetic expression (note code) that reflects whether genes are turned on or turned off. This change has persisted and not yet reversed even after six months of his return.[108]

To counter this ill effect, which carries the risk of cancer and dementia, NASA is contemplating to shield the crew with physical armour or electro-magnetic force field, but this appears impractical. Alternatively, NASA is looking at a range of solutions, from drug therapy to genetic modification. But the solution chosen may have ethical consequences. The matter is under thorough consideration in respect of prolonged mission crew. And to change the DNA of its Mars-mission astronauts to protect them from radiation may be the last resort in the interest of their health and well-being.[109]

Socio-Psychological Effects

Further, Moon Village is a key notion only, but the core concept is the homogeneity of community and congeniality in living that emerges when a heterogeneous group of people live in societal congregation, join forces in one place, albeit not necessarily in one direction and without any common or concrete plans for the future. Harmony does not ooze out from such a disparate society and relations may not always be cordial and convivial. The humans would have simply come together for shared aspiration, common interest and to contribute individual capabilities in support-endemic predicament without much attention to the details of relational contact, gravity of impending hazards, and confidence in solicited cooperation. The chinks in such a normative living are obvious; cohesion and amiability may be missed.

The principle of space village is not sheer cubicles and dormitories in so congested and so claustrophobic enclosed environment but an experiment of living together for common goals and induced unanimity. Whatever is their avocation or interest back on earth, their avowed aim for opting for such living is scientific investigation, technology development, exploiting ambient resources for betterment of their living and common welfare of the local society. It would thus be a community of many nationalities which better discard or leave behind on earth differences of opinion, their worldly mind-set of bigotry and hatred as well as their cultural prejudices and preferences. The aspiration is thus for duty-based society rather than right-centric relationship. Hope for such a Utopia can be sustained only with normal doubts and genuine paranoia.

To repeat the sociological implications of space settlements, it may be reiterated that each settlement would be an eclectic collective of population who would call it their permanent home. They would constitute a heterogeneous, non-cohesive group of people who are from different culture system, linguistic background, religious denomination, racial affinity, educational achievements, and professional leanings. Considering these diverse differences, in the new colonial set up the residents would need to find anew their physical moorings, societal affiliations, psychological bonding, behavioural equations, and emotional support systems. Ergo, the need is to evolve a new eco-system of relationships for space composites of closed-loop habitats. Perforce, integration and cohesion within space societies would be a generational process per necessity.

However, for temporary visitors for short-term stays such a living condition may not be the happiest situation despite thrills and novelty of experience. Limited spaces, limited facilities, and limited comforts in a claustrophobic environment may cause irritability and induce pugnacity. Again, being strapped with attachments or floating for commuting in low gravity condition is not normal to human living and may generate an irksome feeling of being encumbered. Even rigorous training cannot counter the force and conditioning of habits and the resultant discomfort can be disconcerting. Another aspect is staying away from dear ones for relatively long periods may cause pangs and disturb the mind. This may create mental tension and lead to violence and crimes, however minor. In reality, any group of people or community inhabiting certain area or engaging in any activity is eventually bound to have disputes due to clash of egos, behavioural delinquency, conflict of interest, norm violation or legal infringement. This possible predicament leads us to the need for a discipline enforcement authority.[110]

Human psyche is complex and even unpredictable. Polls and surveys throw up surprising results indicating that the human race seems prepared and ready for migration to other celestial bodies in the outer space regardless whether it is a one-way ticket to Mars or a return ticket to the Moon. This implies that humans are willing to go to space jaunts and celestial habitations as leisure tourists, holiday seekers, and temporary visitors, or even for permanent living, forsaking their affection to and affiliations with the mother Earth. This infatuated attraction, changed mindset, strangely stirred feelings, and overwhelming desire to migrate portend a revulsive sentiment, heightened disenchantment with the existing abode, lack of enation with the present social milieu or dis-affinity with the parent nation. Acceptance of space tourism as a social fad is OK but adverse 'psychologisation' of society, even in small part, should be a matter of concern.

Therefore, this crazy keenness and senseless rush to other planets expresses a significant disaffection and utter disillusionment of humans, for whatever reasons, from their mother Earth. Even such intent or propensity for demographic migration to new, unknown and as yet uninhabited, extra-terrestrial locations in societal disgust is indicative of social disharmony and lack of global conviviality. This trend is ominous and disconcerting with portentous implications. It, thus, presents no 'laugh-out-loud' affair that can be viewed in a cavalier fashion. The *angst* is real and it certainly posits a cause of deep concern for the intelligentsia and social scientists to arrest the likely damage to life and society before the point after which there is no road for retreat.

CONCLUSION

It can now be concluded that the humans are enthusiastic and excited about travel into outer space despite high cost of transportation, hazards of space travel, and not yet high safety standards of space worthiness of vehicles. Anyway, these negativities are being improved, rapidly and confidently. Similarly, the human race also seems ready and prepared for fun in space modules, leisure trips to hotels on celestial bodies, and even permanent settlement in the Moon Village or the Mars Colony or the future habitations. This trendy development has come to stay and is bound to get impetus with advancing space technology and consequent cost reductions all around.

At the time of the conquest of the outer space and during the period of negotiations for the OST, it could not be presaged that the exfoliating space technology and its applications will open up the space domain to such varied and variegated opportunities and uses. Therefore, the OST, despite its visualisation of the ensuing predicaments and a futuristic stance, could not foresee the evolution of space applications so fast and so multifaceted. As a result, today, outer space is open to scientific exploration, peaceful uses, military applications, commercial exploitation, private enterprise ventures, space tourism, and for permanent settlement of human race on celestial bodies.

The OST and allied treaties, as the specialised corpus of space law, have handled the changing situation and growing diversity of activities so well for over half a century. The wisdom of the treaties deserves to be applauded and the majesty of space law upheld. But whatever are the high merits of the treaties, their weaknesses and inadequacies are becoming apparent despite twisted 'lawgical' interpretations. In fact, no single law or a small set of treaties can handle such diversity of uses, such multiplicity of players, such divergence of motivations, and such disparate objectives. The disorientation of purpose and lack of sensitivity to each other is obvious in the space arena that hosts strategic interests of militaries, political ambitions of nations, investigative aspirations of the scientific fraternity, and profit expectations of the business community.

Thus, the conflict of interest stares us in the face and cannot be reconciled and harmonized by public international law alone. Understandably, to govern other aspects of space activities, there would be need for other genre of laws to control and regulate different operative elements e.g. scientific investigation, strategic military initiatives, commercial business ventures, conduct of private and corporate players, space tourism operations, and permanent human migration to celestial settlements. Under the circumstances, the necessity for particularized laws for specific activities cannot be wished away, howsoever liberally we interpret the existing instruments.

Therefore, rather than mutate the meaning of current space law or corrupt the space jurisprudence, it would be prudent to negotiate new regulations that are specialized, specific and direct to the object or situation. This cannot be achieved by generic instrument of a single variety but by *lex specialis* tackling each hue of space activity effectively and efficaciously while attending to the working problems of each broad entity. Commercial activities in loosely regulated economies or liberal markets cannot be normative *per se*; and tend to observe scant public morality and profit considerations reign supreme. It, thus, appears imperative that a domain so sensitive, so exploitable, so vulnerable, and so open to a mixed set of players should be protected for its optimal sustainability and regulated in the interest of humanity.

It is understandable that diplomatic negotiation of treaties is so difficult, laborious and time consuming, yet we cannot shirk away from such a solemn duty for the betterment and welfare of humankind. In spite of known handicaps and imponderables, as also the given scenario and the predicament, there is an incumbent yet onerous task of choosing the best solution and implementing it expeditiously with global felicity and confidence building. The frailties of the OST and other space law corpus are now well-known and must be honestly acknowledged because provocative defiance of OST will be least desirable. In the same breath, forced escape medians from the treaties and resort to frail legal sophistry to vindicate individual profit motives is equally condemnable. It will, thus, be prudent to modify and adapt the law to contemporary needs and emerging compulsions. For this purpose, honest cooperation of the space-faring fraternity is sincerely solicited to uphold the majesty of OST and honour traditional precepts of customary space law and build around it legal adjuncts that are suitable and specific, pending a holistic revision of the treaties with futuristic perspective of technology and business initiatives.

The microcosm of space law is sluggish in its metabolism due to UN COPUOS procedures and treaty formation is a notoriously slow process by tradition. These handicaps should neither scuttle the advance of space commercialisation on sheer legalities and a rigid mindset nor at the same time encourage infringements of OST. No wonder, space law is passing through troubled times with pin-pricks from some mis-adventurous countries. Obviously, there is a compelling need to evolve a new legal idiom of governance to handle the flood of space activity in diverse fields and onslaught of new space-users with low threshold of technology as well as private enterprise barging in with profit motive, not to mention the enthusiasm of space tourists and space-settlers.

The new paradigm of space should be able to accommodate second and third generation space activities in commercialisation of outer space and migration to celestial bodies. This calls for professionalised management of celestial real-estate, leasing methodologies for commercial exploitation of natural resources, and immigration regulations for tourists and inter-planetary settlers. Ergo, new space law has to be futuristic in perspective, perceptibly liberal in approach, intrinsically interactive, responsive to contingencies, and conducive to opportunities so that it can assure an all-round unhindered commercial growth, lead humanity on path to an inter-stellar space society, provide the desired economic fillip to exploitation of mineral resources, enable optimal accruals from space business, and ensure distribution of gains 'for the benefit and in the interests of all countries'.

For a task so onerous and multi-faceted and professional, UN OOSA is too skeletal an organisation devoted mostly to secretarial functions. The ensuing space activities with greater private sector involvement are going to turn starkly commercial, to be ventured by corporate conglomerates, for lucrative profit motive, and with business overtones with disregard of common public interest. To interact and handle leases of planetary real estate for touristic hubs and permanent settlements, mining of celestial mineral resources, space travel and tourism, debris scavenging by outsourced agencies, and many others functions are all going to be commercial activities by the private sector. OOSA, in its existing state, can hardly handle such governance efficiently.

It is wisely said that the success of any law is determined by its implementation and the latter depends on the efficacy of enforcement mechanism. The same would apply to treaties, *mutatis mutandis*. But the OST and other treaties provide for no regulatory mechanism nor bear a formal structure embedded in them for proper administration of a domain so vast and bountiful. An externally created secretarial set-up, more as an after-thought, cannot live up to an expectation to restrain a state from doing an act that defeats the objects and purposes of a treaty[111] as well as rein in galloping privatisation of space so that no single state monopolises the easily amenable and lucrative celestial resources and privately appropriate accruals to the detriment of other followers in the race and in denial of sharing benefits with other countries as promised in the OST.

Therefore, to govern and regulate and verify compliance of such activities of diverse nature and content, professionally and competently, there is need for a powerful and specialized institution with broad-spectrum capabilities, say, WSA which could be, if deemed desirable, later converted and upgraded to WSO as an organ of the UN. Hopefully, such a committed and devoted institution will be able to efficiently handle all aspects of all activities in the space domain through its own-evolved criteria, parameters, regulations, modalities and inspection devices; and thus dedicate its services in the interest of common good of mankind and for the common benefit of humanity.

May the road ahead for space activities be full of successful discoveries, cooperative exchanges, business proliferation, industrial initiatives, and societal understanding among space workers and celestial settlers. Let the new era of space activities usher in peace and progress for all space stake-holders, enthusiastic tourists, and permanent space residents with sense and sustainability. Let this slogan reflecting communitarian idealism prevail, '*Astronautica ad pacem, Hominumique progressum*' broadly meaning, let space be at peace and progress for humanity.

NOTES

1. *CNN Television Network,* advertisement appeared on May 25, 1997.
2. Ibid, October 22, 1997
3. *Reuter* release issued on December 31, 1997.
4. "You may plan a space holiday next year" in *The Times of India* (Chandigarh Edition), December 14, 2017, p. 18.
5. Ibid.
6. "Space tourists may not be ready for trip beyond Earth", report from London published in *The Times of India* (Chandigarh Edition), June 26, 2018, p. 14.
7. Sheila Marikar, "For $ 55m, the super-rich can escape this planet for 8 days" in *The Times of India* (Chandigarh Edition), June 6, 2018, p. 16.
8. Ibid.
9. Space.com release on October 24, 2017.
10. Discussed later in the Chapter.
11. Valentina Tereshkova, the first female Soviet cosmonaut, expressed a desire to take a one-way ticket to Mars while celebrating her 70th birthday. Presumably, she was upset with 'post-perestroika' conditions and the 1991 collapse of the USSR. She was dissatisfied with culturally desiccated country and felt a loss of existential foundation. Perhaps, it was an implicit wish for a spectacular form of suicide. Dmitry Shlapentokh (Project Syndicate), "Why Valentina Tereshkova wants a one-way ticket to Mars" in *The Times of India* (New Delhi Edition), March, 2007.
12. "You may plan a space holiday next year" in *The Times of India* (Chandigarh Edition), December 14, 2017, p. 18.
13. Mike Wall, "Luxury Space Hotel to Launch in 2021", in *Space.com,* April 5, 2018.
14. Ibid.
15. The broccoli seeds have been sent in the replenishment shuttle of June, 2018.
16. Herman Potocnik, *The Problem of Space Travel* (1928). The author is also called Herman Noordung.
17. Karl Tate, "A Village in Orbit: Inside NASA's Space Colony Concept" (in Share 2), *Space.com,* August 5, 2013.
18. Ibid.
19. Ibid.
20. The Church of Scientology, too, believes that over-population on planets had occurred millions of years earlier also which led to migration to other planets. This belief is discussed later in the Chapter.
21. Harrison Tasoff, "Smithsonian Channel Specials Tell Humanity's Story, From Big Bang to Colonizing Space", Space.com, March 23, 2018.
22. Ibid.
23. Mike Wall, "Mars Colony Would Be a Hedge Against World War III: says Elon Musk" in *Space.com,* March 28, 2018.
24. Ibid.
25. "Hidden lava tubes on Moon and Mars can serve as human habitats", PTI report from London in *Times of India* (Chandigarh Edition), October 1, 2017, p. 7.
26. Data sent by Indian satellite *Chandrayaan-1* proved beyond doubt the existence of water on the Moon.
27. Peter B. de Selding, "Europe Hits Snooze on Woerner's The Moon Awakens Push", *Space News,* January 8, 2016, available at http://spacenews.com/europe-hit-snooze-on-woerners-the-moon-

awakens-push/last visited 4 February, 2017. Dietrich Johann Woerner is the Director General of European Space Agency.

28. "Moon to get its first 4G network next year" in *Times of India*, March 1, 2018 (Times Trends), p. 16.
29. Ibid.
30. Harrison Tasoff report in *Space.com,* October 17, 2017.
31. Ibid.
32. *Space.com* report posted on January 18, 2018 by Patrick McClure and David Poston.
33. Meghan Bartels, "Scientists Discover a Lake on Mars" in *Space.com,* July 25, 2018.
34. "Hidden lava tubes on Moon and Mars can serve as human habitats", PTI report from London in *the Times of India* (Chandigarh Edition), October 1, 2017, p. 7.
35. Ibid.
36. Alex Knapp, "*Dennis Tito's 2018 Mars Flyby is on the Ragged Edge of Feasibility*", available at <http://www.forbes.com/sites/alexknapp/2013/02/27/inspiration-mars-aims-for-2018-flyby-of-the-red-planet/#7ce40869247f>l, last visited on 4 February, 2017.
37. Statement made by Charles Bolden, Director, NASA. See Trent Gillies, *NASA's Bolden: Mars Mission is Closer than Ever,* available at http://www.cnbc.com/2016/04/02/nasas-bolden-mars-mission-is-closer-than-ever.html . Last visited 3 February, 2017.
38. Report by Mike Wall in *Space.com* on 5 February, 2018, on the eve of the Launch. Also refer *The Times of India* (Chandigarh Edition), February 8, 2018, p. 16, Times Trends.
39. Comment by Jay Melosh of Purdue University, "Musk's car carried bacteria to space" in *The Times of India*, March 1, 2018, p. 16. It has been alleged that the payload of the car was not properly sanitized and may have carried microbial infections from the earth contrary to the stipulation of the OST. It is feared that Earth's native terrestrial organisms could interfere with indigenous Mars biota.
40. Plan was announced at 68th International Astronautical Congress at Adelaide on 29 September, 2017.
41. Full form of the codename BFR is Big F_ _ _ing Rocket. This system can operate in the earth's atmosphere also and can carry passengers round the globe in an hour.
42. Adelaide announcement by Elon Musk on 29 September, 2017, n. 35 supra.
43. Mike Wall, in *Space.com* on 5 February, 2018, on the eve of the Launch on 5 February, 2018.
44. Leonard David, *Humans to Mars by 2028? Checkout Lockheed Martin's Red Planet 'Base Camp Idea,* available at <http://www.space.com/32963-mars-base-camp-lockheed-martin-video.html> last visited 4 February, 2017.
45. Elizabeth Howell, "SpaceX and Boeing Test Parachutes for future Astronaut Space Taxi", in *Space.com* April 4, 2018.
46. Discussed later under Psycho-Sociological Vulnerabilities.
47. Report by Elizabeth Howell in *Space.com,* February 14, 2018.
48. *Washingtonpost.com*, January, 2018
49. Mike Wall, "NASA looking at a way to Commercialize International Space Station" *Space.com,* March 5, 2018.
50. Ibid.
51. 'Alief' as suggested by philosopher Tamar Gandler, is opposed to 'belief' in that it makes you shrink from accepting the cognitive obvious. For example, alief is the initial hesitation in stepping on a glass bridge across a canyon despite the knowledge that it is perfectly safe and being used by many every day.
52. Details published by Callie Stewart in "*Wikimedia Commons*" on May 16, 2016. Later updated in 2017.

53. L Ron Hubbard, *Dianetics: The Modern Science of Mental Health* (1950).
54. Virgilliu Pop, Who Owns the Moon? Extra-Terrestrial Aspects of Land and Mining Resources Ownership (Springer, 2009), p. 3. For a more detailed discussion on the subject refer G. S. Sachdeva, *Outer Space: Law, Policy and Governance* (New Delhi, KW Publishers, 2014), p. 165ff.
55. http://asgardia.space/en/word.
56. Ibid.
57. This status was granted at 61st session held in June, 2018.
58. Outer Space Treaty, Article II.
59. Ibid, Article VI.
60. Ibid, Article I, second paragraph.
61. Ibid, Article IX.
62. For a detailed discussion on the subject, refer G.S. Sachdeva, "*Jus Cogens* of Space Law: A Proposal" in his book, *Outer Space: Law, Policy and Governance* (New Delhi, KW Publishers, 2014), pp. 1-29.
63. Alan Wasser and Douglas Jobes, Space Settlements, Property Rights, and International Law: Could a Lunar Settlement Claim the Lunar Real Estate it Needs to Survive?" in *Journal of Air Law and Commerce,* 2008. Vol. 73, No. 1, pp. 43-47. Cited in B. Sandeepa Bhat, ed., *Space Law-The Emerging Trends* (Kolkata, Eastern Law House, 2018), p. 11.
64. G.S. Sachdeva, *Outer Space: Law, Policy and Governance* (New Delhi, KW Publishers, 2014), p. 166.
65. For a detailed discussion on the subject, refer G.S. Sachdeva, ibid, pp. 165-204.
66. Incidentally, it was reported in newspapers in 2011 that Ms. Mayawati, President of Bahujan Samaj Party and then Chief Minister of U.P., India was gifted one such plot on the Moon by her followers.
67. Refer http://www.lunarembassy.com last accessed on 10 April, 2016.
68. Virgiliu Pop, *Who Owns the Moon? Extra Terrestrial Aspects of Land and Mineral Resources Ownership* (Berlin, Springer, 2009).
69. Medieval traders visiting foreign countries used to buy rights from the native ruler to establish suzerainty without national sovereignty.
70. Gregory Nemitz v/s the US and another (2004), US District Court, Nevada.
71. Gregory William Nemitz v. The United States of America, et al, 9th Circuit Court of Appeals, Nevada, Case no. CV-N-0300599-HDM (RAM), reported in Westlaw.
72. Virgiliu Pop, *Who Owns the Moon? Extra Terrestrial Aspects of Land and Mineral Resources Ownership* (Springer, 2009), p. 38.
73. In *re Langevin,* 2012 QCCS 613.
74. Carol R. Buxton," Property in Outer Space: The Common Heritage of Mankind Principle versus the "First in Time, First in Right" Rule of Property Law", *Journal of Air Law and Commerce,* 2004, vol. 69, p. 689ff.
75. Ram Jakhu, "Legal Issues Relating to the Global Public Interest in Outer Space", in *Journal of Space Law,* 2006, vol.32, pp.31-110.
76. B. Sandeepa Bhat, ed., *Space Law: The Emerging Trends* (Kolkata, Eastern Law House, 2018), p. 11 ff.
77. Moon Agreement, 1979 with its "Common Heritage of Mankind" has not been drawn in detail into this discussion because many scholars may object to its tenets because most of the major space-faring powers have consciously refrained from joining and only 14 states have ratified this instrument till 2017.

78. Alexander William Salter, "Ordering the Cosmos, Private Law, Celestial Property Rights" in *Journal of Air Law and Commerce* (2017).
79. Outer Space Treaty, Article III.
80. *The Times of India* (Chandigarh Edition), February 16, 2018.
81. Ibid.
82. "Eight events that will shape the new space race" in *The Times of India* (Chandigarh Edition), November 23, 2017.
83. Ibid.
84. The Times of India (Chandigarh Edition), February 5, 2018. <Surendra.Singh@timesgroup.com>
85. Report by Chethan Kumar from Bangaluru, "Isro working on 'igloos' for future outposts on moon" in *The Times of India* (Chandigarh Edition), February 26, 2018, p. 7. Incidentally, astronauts inform that lunar soil is soft and dusty and smells like gunpowder.
86. Report by Srinivas Laxman from Mumbai, "Water distributed across lunar surface: Nasa probe on Chandrayaan-1" in *The Times of India* (Chandigarh Edition), February 26, 2018, p. 7.
87. In India, it is customary period for land leases. It is extendable to 99 years.
88. Incidentally, this principle of inclusivity of interest and benefit of all countries is mired in a maelstrom of controversy as unearned profit that is unconscionable on justice and equity. Instead, it could be for collective good of mankind and common benefit of humanity. This aspect has not been discussed here as being out of scope.
89. Agreement on the Rescue of Astronauts, the Return of Astronauts and the Return of Objects Launched into Outer Space, 1968.
90. Convention on Offences and Certain Other Acts Committed on Board Aircraft, signed at Tokyo on 14 September, 1963.
91. There is litigation by a lady in the US, in a case of rejection after undergoing physical tests, training and indoctrination. The disappointment in rejection at this stage is understandable. More suits of this nature and for this cause can be expected in the future.
92. Convention on International Liability for Damage Caused by Space Objects, 1972.
93. "Space tourists may not be ready for trip beyond Earth" PTI report from London in The Times of India (Chandigarh Edition), June 26, 2018, p. 14.
94. Megan Gannon, "NASA Astronaut Jeanette Epps speaks about her Puzzling Removal from Mission" in Space.com, June 22, 2018
95. "Space tourists may not be ready for trip beyond Earth" PTI report from London in The Times of India (Chandigarh Edition), June 26, 2018, p. 14.
96. Information from Wikipaedia.
97. Jesh Gabbatiss report, "Astronauts battling space fever in zero gravity" in *The Times of India* (Chandigarh Edition), January 8, 2017.
98. Peter B de Selding, "Europe hits Snooze on Woerner's 'The Moon Awakens' Push" in *Space News,* January 24, 2016.
99. As of April, 2017, NASA Opportunity Rover had travelled 27 miles (43 km) and Curiosity nearly 10 miles (16 km).
100. Mike Wall, "Mystery on Mars: Does Methane Really Indicate Life" *Space.com,* December 18, 2015.
101. Fabio Tronchetti on *Sputniknews.com,* December 3, 2017. Prof Tronchetti is Law Professor at Harbin Institute of Technology in China.
102. Comments in a blog notification on LinkedIn in March, 2018.
103. Jesh Gabbatiss, "*Astronauts battling space fever in zero gravity*" in *The Times of India* (Chandigarh Edition), January 8, 2017.

104. Note 97 *supra.*
105. Chelsea Gohd, "A Radio-active Molecule Detected in space-An Incredible First", in Space.com July 30, 2018.
106. "*Does Living in Space Change How Genes Work?*" (Sourced from NASA, Time, NatGeo), published in *The Times of India* (Chandigarh Edition), March 20, 2018 on Times Special Page.
107. Elizabeth Howell, "NASA Twins Study Verifies Long-Term Health Effects of Space Travel", Space.com, March 12, 2018.
108. Note 86 *supra.* Elizabeth Howell, "NASA Twins Study Verifies Long-Term Health Effects of Space Travel", Space.com, March 12, 2018.
109. Daily Mirror, "Why Nasa may alter astronaut's DNA" in t*he Times of India* (Chandigarh Edition), October 15, 2017.
110. Discussed earlier in section on Legal Implications.
111. Vienna Convention on Law of the Treaties, Article 18.

CHAPTER FOUR

Commercial Order of Outer Space

Quest for Ethical Norms*

INTRODUCTION

Science and technology have amply proved the availability of a vast treasure of natural resources in the celestial bodies, like asteroids and planets and moons, which have since become scarce on the earth and are direly needed for use to sustain and benefit humanity. These are many and myriad. Some uses of outer space relate to situational advantages like geo-synchronous slots for communication and broadcasting or availability of 'astro-estate' for excavation of minerals or as real-estate for tourism infrastructure and for residential settlements on the Moon and Mars, at least for the present. Technology has confirmed the feasibility of their beneficent utilisation and peaceful uses and we already are enjoying some of the results of these applications in our daily lives, though less for convenience and more as progressive addiction.

Motivated by strategic concerns and national security, governments, till recently, have been the sole players in the space arena but are now progressively reducing public funding in furtherance of commercial applications and civil-use technologies. This trend to prune budgetary allocations for research and development of non-strategic objectives has been apparent for some time. Budgetary cuts in the funding of NASA for the year 2019 and pruning of their missions as well as commercialisation of ISS to make its operations

* This is revised and enlarged version of a chapter with similar title in G. S. Sachdeva, *Outer Space: Law, Policy and Governance* (New Delhi, KW Publishers, 2014).

financially self-sustained by the year 2025 are all supporters of this tendency. Some other space-faring countries are adopting this logic and thinking and are inclined to slash their exchequer expenditure except on strategic initiatives with national security importance.[1]

Therefore, space commerce, business and industry by private sector players, is thus next thing in the offing whether for reasons of economic profitability or entrepreneurial vanity or business aggrandizement or commercial adventurism. Fortunately, space technology for civilian peaceful purposes like global communications and broadcasting, remote-sensing and geo-spatial applications, space travel and tourism, space residential settlements, industrial manufacturing in spatial environment, and commercial mining of space resources among others, are also advancing in step with equal rapidity and viability, as well as becoming affordable too, to attract customers and to make business visions feasible and actualize soonest.

It is obvious that enterprises in the outer space and on the celestial bodies would entail colossal outlays of capital and operating liquidity, *albeit* with unforeseeable risks, unknown imponderables, and onerous hazards. Many giant corporations, business conglomerates, and *entrepreneurs extraordinaire* have billions in corporate funds and personal accounts, bear excellent business credit-ratings, and control commensurate infrastructure to muster resources to make space commerce a reality much sooner than anticipated. In fact, this visualisation has been partly realised in commercial space transportation with fare-paying passengers commuting to the ISS and NASA outsourcing transhipment of astronauts to private behemoths in the field like SpaceX and Blue Origin. Therefore, while the players are getting ready fast enough, the rules of the game of space business, industry and commerce have neither been pre-fixed nor adequately addressed. Governmental concerns for public interest and Treaty obligations are compulsive and well established but motivations and dynamics of private astro-players are governed by different considerations and compromises that are not always conducive to societal welfare and international obligations. The divergence is conspicuous and could be internationally embarrassing.

Human beings have not exactly covered themselves with glory in commercial and business activities on Earth. Driven by unquenchable greed for profit and cut-throat competition for egoistic advancement; business values, ethical trade practices, and commercial morality have, in the process, been badly mauled and, often, even sacrificed. Consequently, while commerce has quantitatively increased exponentially on the earth, yet qualitatively it has caused no amelioration in the welfare of humanity. Neither have humans attained any greater peace of mind nor have their sense of satiation for wealth been doused. This hypothesis can be vindicated from the preaching on the art of living, human welfare discourses, and economic history of humankind. The collage reveals exploitation by all, from human slavery to self-centered entrepreneurs to labour chauvinism to profit-sucking by financial wizards. Therefore, let us not cling to our behavioural imperfections; and to carry this commercial mind set and economic culture to the outer space would be hardly complimentary. The signature characteristics of the new economic order of outer space should be equity, equality and humaneness on a level playing field.

The matter is urgent as space industrialisation may be close at hand. Products have been identified that require microgravity conditions or super-cold temperatures or sterile environment of outer space for their manufacturing and processing.[2] In the not too distant future, space laboratories may be set up and specialized workers posted there. Industrial relations between labour and management may not always remain cordial. Safety and welfare of employee should gain primacy rather than profit on invested capital. Further, the law relating to intellectual property rights in outer space is nebulous and needs to be updated so as to conform to supporting global state practice to obviate avoidable legal conflicts.

Now at the threshold of launching on space commerce, with such vast potential, *albeit* with ominous risks, humankind would be wiser to consciously and universally mandate acceptance of new business values, industrial code of conduct, commercial ethics, and trade discipline while harnessing his commercial instincts and business acumen for activities in outer space. In fact, there are already stirrings of a new economic order in outer space which need to be stimulated and nurtured appropriately. It is, of course, conceded that the economic challenges in the outer space market may not be simple or easily assailable. There is also no denying that commerce and industry have their own rules of the game. Yet, it certainly behoves humankind to evolve a New Ethics of Commerce for Outer Space striking a harmonious balance between business management, societal sensibilities, and ecological sustainability. This should then act as Charter of Change for commercial and business activities in space domain. The pillars for such ethics should be justice, fairness and equity based on eternal truths, traditional morality, established values, sensitive inter-relations, co-operative attitude, and Conscious Social Responsibility.[3] The evolved culture, in the absence of a mandate, would require normative self-volition and voluntary adherence. Fortunately, at present, we have the opportunity to usher in necessary reforms, before the economic ills and existing faulty working culture take root, provided we have the political will and a sincere determination to do so.

The above proposition begs a question about whose ethical norms or espoused morality should be emulated. These differ widely even within each nation and international variations are marked and conflictive. Shall that be the cult of consumerist materialism of the West with disregard to humane considerations or the Eastern haste for development with disregard to concomitant ecological consequences? Or should these be values of economics or sociology or theology? Alternatively, this may embody the ethics of an idealist or humanist or an academic philosopher. Economic prudence is too objective and profit-motivated to brook sympathetic approach or sensitivity to worker's woes; and experience advises that societal altruism is not the best friend of hard core economists. These near-opposites and incompatibilities deserve to be reconciled and harmonized for peace and stability in space.

In nutshell, the space age is likely to be dominated by space commercial activities and interplanetary human transportation. As these activities develop, it is important to consider business values, commercial ethics, and trade discipline. The failure to do so could result in space commercial development taking place imbibing the attributes and practices and mind-set of similar activities on Earth like greed for profit and competitive advantage for advancement. To better prevent this possibility, this chapter proposes that there is the need to develop a new ethics for commercial order of the space based on high standards of business morality and commercial honesty, with due consideration for CSR, welfare of the space workforce, and due regard to ecological sustainability of space environment.

There is no denying that commerce has its own rules of the game that require consummate skills, aggressive attitude, and intuitive foresight. Further, the economic labyrinths of the commercial market of the outer space may not be straight or placarded. Unpredictability, volatility and risks are understandable. Therefore, entrepreneurial decisions would sure require an uncanny business acumen and risk-taking aptitude that merit special recognition and exemplary reward. Nevertheless, a *Commercial Order of Outer Space* based on high standards of business probity, primacy to worker welfare, common benefit of mankind and commercial honesty with moorings in Conscious Social Responsibility,[4] as well as due regard to environmental sustainability seems sagacious and well advised. This chapter will launch a quest for germane parameters and evolve select tenets as Ethical Norms for Space Commerce.

SOME PEACEFUL USES OF OUTER SPACE

Humans ventured into outer space for security and curiosity[5] but have found vast vistas of economic potential that lay bare for peaceful utilisation and human development promising an exciting future for humankind. Of course, governmental funding has pioneered strategic objectives and scientific exploration in the space arena but states may not continue to finance non-military and exclusively civil use activities from public exchequer any longer, as is the visible trend. The military utilities have started yielding diminishing returns.[6] Consequently, strategic experimentation and applications have reached a plateau. Nevertheless, the technology threshold lends itself to diverse civilian uses and commercial applications for which the private enterprise has come of age to take over and exploit.

Today, human odysseys into outer space for commercial purposes, business economics, space tourism, industrial ventures, and celestial settlements may not be large in numbers but these are going to increase substantially in the near future. A few examples will illustrate the potential of the vistas that are opening up. The areas with galloping growth are communications and networking, broadcasting and television, and remote sensing and geo-spatial applications. The space communication has manifested itself in Global Positioning System (GPS) and its equivalents by other countries, which has world-wide uses in traffic control of ships at sea, aero planes in airspace, and vehicular traffic on the earth. The GPS system is operated by the US with a set of 24 satellites geo-synchronously positioned and orbiting the earth to provide real-time information, command and control. Similar systems, namely, Glanoss by Russia, Galileo by European Space Agency, BeiDou by China and GAGAN by India are also independently operational for specific objectives.

The next space major is broadcasting and television and internet streaming. Space satellites are positioned in geo-synchronous functional orbit over the Equator to beam radio and television programs with wider footprint, diverse content, for different audiences and to satisfy varied needs like entertainment, information, education, societal uplift, rural development and financial services, to mention only a few. And, the demand for diversified applications and broader coverage for these facilities is bound to increase in the developing countries of Asia, Africa and the Latin America while geo-sync slots are already over-crowded.

The technology of remote sensing and geo-spatial data generation has made significant strides in high-speed and high-resolution photography. As a result geodetic surveys, sensing of natural resources, determination of water table, changes in glacial surfaces, mapping of forests, and other cartographic uses have emerged and multiplied. This benefit assumes great importance for developing countries where wealth of natural resources, including forests, remains untapped and unmanaged. This will open up vast opportunities. Apart from these, remote sensing in meteorological applications, weather warnings, and disaster management has shown great promise. Newer developments like hyper spectral sensors and synthetic aperture radars are being harnessed for relevant usages. The latest techniques with infra-red sensors capable of night vision are being put to myriad uses for dual-purpose technologies. Scope for further developments almost seems endless and equally variegated.

The space travel and tourism are poised for take-off. Space travel has already become a reality and over two dozen fare-paying tourists have orbited the earth and visited the ISS. They have brought nostalgic memories and exhilarating experience of viewing the mother earth from the outer space, apart from so-claimed scientific experiments. This has spurred a new aspiration among the expanding middle class and as a result novel tourist jaunts and new tourism destinations on offer are for exotic experiences, adventure sports, honey-mooning in zero-gravity environment, and pleasures of stay in floating hotels to enjoy the vision of *lumiere splendour* of the visible universe including the mother Earth. This may not yet be the ultimate in space sojourns, entertainment and hospitality services. More imaginative and innovative offers may be forthcoming in advertisements. This vista with esoteric facilities just seems to have opened up with great potential and vast opportunities for leisure and pleasure coupled with thrills and adventure.

Apart from tourism, there is a segment of earthlings who are keen to live in celestial settlements like the Moon Village or the Mars Colony for a short or long stay. Their motivations for a visit are different from the space tourists and there are those who wish for a one-way ticket to the other planet and intend staying there as permanent residents with no intention or plan to return to Earth in the foreseeable future. They are willing to abdicate their country nationality and dis-affiliate themselves from their kin and the global community. This speaks of a dangerous portent of societal dis-affection from their existing community, possibly because of lack of conviviality, social turbulence, rampant terrorism or loss of peace and tranquillity in life, for whatever reason. Such migration is bound to have serious impact and multiple implications familial, sociological, relational and juridical concerning emigration as also immigration formalities. Asgardians and followers of the Church of Scientology, though espousing peace for humanity in the universe may instead create dissent and discord. We are certainly not prepared for either of such an oncoming upheaval or impending exodus, neither mentally nor legally nor with requisite regulations.

In a relatively not too distant future, establishment of suitable industries in the outer space appears a profitable option as supported by state-of-the-art manufacturing technology and on a reasonably large production scale to meet splurging demand. Captains of industry have identified products that require the gravity-free or super-cold or sterile environment of outer space for fabrication, manufacturing and processing, for example magnets or crystals or vaccines respectively. Factories and laboratories may soon be established in space and qualified workers stationed there in appropriate numbers. Cargoes of raw materials and component kits will have to be transported to these sites and manufactured goods brought back to the earth for use or sale. Despite best intentions of a professional corporate management, industrial relations between labour and organisation may not always remain conducive or cordial. Hence, safety and welfare of the employee should remain the prime concern rather than returns on capital investment.

Outer space environment may be harsh for humans but for manufacturing it is incredibly favourable. Materials processed in space gain multiplied strength, acquire tensile qualities, gain alloyed uniformity, can transfer data with clarity and without loss in transmission, and form clear flawless crystals that grow. Processing media and techniques can also be changed. For example, heating of steel to strengthen it or cooking of food on fire can be substituted by quenching.[7] Ultra-high vacuum and sterility of space environment helps things form without impurities and avoid contamination like vaccines and stem cells. Microgravity allows metals to mix evenly, to hold together without traditional supports, and even facilitates metals grow evenly in all directions without encountering walls or limits. Thus, microgravity is of particular importance in computer parts, miniaturised devices and nano-technology. This environment is also conducive to manufacturing with higher resolution, faster processors, more bandwidth, and greater precision through novel materials, unique alloys, innovative processes with higher energy efficiency and elimination of processing defects.

First experiment for such manufacturing relates to fibre optic cable, called ZBLAN. Under the effect of microgravity, liquid metallic glass and other metals can be mixed to derive strength twice that of titanium. This hardness is suitable for debris shields, panelling and mirrors. Similarly, fibre-optic cables when manufactured in space (on ISS), the high quality fabrication is less prone to develop crystals that cause loss in transmission; and tends to be more suitable for laser telecommunication and hi-speed internet. The advantage achieved is that heavier metals do not sink to the bottom and mix uniformly, that is not possible on earth. It may be expensive today but with developments all around, it will eventually become cost-effective vis-à-vis quality performance and may be labelled and globally sold as "Built-off-Earth" product.[8] There are a lot of other potential applications like fibre amplifiers, laser products, drilling equipment, surgery devices, infra-red imaging, and remote sensing. This may, therefore, turn out to be first real space-based manufacturing industry.

Another line of manufacturing concerns gallium nitrate that is used for LED's but is difficult to solidify on the earth; it can be beneficially handled in space. Processed in space, different metals attain multiple properties. For example, iron gains strength and flexibility; and when alloyed with other metals, it acquires a homogeneous blend because due to microgravity heavier metals do not tend to settle at the bottom but mix uniformly. Thus in space, it is possible to remove convection, buoyancy and sedimentation to reach a desired property or propensity of the metal. Space environment also permits researchers to test alloyed materials as to how they withstand the harsher ambient conditions of powerful radiation and extreme temperature changes. A company by name and style of Alpha Sciences is into such experiments with 3D Printer and its future vision is much grander than the imagined possibilities.[9]

The advantage of microgravity can be adduced for still another application on protein and virus crystals that can grow larger and purer than on earth. This is because gravity does not pull them down or apart nor air pressure keeps them compressed and constrained. These crystals determine the 3D structures to aid analysis of virus characteristics and accordingly help inform new strategies for drug discovery. Allied to this is the fact that cells are not smart but are adaptable and if they touch the side or a surface, it gives them a message that is biologically misleading. For this important phenomenon, growing cells in space, though still speculative, yet is beneficial. So the possibility itself provides a good and cogent reason for research in space, particularly for organ cells, e.g. heart, lung, kidney, liver and muscle tissues.

Manufacturing *in situ* with locally available materials is another option opening up soon. Celestial bodies are believed to be rich in natural resources which can be excavated, processed and utilised locally for infrastructure construction and incumbent requirements of the permanent settlers on their respective planet. Fortunately, such use of celestial resources for local needs does not foul with the existing space law enshrined in the OST. Another state-of-the-art manufacturing process, most suitable for outer space, is 3D-Printing, that can be designed and controlled through computers and communication from the earth. An additive manufacturing digital device, 3-D Printer, embodying this technique of printing in zero-gravity was sent to ISS in September 2014 and it printed first part in orbit on 24 November 2014. It is an important milestone that has ushered in an era of IN-space Manufacturing.[10]

This successful demonstration of ability to manufacture parts in space has changed the world and is a stepping stone to the future. More so, because experiments have been successful to form items such as crystalline structures and latex spheres as also assembly type construction. This Additive Manufacturing Facility (AMF) at the ISS will offer a great advantage of obviating the necessity to fabricate a part on the earth and its transportation, with associated supply chain, to the ISS. It will also help trouble-shoot potential problems. Thus, this technology will afford tremendous saving in time and expense as well as attendant botheration and anxiety. The novelty and versatility of this digital manufacturing device have not yet been fully visualized. In fact, it is often difficult to appreciate the importance and utility of inventions that eventually solve larger problems. Thus, a ground-breaking endeavour deserves a lot of trust and understanding in the beginning; just as in the past, conceived ideas took time to actualize into commercial realities and eventually into business successes. It is also proposed to commercialise this digital technique for innovative applications and wider end-use.[11]

The future of space manufacturing may be relatively distant in commercial operationalisation and may need large amounts of research inputs as well as effort towards development and refinement but it is certainly achievable and possibly, is going to be fruitful with multitude of opportunities. Similarly, the technology though still at low maturity, yet can guide in the right direction for imaginable results. It is wisely said by a technologist that the progress of a new technology develops along interesting paths, many of them uncharted and unintended, that can innovate and create a multitude of possibilities. Same way, for this technique also most advantages and future uses are yet to be conceived and fructified. We have not yet plumbed the depth of possibilities and the visualized potential in manufacturing arena is not mere dreams or sheer ideas, it is happening and more exciting events are yet to unfold. Most often, challenges get converted into opportunities.

It is now well confirmed by scientists that the Moon is rich in mineral ores, crusted Helium-3, and ice water deposits. Astronauts also confirm that the surface layer of the Moon is soft and dusty. It is, therefore, not unlikely that resources for our future energy needs may be obtained from there. Excavations on the surface and even below the surface may seem a viable option technologically and economically. Transportation of the mineral ores and helium-enriched dust though may be the easiest yet the most expensive part of the operation. Nevertheless, rich dividends are expected from such mining activities. Further, the Moon Treaty,[12] at present, legally permits excavation and removal of materials from the Moon. Hopefully, this stream of mining industry would flourish on the Moon and prospected asteroids, rather rapidly and may even broaden its reach, scope and operations to other celestial bodies. For example, the feasibility of harnessing solar energy in space and beaming that to the earth does not appear insurmountable or its possibility so remote. Russians are leading on this front.

There is, thus, no doubt that outer space and celestial bodies can afford immense opportunities for profitable business, broad-spectrum commerce, specialized yet viable industrialisation, varied tourism offers and terminal settlement possibilities that can be utilised for the welfare of mankind and improve the quality of life of man on the earth as well as in outer space. Such a bargain should not go waste or be stifled for lack of political will or legal hitches or vested national interests or the banal propensities of man. There is need for change in mind set and adaptation of existing space law. We should wish to foster an Elysian environment of peace and harmony in space. Hence, *New Ethics for Space Commerce* is imperative and a call of the day.

ECONOMIC HISTORY OF HUMANKIND

Humankind is now poised for a giant leap into the outer space for commercial ventures, industrial establishments, tourist opportunities, and self-sustained celestial settlements. There is no doubt that commerce and industry have their own operational mechanics and profit calculus. But devoid of ethical moorings and normative compulsions, business loses its true public object and social purpose. It may seem a truism, yet deserves reiteration that all economic activity should aim at maximum pleasure of participants and, in general, optimum welfare of all. These homilies should not be forgotten or forsaken under the stress of competition or profiteering. Even for personal actions, humanity and humaneness are all intimately linked and the nexus is remarkably resilient. These rise and fall together. Hence, humans must carry ethical norms to the outer space even for mundane economics and elementary commerce.

A walk through the gallery of economic history of the world bares an ugly face of humankind blemished with insatiable greed and stark exploitation; ruthless competition in complicity with political power centers and adoption of unfair means. The economic psyche of humans has always been flawed with self-interest and vested motivations. They seem to confront a delusion caused by the traditional economic paradigm that more wealth gives greater satisfaction and consequently proportionately higher happiness, often confused with peace of mind. In fact, internal happiness is confounded with external comforts, conveniences, and luxuries while an old adage with wisdom is forgotten that happiness cannot be bought; it only oozes from inside of the mind and contrarily, satiates the needs.

Human behaviour has not always been just, equitous and righteous and nor have its actions exhibited an instinctive sense of business morality or social responsibility. On the contrary, human actions have been mostly prodded by banal interests and worship of wealth alloyed with unabashed display of ego and promiscuous flaunting of possessions. Thus, the deity has been mammon and its propitiation only for profit. It is no gratifying scenario to boast about in the cosmos or to the aliens. In fact, it should make us repentant and penitent. The intention here is not to express *angst* that illustrated practices and impugned attitudes would be carried to the outer space; but have been recorded to highlight human propensities and economic proclivities. Nevertheless, it would be worthwhile to avoid such attitude, mind set, modus and motivations. The narrative is neither critical nor baseless; it consequently prods that amends are recommended for space commercial development, concerns for human welfare, and peace in planetary settlements. Umpteen instances can be adduced to vindicate the above point, but a few should suffice and are briefly discussed in succeeding paragraphs.

The Practice of Slavery

The practice of trade and trafficking of human beings is not too ancient in human history and still continues in different forms in many parts of the world. Subjugation and inhuman treatment have really been deplorable and reprehensible on social ethics and humanitarian benchmarks. Nonetheless, sheer force of economics impelled this trade that still persists in certain variants like bonded labour. Unfortunately, despite vigorous campaigns and near-mandatory *Universal Declaration of Human Rights* of 1948 and its supporting covenants, this scourge has not yet been completely banished from the face of the globe. Its discernible remnants exist scattered under different mutations.

A deeper scrutiny of the causes of slavery reveals that among others, a prominent reason for the origin of this practice has been poverty leading to a trap of indebtedness coupled with unconscionable greed of the rich and powerful abetted by state patronage. The labyrinth of debt-trap could not be negotiated to freedom or the alleys were blocked deliberately to keep the slaves almost legally confined. The banality of man, for sheer economic considerations, was perpetrated atrociously on the rebellious; it was a macabre dance of inhumanity. The shackles have slightly released but not fully broken to freedom with dignity.

It is not unlikely that the workers transported to the outer space and celestial bodies may experience similar helplessness under contractual obligations, familial isolation, no-escape transport facilities, and inhospitable environment. The labour in the outer space may find itself in no better situation than indentured servitude, perhaps, a shade worse for being in a laboratory orbiting around the earth or to be stationed in a manufacturing hub on a planetary body and may be, living in a celestial ghetto. In such a predicament, workers plight should not be exploited to adversary's benefit and they be treated compassionately and humanely. Their welfare should take primacy over other business considerations, a feeling of empathy in human relations and good conscience should govern supreme in the outer space.

Colonialism

Another historical fact that shames mankind is colonialism by imperialist powers that spread its tentacles far and wide. It was not the annexation by one country or by one politically and militarily strong nation but the rule of some over many annexed countries on the different continents. There was an inexorable race to capture the hapless countries and sometimes fights between the competitive captors to decide superiority and control; and in the bargain natives were killed and the country was ravaged. The empires of influence and reign expanded and persisted by political vile or military campaigns. Thus, the shackles of colonialism have persisted for more than a couple of centuries and its visible retreat started in the twentieth century.

Colonialism was no benign system of rule and governance. The rulers never identified themselves with the interests of the ruled and there was no feeling of empathy; having come from so far away from their native country and with their aims transcending from commercial trade to forcible governance. The ultimate purpose of colonisation was exploitation of the resources, human and material, from the colony in utter disregard of environmental sustainability or wellbeing of the natives. Minor and sporadic acts of benevolence bestowed on the locals as palliatives do not count for much. In general, the colonies remained underdeveloped with little to claim as infrastructure, and the colonized masses steeped in poverty, near total illiteracy, stark social inequality, and no political manoeuvrability. Governance was strict, ruthless and infused fear for life. The natives seemed helpless with no viable choices.

Many who survived the colonial times, and are still living, have witnessed the macabre dance of rulers' whims and fancies and suffered many an individual scars, physical injuries, and personal insults. They have seen, from close quarters, the ravages of economic exploitation, looting of royal treasures, the shipments of wealth out of the country, and atrocities on the few brave dissenters. There was hardly any remedy or relief to escape the wrath of the heartless rulers. This reign of terror has lived for over two centuries in India and in large parts of the world. The British prided on the fact that they had so many colonies spread all over the globe that the Sun never sets on the British Empire. The economics of colonialism had nothing to commend as a system. It was an era of illegal transfer of unearned wealth with no compunction or scruples and no remorse either. Fortunately, it has mostly ended, though, in some cases with rebellions, heaping ignominy, and disdain on the rulers. A few of the erstwhile colonies are now picking enough courage to demand reparations for their depredation. Such a situation should not prevail in space trade and celestial settlements. Hopefully, wisdom will be on our side.

The Faces of Capitalism

The mosaic of economic systems is primarily in two colours, capitalism and communism.[13] The true spirit of the latter has enamoured the world for a couple of centuries but has ruled the minds of people and their governance philosophy for just over a century. Fundamental communism has since diluted itself beyond recognition and taken different hues of capitalism. Russia and China make classic examples of the growing disenchantment with this ideology. On the other hand, almost the entire world, today, prides on capitalism, but its history has shown ebbs and flows. Its weaknesses have lately become apparent and it has now nearly touched its nadir and is facing insurmountable threats and challenges as a viable economic system of the future. Perhaps, it needs a new incarnation with the best features of both systems and an adaptation to the new business economics free of ego and irrationality.

Capitalism was an excellent economic system with free play of market forces that had an innate tendency to appropriately interact and make self-corrections to reach the state of equilibrium and stabilize at that till upset by other economic factors or impulses. But over the centuries, increasing inroads by state regulation and overleveraging corporate giants and skewed labour preferences have shifted the fulcrum of balance and rendered the system unstable. The major maladies of the system can be identified as aggravating income inequalities, deteriorating ethical governance, and lack of transparency in corporate decisions. Business leaders have strayed from the chosen path of business as societal task to get struck in the mire of disproportionate wealth accumulation, brazen promiscuousness and ostentatious self-aggrandisement[14] whereas the ultimate goal of business is self-actualisation. They would immensely benefit by adopting trusteeship model for corporate governance and management by considering themselves as stewards of the enterprise and, thus, appreciate that profit accrued is due to the contribution of many and not generated solely by their wisdom and effort alone. Moreover, that it deserves to be shared in some determined ratio of contribution and not be disproportionately appropriated by a few in denials to deserving others.

The business community, somewhere or somehow, has lost the focus on building great business houses anchored on cherished values; and espouse concern not just for the coterie of shareholder but that of all stakeholders at large. They failed to visualise societal problems as opportunities for entrepreneurial development as also concurrently improve the standard of living of the client community. Besides, they also acted myopic to fully envision environmental depredation and jeopardy to sustainability caused by their uncontrolled exploitation of natural resources as raw materials. The result has been utter depletion, unsustainable growth, and widespread pollution all around causing dwindling of profits. The monster had been unleashed and it has struck back. A common lament is that capitalism has failed.

Nevertheless, capitalism can be a legitimate, viable and enduring system if tempered with humaneness, ethics and morality. One may tend to agree with Arthur Clarke that one of the greatest tragedies of mankind is that morality has been hijacked by religion and has been preached exclusively as its preserve. This unfortunate refrain and its ground reality have to be corrected by oriented action and objective dedication. Morality must become secular again and conscience must triumph to guide professionalism and rule all human endeavours in different domains. The salvation of humanity lies in honest acceptance and sincere practice of ethical morality that is general and universal.

Exploitation of Labour

Classical economic theory teaches of division of labour[15] and that there are four factors that must join together to create economic production or "wealth".[16] These are land, labour, capital and entrepreneur and their returns are rent, wages, interest and profit respectively. Land, labour and capital are almost always available with some in every society, but their association and integration is initiated and assured by the entrepreneur, who is the risk-taker and, thus, the catalyst for economic activity. He harnesses the other factors to cooperate in a productive manner to achieve production that has economic value. He is thus, generally, the greatest beneficiary from the produce and profits. He being the coordinator and controller is in a position to take undue advantage of the needy or exploit the other factors and can deny them their due share in the distribution of wealth. He may as well be, by intent and desire, fair and equitous.

Over the centuries, the distinction and boundaries between these four factors of production have blurred and their roles have not remained straight-jacketed. In the process, entrepreneur over this period has assumed the face of management and has taken over the responsibility to invest, at least, a part of the capital to begin with and muster the rest of the requirements by cooperation or coercion. Landlords have created disputes and similar confrontations between labour and management have become common and repetitive for various reasons—legitimate or untenable.

At the same time, corporate history of India is replete with stories of industry leaders whose honesty and dedication created durable institutions of repute manufacturing quality products, practiced and established cherished values that furthered social growth and national economic development. They engineered socialist work culture and espoused near-equitable distribution of wealth. They established organisations where workers were emotionally attached and bore generational loyalty. The miracle of labour-management cooperation had materialised. This sentiment has widely existed in the industry in Japan and Korea also.

Of late, labour has come to be euphemistically called and treated as human resource. There is growing awareness that this resource is precious and vital to production and productivity and hence needs to be developed and nurtured to fit into company work culture and adapt to the corporate objectives. This perception, this understanding, and this attitude towards erstwhile working labour has led to a realisation of its valuable contribution to the profit kitty and has encouraged harmony in mutual relationship. Nonetheless, disputes concerning exploitation of workforce still occur, however minimal. The intention here is to counsel that the 'space workforce' that would be literally captive, be treated humanely, empathetically and compassionately with an appreciation that they work under harsh conditions, in inhospitable environment, emotionally lonely from dear ones, and on a celestial body with no possible escape opportunity.

Excesses by Labour

The history of hate between labour and management dates back for centuries but investment in this banal emotion never pays good dividends. With experience of marginalised existence and unequal treatment for over centuries, labour has found its own defence mechanisms and honed its weapons to fight back and, to some extent, eke out its due. The first was unity in workforce and unionisation. With this, the labour augmented its bargaining power and collective strength to stand firm for its legitimate rights and conscionable demands. Exploitation reduced to a great extent, though did not cease altogether. A lot more had to be done.

With this changed stance, character and behaviour, the next weapon innovated by the labour was strike from work and suspension of work. It became a potent tool for negotiations and gradually became a constant threat to the management. The concept of work discipline had to be revisited and revised. Soon workers' unions found lethal power in their hands, and it was much more potent than they could sensibly wield. The tables had nearly turned and the management was in a quandary. They had a new problem on their hands for which no textbook solution was to be found.

There is a legal maxim that you come to equity with clean hands, and this was not to be with labour. The image of labour was not entirely clean and untarnished. The history of excesses by the labour can obliquely be reminisced from the, still not forgotten, French Revolution. Labour had gone berserk indulging in violence that resulted in chaos and bloodshed. The sullied image of labour bore further gashes. A similar volatile situation arose in England with introduction of textile machines in the nineteenth century (1811-13). Skilled workers were progressively laid off and it was these unemployed textile artisans, who had suffered starvation with their families, started the Luddite movement. In violent protests they destroyed automated looms and wool and cotton mills in Nottinghamshire, Yorkshire and Lancashire. They fought pitched battles even with the British Army. Unfortunately, it was the workers who bore the major brunt of loss in their agitation.

In India also, there were widespread protests by labour on induction of computers, towards end of twentieth century, fearing lay-offs and apprehending wide-spread unemployment. But this was not to be and on the contrary employment opportunities increased in newer skills. Frankly, this is the other face of labour that should impel for conscious cogitation to reinvent its inner aspirations and identify with the desired goals. Workforce should desist from creating such 'dilemmic' predicament in outer space. Cooperation and amiability should be the watchwords for workers' conduct and mutual relations.

Monopolies and Cartels

Economic theory teaches the casuistry that commerce has its own language and is regulated by the causal interplay of demand and supply. But these naturally interactive and self-equilibrating market forces can be adversely influenced and distorted by aberrations like monopolistic trade practices and cartelization for tariff fixation and other unethical overtures. In fact, brand advertisements and addictive preferences make a person less rational on prices and more prone to defy fundamental economics of consumer satisfaction. Corporate world knows the ropes of business and can quite often create a façade of unimpeachable conditions to skew the market forces, apparently legally and rightfully, yet not righteously and morally.

A bane of competitive market and declining business values has led to monopolistic chauvinism and restrictive trade practices in detriment to the best interest of the hapless consumer and to deny him his right to choices and undermine his freedom of selection in the free market. The probable abuses of these practices can stifle the free enterprise system and distort the market to the seller's advantage. Many countries have banned monopolistic practices by law yet it rises in different incarnations like a phoenix. The business mind is innovative in a twisted sense also. Naturally, when the interests of producer and consumer are conflicting, this game shall continue with ebbs and flows.

The other banality is cartelization and the malaise of buy-outs and mergers. Whatever the supportive logic be, in the end it works out to edging some corporate out of the arena or swallowing of small entrepreneurial ventures by the business oligarchs and industrial tycoons. Such decisions of existential annihilation may claim good economic sense yet many of these, under context and circumstances, would be indictable and may not stand firm on ethical scrutiny or the criteria of equity or serve the enduring interests of larger community. These market devices and business practices have not much to commend for and better be discarded on the globe itself rather than loftily carted to the cosmos. In the context of quest for New Ethical Values, negative points better be shunned and jettisoned here on the Earth itself rather than emulated for space business.

RATIONALE FOR THE ETHICAL NORMS

The age-old confrontation between labour and capital is almost legendary that has hardened into antagonism over the years. This thesis, in historical context, has been proved by Karl Marx and Lenin who have highlighted the dichotomy between bourgeoisie and the proletariat; and this fundamental struggle for a clutch of rights became the pivot for communist movement that has enamoured more than half the world for over a century. Perhaps, initial thrust was necessary for reform but this hardened into confrontation and overzealous espousal of perceived rights of the proletariat. However, history views intemperance with disdain. Therefore, it emerges as a hard lesson that capital and labour need to foster harmony and amicability for better welfare and mutual good of each other.

The purpose of this recapitulation is to learn from experience. Workers deployed in the outer space and on celestial bodies living in prolonged loneliness, trying working conditions, and inhospitable environment may develop physical ailments as also can get mentally restless or develop phobias or attendant psychological disorders. These are the hazards of working milieu and 'un-ergonomic' conditions which command utmost consideration and sensitivity for the well-being of the worker in outer space. This mandate must be respected even in preference to the profit accruals. It, therefore, becomes equally incumbent on labour employed in outer space to behave in most responsible and disciplined manner and strive towards highest standards of productivity in a convivial relationship of camaraderie and mutual harmony.

At the same time, it is equally pertinent to mention of the discord between capitalists as members of own fraternity in cut-throat competition or in crass cartelization or other devious business practices. Similarly, cat-fights between sister labour unions within the same organisation or sabotage of espoused causes by the union leaders for personal or vested interests are too well known for elaboration. It is, therefore, suggested that we abdicate conspiracy, deceit, back-stabbing, and other banal games here itself and carry only nobler instincts and ethical values to the outer space and celestial bodies for conduct of business and operation of industry there. Thus, our image would be clean and our heart pure in the sublime serenity of the cosmos. Humanity shall outshine in its qualities compared to other sentient beings in the universe.

Economics, being a rational science, assumes prudent propensities for its equilibrium mechanics but it still succumbs to the prime objective of maximisation of profits by artificially inflating prices or cutting costs on all sides. The principle of optimisation is often side-lined in the production activity. In fact, economics intersects business sense at obtuse angles disregarding other equity parameters and social indicators. This approach and orientation may not always be ethical or conform to etiquette to promote the respective best interest of all or any facilitator of economic production. As a result, business calculus may get skewed from objectivity, equity or inclusivity thus, perpetrating injustice and unfairness. Hence economic quotients should be tempered with basic human values and commercial morality to ensure optimum welfare for all, discharge of social responsibility, and assure pervasive justice.

Many commercial activities are already operational in the outer space such as in the fields of telecommunication, television, transportation, remote sensing etc. but have been at times influenced by vested interests of the operators and available facilities have not always remained democratized for use by all. A couple of examples in illustration will suffice. First, the US has been motivated by national interest in selectively denying GPS facility even to the West-European nations in times of 'alert, emergency or war' as per its own regulations. In this context, India, too, has suffered uncooperative refusal from the US during the *Kargil* Operation in 1999 which was aimed to oust Pakistan forces that had illegally infiltrated into Indian Territory and temporarily stationed there. India could not tolerate this denial of remotely sensed data in respect of its own sovereign areas. This impelled India to develop and operationalise its own GPS-like facility called GAGAN. Success came to India and thus the US has created its own competitor, among others, by default.

Thus, the unscrupulous withholding or denial of information and data collected, over the country remotely sensed, and instead offering suspect reasons and lame excuses like camera malfunction or cloud cover or poor resolution have become trite and routine. It is also pertinent to mention that raw data, even if made available, will be of little use unless analysed results are provided. Again, space tourism and planetary colonisation may bring to fore the customer-operator clash of interests. The individual traveller, as consumer of the service, may be treated shoddily by the potent transport-cartels and as a result liability disputes may turn one-sided to the patent disadvantage of passenger or celestial inhabitant. Copious illustrations can be piled up to buttress the above assertion from the aviation domain which seem fairly similar. Therefore, vested interests must be sacrificed at the altar of fundamental business values, traditional trade ethics, and the majesty of commercial discipline in service of humankind in the outer space.

QUEST FOR VALUES: A DILEMMA

Now, at the threshold of a vigorous launch of space commerce, space tourism, and planetary settlements, we should desist from carrying our undesirable baggage of controversial corporate culture and condemnable labour chauvinism to the outer space. Man would be wiser to consciously mandate itself and universally accept new business values, revised commercial ethics, and desirable trade discipline while harnessing his commercial instincts and business acumen to promote a myriad activities in outer space. The sermon appeals to heart and the rhetoric makes sense, but this proposition begs a question that whose ethical norms or espoused morality should be emulated. It is a dilemma of many choices and the criteria for selection.

Let's first discourse on morals, ethics and norms. These terms do not connote the same meaning, nor are interchangeable. By doing so, advertently or inadvertently, we add to our personal fund of biases and prejudices, this mind-set has to be cleansed. So there is need to check the true import and fine distinction between them. Let's first take morals. Morals are the codes of behaviour that we can, and indeed, must apply to ourselves. Our codes of behaviour, defining our sense of appropriateness or otherwise, are evolved from the faith system we believe in as also from our social and familial environment. Thus, morals can be termed as 'facticity' of our individual situation. This depends upon a person's religious belief or agnostic notions; ones deemed social obligations, and the choices one makes in personal life. This orientation or preference can aggregate to groups of like-minded people that may constitute a society. Morality is, thus, the pinnacle of human evolution; and individualised or society-specific civilised living. And applying it to space commerce, even if an argument is proffered that economics and morality are strange bed-fellows, it should still be sincerely strived to marry them to inculcate harmony and compatibility.

Ethics are the codes of conduct and behaviour that we apply to all societies, in general, including those which are totally foreign and unfamiliar. In many cases, the two codes of morality and ethics may coincide and concur. These could as well differ widely. For example, to kill a person is deemed to be wrong morally and ethically. But there could as well be divergence of views between both. For example, to defend yourself and your country from enemy aggression by conscription would be an ethically sanctioned duty, also called patriotism. But it may conflict with individual morality. Similar irony occurs when individuals and societies seek to project and impose their moral codes as ethical obligation on others. This is transgression of freedom or could be dubbed as moral hegemony or ethical imperialism.

Thus, in the interplay between morals and ethics, there are no right answers, only right questions. And from here, we commence our journey to pick the best of ethical values, the haloed precepts of morality, and revered axioms of justice that can be superimposed on the template of economic theory and practice. Let none subsume the other but only lend a hue of purity and sublimity to make it right and righteous for both streams. In a way, it compels us to evolve and enunciate specific and relevant ethical principles based on contemporary values and ensuing human needs especially for space persons, in space age, and for space domain. Existing principles and established norms of space law may be of help. This can usher hope for humanity in outer space.

Rationality, ethics and morality are not always compatible or congruous. There can be contextual differences on rational considerations, variations in ethical prioritisation, and conflicts over moral values. These differ with different communities, cultures and customs. Variations exist even within each nation while international divergences can be markedly distinct and conflictive. The choices are many and myriad like the cult of consumerist materialism of the West with disregard to ecological considerations or the Eastern philosophy of placid peace, mental serenity and material contentment or "*shubh laabh*"[17] of Indian businessmen or the precept of *Daswandh*[18] in Sikh community or economic postulates contained in the *Shariah* of Islam;[19] or haste for development with oblivion to concomitant consequences and political discontent, as is the case with many developing states. Alternatively, should these values be drawn from the disciplines of economics or sociology or theology? Or that these may embody the ethics of an idealist or empathy of a humanist or rationality of an academic philosopher? Whichever values may be selected, these should quintessentially be eternal or at least enduring.

It is a complex question endemic with different cultural convictions, societal mores, multiple beliefs, controversial opinions, and subjective biases. However, the point at issue is rather subtle yet abstruse, more like the moral of a Buddhist *koan*,[20] which is difficult for normal understanding or comprehension by logical deduction; and is only revealed to an enlightened mind. That is the crux of the difficulty and as a result differences persist and perpetuate. On the other hand, selection of standards of business probity, commercial transparency, industrial discipline, and trading honesty may not be an easy task. This is conceded unconditionally. Nevertheless, every business fraternity evolves its own rules specific to the peculiarities of the business and the domain traits which are adhered to by the players in the arena, voluntarily and cooperatively. This acts as a non-legal mechanism of approved behaviour generally called as norms.

Norms are not positive laws but are effective in societies to curb aberrative and anti-social behaviour. Society, thus, has a tacit understanding and approval of good conduct and members generally tend to cooperate without coercion and do not like to fall out of line, for fear of stigma or ostracisation. The results of compliance are encouraging, therefore, sociologists treat "the government as an exogenous force that intervenes to deter socially"[21] and thus be coercive legally. This brings us to a hierarchy of enforcement. State enforcement agencies ensure compliance of statute laws, regulations, controls and standards. Policy, guidelines, principles and advisories are optional for adherence; while norms and ethics are self-regulatory and assure obedience by voluntary behaviour and desire for conduct in conformity. Thus "the cooperation theory holds that people will always follow their intrinsic preferences..."[22] and avoid deviant behaviour as it may attract social condemnation or community sanctions. Ergo, commercial ethics and business norms of self-regulatory nature may have a better chance to cleanse baser global business practices and transport the purified concepts and a clean mind-set to the outer space and the celestial bodies.

Understandably, the answer may be hard to find but search for 'legal-*koans*' should not cease. One may not bemoan our myopic vision for groping common ethical values but what distresses is that while humanity possesses the intellect to seek out a viable and durable answer, it has so far failed to find one. Nevertheless, collective human wisdom under the aegis of the United Nations can arrive at a negotiated, common-denominator solution that is reasonable and acceptable. This task should be taken up pro-actively and not be procrastinated indefinitely to wait for an epiphany. It may be too late then. Urgency stares us in the face.

TENETS OF NEW ETHICS

The dilemma, discussed earlier, is obvious but the conundrum must be solved. In the Babel of ideals and values touted from all over the world, the choice is difficult but has to be exercised. Perhaps, one stream of thought leads to eternal truths and traditional values nurtured by civilisations, across the world and for centuries. Some of these are age-old precepts of wisdom which have survived over time to become ageless and haloed. It is these, that have to be identified and isolated for our purpose to compose new anthems of economic behaviour in outer space that also conform to legality.

Therefore, an effort has been made for a tentative selection of espoused objectives, as part of our quest for the new Ethical Values for

Commercialisation of Space. It would be pertinent to highlight that the norms articulated here are not extraneous to the existing law and legal idioms facilitating governance of the regime of the outer space and have been culled out from relevant conventions and treaties that have stood the test of time. These 'ethico-legal' principles have been reiterated with contextual reformulation. These are discussed in succeeding paragraphs.

Law and Justice

The first and foremost tenet should be adherence to law for implicit and explicit justice and it should emerge from self-will. Statutes overflow with legislations that regulate and control economic activity and prescribe sanctions for violations also. But, their existence and concomitant fear has not banished illegal actions nor curbed violative behaviour. This calls for serious introspection and hints towards innate discipline for voluntary economic decisions within four corners of the law though tempered with business gut-feel. Hence, there is need for re-baptism of business fraternity into 'legal economics'.

Apropos the abovementioned aspect, it surprises to learn from empirical studies that normal human behaviour is much less rational than that has been assumed or taken for granted.[23] In other words, normal human behaviour is rather irrational than the celebrated assumption of economic theory. This revelation has shaken the basic premise of 'an economic person' that abides by prudent preferences. The classical economic theory seems to be crumbling under this reality check and benchmark of rationality. Consequently, the dynamics of economic relations has been put in disequilibrium. Whatever may be the acceptable truth, conventional wisdom is at stake. The allegation is serious and arraignment must be sustained on valid grounds.

It is axiomatic that law leads to justice and it treats all equally and assures equality. Law is just and protects the assured rights and legitimate interests of all concerned judiciously. It is non-partisan, does not discriminate, and operates objectively. But law and justice are not enough by themselves and do not work in a vacuum. A shrewd businessman or a skilled economic operator can many times disguise dubious business intentions and vested economic decisions, with concealed exploitative designs, under the garb of good economics, valid law, and mutual interests. In fact, it is for this very reason a lament is frequently heard that capitalism is not working. Good Conscience should be superimposed on capitalism to make it humane and fit for the outer space.

It seems important to announce that all economic activity in outer space, perforce, has to be in consonance with the legal regime of outer space as contained in the Outer Space Treaty[24] and other germane Agreements as also international law and Charter of the UN. The mandate requires that activities shall be peaceful and "...carried out for the benefit and in the interest of all countries..."[25] and "...in accordance with international law, including the Charter of the United Nations and the Statute of the International Court of Justice..."[26] and for promoting international cooperation and understanding. Thus, the altruistic motive of activities comes in sharp relief and needs no further emphasis. Therefore, business economics of outer space needs to adjust and abide by this tenet of common benefit of humanity and ultimate welfare of humankind.

Equity and Fair Play

Equity is not an established concept of economics nor is fair play an honourable principle of economic prudence; but their importance and relevance cannot be belittled in the new order of Space Ethics. Equitable share of each factor in the accumulation of wealth should be the norm and the game should be played fairly on even rules in the truest sense. Equity, in a way, is social justice for all. Same way, entrepreneurs should also be provided with a level playing field for their activities to ensure equal opportunity for unfettered performance and metrics of comparable results.

Equity introduces morality in law and is generally considered to be, "The body of rules considered as governing all on account of their excellence and universality".[27] Fairness implies economic interaction with equal and indiscriminate applicability of rules of the game with an attitude of willingness to abide by the result, whatever the outcome be. Success may not be the sole motive of every endeavour and, that too, in utter disregard to the means or methods of achievement; instead righteous attitude with sincerity of purpose and fairness in treatment should govern all activity. There should be no tinge of fraud or cheating or deceit or malafides; but an ability to tolerate and absorb circumstantial and providential failures. Truth should prevail and our endeavour should to make a tryst with transparency.

This parameter gains sustained importance in view of multinational and global conglomerates taking up space commerce and service industries. Their operations and management involve cross-cultural values and parochial mind-set that may lead to misgivings and trust-deficit due to differential perceptions of the same event. This brings us to the seminal role of reflected knowledge in nurturing global trust and summation of varied potentialities to common advantage. Further, greater transparency in dealings and broad-spectrum accountability is recommended to foil international misunderstandings and ensuing repercussions.

Here again, a reference may be drawn to the germane law. "Outer Space, including the Moon and other celestial bodies, shall be free for exploration and use by all states without discrimination of any kind, on a basis of equality and in accordance with international law, and there shall be free access to all areas of celestial bodies."[28] The essence of this provision stresses equity and fair play in ample measure. Further, since monitoring of activities and verification of compliances is going to be difficult for some time and expensive proposition for a long time to come, transparency assumes greater significance and demands voluntary obedience with utmost honesty.

Many pedagogic economists and 'astro-entrepreneurs' are bound to vehemently differ with this stand and would argue that economic decisions cannot be taken so openly under the Sun. The primal considerations in commerce and industry centers around being the first to move in before others think of the same. Time is of essence here and the first to seize the opportunity is the winner. No doubt so, but this race to reach the goalpost should not jostle others unduly or make them fall unfairly. Wild economics and berserk commerce must be shunned. Honesty still remains the best policy, whether in business or commerce or industry, and certainly for the outer space domain.

Corporate Social Responsibility

Corporate Social Responsibility (CSR) means social service activities undertaken by business houses that enhance their value in community and society at large and in return benefit their reputation and brand value and gain dividend by increasing their clientele.[29] Whatever be the merits of this trend, it has become fashionable in the business teaching to stress on CSR to remind corporate houses that their business and resultant profits emanate from the addicted consumers in contiguous populations and captive base in social groups; and that they need to empathise with and plough back a part of profit surpluses for transformation and uplift of this devoted clientele. Anne Frank rightly said, 'No one ever become poorer by giving' and least so, rich firms and countries. But this mind-set does not fit with business economics. As an extension to this, the corporations should be exhorted to adopt appropriate strategies and policy bundling techniques that reach out globally to provide social add-ons in loyal communities and population aggregates that have international dispersal. This has come to be regarded as business discipline and social obligation that must be practised with professional rigour at stipulated periodicity and ground delivered with focused and structured mechanisms.

It deserves clarification that this responsibility is of non-financial nature and tends to create a balance between economics and ecology, social affairs and good governance.[30] In nutshell, corporations are striving to harmonise and promote aspirations of the society with economic reality and trying to assure a healthy and sustainable lifestyle. Fortunately, businesses are hearing, and heeding, the signals. CSR has become a core value of business brand whereby companies integrate social and environmental concerns in their business operations and interaction with stakeholders. There is, thus, a growing trend to absorb and integrate this informal liability into 'Company Belief System' as a constant and permanent objective. Thus, the emerging global reality for business is that CSR can no longer be viewed as an optional project of philanthropy but has to be treated as intrinsic part of core business with analogous vision and goals for the targeted society. This trend is indeed laudable.

One of the reasons for the enlargement of CSR is the receding frontiers in the service sector by governmental agencies and increasing withdrawal by the government from the social sector of responsibility. Howsoever uncomplimentary is this trend, public governance is making way for corporate sector to take over in this regard because its sustenance emanates from the community. Private enterprise is, thus, understood to mean responsible and accountable management of business with profit potential to spare for this purpose. A fundamental change in organisational values is discernible. Some international companies are continuing with longstanding and excellent tradition of returning its social debt to the community. Many terminologies have been used to accord international rankings and ratings on CSR to global industries and multi-national corporations but due to lack of accredited criteria and reporting standards, reliable benchmarking still remains a problem area.

It is humbly proposed that such traditions of altruistic service for the welfare and betterment of community should be carried as an exalted virtue to be part of our genetic baggage to the commercial arena and industrial niches in the outer space. Such a conviction of ethical values in business philosophy is bound to herald goodwill, harmony and peace among all inhabitants of the outer space and those residing on the celestial bodies. Wisdom ordains to invest in values of core social purpose for the future so that we do not get on the wrong side of history once again. Further these values of social responsibility (CSR) should equally apply to individuals and other entities and should emerge as Conscious Social Responsibility and not merely be considered binding on corporations only.[31] The obligation appears ethical and reciprocal for all entities and individuals equally.

Compassion towards Workforce in Space

It is a fundamental economic truth that labour is an important contributor in any activity leading to generation of wealth. But lately, workforce has become aware and has understood the importance and vitality of its contribution and share in the economic produce. As a result, it has unduly inflated its ego and weightiness beyond reasonable cooperation. This has generally led to strife between classical economic factors of entrepreneur and labour. At the same time, the working class has also been exploited unfairly, has suffered abuse in many ways, and has faced institutional neglect. Thus, managements have denied them their proportionate share equal to contribution in production. This discrimination, exploitation and injustice cannot continue till perpetuity and should gracefully convert to equity, equality and fair play.

Both parties have soiled hands and cannot plead equity. Besides, this attitude and mind-set should not creep into space activities or be transported to the space domain. Besides, the workforce in outer space shall have to bear conditions of hardship and harshness of spatial environment. Apart from this the worker will be more vulnerable and dependent on management, economically and emotionally. In all fairness and equity, the management should be sensitive to the peculiar concerns of space workers; and consider and address their problems compassionately and humanely. On the other hand, the labour should work sincerely and productively, as also not resort to unionist tactics of striking work or uncooperatively create unrest. Antagonism seldom pays while dialogue is the best means of resolution of disputes and misunderstandings. Mutual cordiality and high conviviality in relations will benefit both, and generally be conducive to maintain stability and peace in the space domain.

Safety from Space Debris

Last, but not the least, important pillar of New Ethics relates to sustenance of outer space environment and this is part of sustainable development goals (SDG's) prescribed by the UN. This guarantee is important and must be factored into business decisions that are generally blind to social and ecological parameters. The motive of commerce is profit and business seeks out economic benefit and in this stark analysis, environmental concerns tend to be either ignored or get relegated to a much lower priority due to lack of clear perception of or concern for the consequences that would be inevitable. This sort of myopic business deliberations must be adjusted and oriented towards environmental realities of the future.

The first man-made object to despoil the pristine environment of the cosmos was the Soviet *Sputnik* in October 1957 and since then, thousands of satellites have been launched by many countries and the corporate world. According to US Surveillance Report, as on today, nearly 10,000 objects are being tracked in orbit in the outer space. Considering the progressive increase in launches, this figure is bound to grow rapidly. Besides the satellites, there are other causes for escalating number of objects in the outer space. First, multi stage rockets shed off their parts like motors, fuel tanks, shrouds, fairings and fastening material till positioned in planned orbit. Secondly, motors and fuel tanks detached from rockets do not completely exhaust their fuel content and tend to explode creating splinters, big and small. As per one estimate, over a hundred such explosions have been recorded and the number of unrecorded ones may be much more. Thirdly, controlled blasting of rogue satellites or secret mission vehicles or for technological experiments are also on increase thus littering the outer space.

With cumulated clutter mounting in the outer space, vehicle safety, collision risks, and economic viability of operations is bound to be adversely affected by higher risk quotient and attrition factor. Further accumulations of debris and continued deterioration of space environment may even boomerang to the earth. The threat is valid and risks foreseeable. But principles of economics, parameters of business or inputs for commercial decisions take no cognizance of such critical factors or cataclysmic possibilities. Nor does the profit calculus of businessman acknowledge such non-fiscal probabilities or non-revenue considerations. His denominators are subjective and his quotient is profit.

We need to guard against such abstract and mechanical decision-making devoid of societal concerns, ecological impact, and environmental pollution or the survival of humanity itself. And it is here that the UN has a significant role to play in regulating activities in the outer space. First, with increasing number of commercial launches, the UN may consider imposing a levy based on type of use, period of life, disposability plan or an estimate of profitability accruable from the commercial satellites. Secondly, as far as possible, all space vehicles should return to the earth in a controlled manner on completion of mission. And in case of failure to do so, a pollution cess be levied on the operator and the launching state to be paid to the UN jointly or severally. This fund could be utilised for research and development of space scavenging technologies.

Lastly, the UN may take it on its agenda to seize jurisdiction and obtain an enabling provision to legalise commercial retrieval of defunct and non-functional satellites by commercial debris remover corporations. Business assessments reveal satisfactory profit potential on retrieved objects that can be cannibalized for expensive rotables for reuse, recycle costly material; and from the remainder salvage, fabricate souvenirs for sale in global market. One would sure like to flaunt a bit-piece of space-returned satellite on ones coat-lapel or as a vanity brooch. These are ego items of distinction and exclusivity for the elites. A serious consideration and endeavour in this regard is sure to yield profits over the costs of retrieval, in the true economic sense of the enterprise.

LEGITIMACY OF INTERNATIONAL CODES

Having enunciated the tenets as the four pillars of the New Ethics for a New Economic Order of the Outer Space, it is, with due humility, proposed that these may be formulated into UN Guidelines and promulgated as Code of Conduct for Business and Industry in the outer space on similar lines as that for use of Nuclear Power Sources[32] or Prevention of Space Debris.[33] The proposal assumes importance as commercial footprint in the outer space is increasing and expanding, hence, the urgency in ushering the new economic code. It is conceded that principles and guidelines are non-mandatory and not legally binding but it appears the best option under the circumstances and can be hoped to usher in a new culture of business norms that will grow on its own pollination.

Experience vindicates that unwritten and written codes of conduct have magnificently served their avowed objectives over many millennia for moulding and nurturing recommended behaviour among groups and communities for a long lineage of generations. In tandem, one can seek succour from the research of Eric Posner[34] that has confirmed from anthropological studies that social norms of tribal communities are strong in "routine compliance" and have shown much fewer aberrations or acts of defiance due to "the collective infliction of sanctions...including stigmatisation of the deviant and ostracism of the incorrigible"[35] than in societies with legislated and enacted laws with stringent sanctions.

Similar situations have existed in international relations and the world comity even in recent times.[36] Excepting minor aberrations, the results achieved have been compliant and compulsive. Nonetheless, it is to be expected that a part of international law laity would be sceptical about the utility and efficacy of such guidelines. There is even a school of thought that holds the argument that international law lacks legitimacy in comparison to statute municipal laws. Their opinion deserves reverence but would appear valid in parts only. A holistic approach would reveal a different perspective altogether.

In modern governance with globalised developments, sovereignty is being progressively eroded and international institutions, with the consent of the states, are assuming greater regulatory authority and governing competence. Apt examples could be the UN and the European Parliament and, to a lesser extent, Organisation of Islamic Countries or African organisations. Consensual mandates have legitimized their authority and provided symbolic validation to their existence and controlling prowess. Consent of states has reinforced *pacta sunt servanda* to accept and honour international obligations emanating from these organisations *vis-à-vis* other state-parties. The legitimacy deficit is more than made up. And, from this stems the aura of mandate upon the states, whether in the form of international law, conventions, treaties, agreements or global codes of conduct. Delinquencies and violations, though rare and minimal, really prove that rules do exist of which cognizance is taken and others are willing to abide by these.

CONCLUSION

Countdown to commercial exploitation of the celestial bodies for natural resources and of celestial real estate for tourism infrastructure as well as planetary habitats has begun. Development activities are in different stages of experimentation, testing and completion. Operationalisation of space travel services may happen sooner than believed and excavation of mineral resources slightly later. The designs of Moon Village and Mars Colony are under scrutiny and may soon start taking shape on the ground. Despite imponderables, promises of the space behemoth may materialize as scheduled with no major delays or hiccups. Thereafter, once the services are ready to commence and are offered to the public, the costing dynamics will patently favour high profits on investment and gestation. Formats of business and ethical values of space commerce will tend to harden and crystallize. Change in contoured mind-set will be difficult thereafter.

Today, we have an opportunity to create a template of benign economic culture and evolve norms of social obligation for righteous distribution of resources, with the object of common good of humanity and optimum welfare of all stakeholders leading to peace and pleasure in the universe. This vision in the face of present human paradox is unreal. The irony is that today we have multiple choices, greater opportunities, more wealth and high economic prosperity than at any other point in history, yet at the same time we are more depressed, dissatisfied and despondent. Hence, let us not strive for sheer brilliance of activities or ultra-prosperity for the rich and the powerful without equitable sharing. The proposed postulates with induced force of legal mandates would go a long way to save man from perpetrating dishonesty and deceit in commerce in outer space and thus, enjoy social conviviality, inner happiness, and peace of mind.

It would be, perhaps, too much to expect from the old order to cede so easily, and without resistance, to the new legal economic order in the outer space. The 'lackings' have been stated explicitly and often enough. But what disturbs is the evident lack of determination in closing the discernible loopholes or applying appropriate stimulus to stir the society and divert its traction in the right direction. These efforts, if serious and concerted, are bound to cause awareness in a critical mass of intelligentsia who can stand up for change to create a ripple effect in society. For this we would need to refurbish our mind-set and traverse to a voluntary accession of the new tenets so as to reach the discretionary threshold of new economic space order. The engines of change are revving up and take-off to new ethical values just needs positive determination.

It seems equally pertinent to suggest that the pillars of New Ethics may be elevated to the exalted status of *jus cogens* of space law to bear peremptory compliance by all nations and all operators in the outer space where activities perforce have to prosper because of immense benefits accruable to humanity. This vision may materialize, but there is dire need for simultaneous emphasis on ethical content and quality of activities, undertaken with integrity and honesty, so that competition gets transformed into cooperation, greed gets alloyed with altruism, and consumerism gets tempered with sustainability. Fortunately, all these do not appear so incompatible and can co-exist and even synergise for collective happiness.

It is humbly submitted that to begin with, the UN, or any other appropriate international organisation, should take initiative to enunciate ethical commandments for regulating commercial conduct and to inculcate good business behaviour and industrial discipline among nations, corporations and entrepreneurs in the outer space. An opportunity to indoctrinate into a culture of benign economics and perpetuate social obligation for righteous distribution of resources, with the avowed object of common good of humanity and optimum welfare of all countries, exists now. Let's confront the challenge and achieve the desired. Of course, for the intended purpose, negotiations may be protracted and difficult yet, cannot be put off for long. Confidence impels that collective wisdom can identify good economic virtues, commercial ethics and industrial practices; and elect the best suitable and acceptable for institutionalizing into a common code of conduct.

Let's conclude with faith in the new Commercial Order of Ethical Norms for Outer Space as a code of conduct and believe in the goodness of humanity to follow these precepts to realize its innate potential and benign graces for the optimum welfare and common benefit of mankind. It needs to be emphasised that the moral of the story is more important than the story itself. We may, therefore, do well to pray with Einstein, in his strain of emotions, to seek goodwill among men, sanity for humanity, and peace in the universe to enjoy the united colours of economic happiness and social development.

NOTES

1. Some states like China and India may not adopt this model of state funding for space activities for some more time. Though this may remain the basic policy, yet China has started encouraging private enterprise in space activities. A private sector Chinese company , OneSpace, was founded in 2015 and its progress is often compared to SpaceX. OneSpace has launched a 30 foot long rocket on May 17, 2018.
2. Russia has experimented on processing of life saving vaccines in the sterile environment and the US has conducted experiments in fabrication of super conductors in the hyper cold environ of outer space. Experiments by other countries on additive engineering, bionomics and stem cells are also in progress. All countries have found highly encouraging results.
3. It is also referred to as Corporate Social Responsibility (CSR). The word 'Conscious' has been deliberately chosen not to restrict this concept to corporations but to make it more pervasive and to include individuals and Non-Governmental organizations (NGOs) in its ambit.
4. Ibid.
5. Initial space activities of super powers were extensions of military objectives and subsequent deep outer space probes have been prompted by quest for knowledge.
6. This can be attributed to altered political compulsions and lessened strategic security concerns in a uni-polar world coupled with economics of escalating costs. Even the recent US-Russian Agreement of 2010 to reduce stocks of nuclear warheads has also decelerated belligerence. Political environment is, no doubt, subject to change and priorities may shift.
7. Sarah Lewin, "Making Stuff in Space: Off-Earth Manufacturing is Just Getting Started", in Space.com, May 11, 2018.
8. Ibid.
9. Ibid.
10. Report by Mike Snyder, Lead Engineer with Made In Space, in Space.com, November 25, 2014.
11. Ibid.
12. Agreement Governing the Activities of States on the Moon and other Celestial Bodies, 1979, popularly called the Moon Treaty. This agreement, however, as yet, has been ratified by just a dozen states. Further, germane regulations in amplification of basic provisions need to be drafted and approved.

13. It is a broad dichotomy to bring home the point and not a fine discussion of nuances.
14. Excerpted from the Harvard Business School proceedings of Business Summit: The Role of Business Leaders in Sustaining Market Capitalism, held on 14 October, 2008.
15. Adam Smith, *The Wealth of Nations* (Great Britain, 1776).
16. Ajit Bhalla, *New Wealth of Nations* (2018). Dr Bhalla has added 'education' as a factor for growth of wealth. He has analysed the education level of societies and related it to their wealth formation and has come to this conclusion. Empirically also better educated communities are richer than less literate ones. This correlation appears valid.
17. Hindus worship *Lakshmi*, goddess of wealth, invoking *shubh laabh* or auspicious profits in business. This can be interpreted as divinely legitimate profits or conscionable returns.
18. There is a practice ordained in Sikh religion that urges its adherents to donate/voluntarily contribute 10% of their earnings/ profits towards religious/charitable causes. This mandate is thus applicable, both to individuals and business houses, as Conscious Societal Responsibility. This term has been used in preference to Corporate Social Responsibility (CSR) because of its wide ambit and applicability. This practice has been prevalent among Sikhs for nearly five centuries.
19. The Islamic Law in *Shariah* prohibits interest (*Riba*) on borrowings and lending, speculative transactions or gambling (*Maysir*), selling something with uncertain outcome or subject matter or date or delivery (*Gharar*), and investments in businesses which deal in alcohol, drugs, pornography, gambling, manufacture of weapons, among other restrictions, are treated as *Haraam.*
20. *Koans* are Buddhist parables with a moral that defy normal understanding and can be comprehended at a higher echelon of the enlightened state of mind.
21. Eric A Posner, *Law and Social Norms* (Harvard University Press, USA, 2000), Indian reprint, Universal Law Publishing Company, 2009), p. 4.
22. Ibid, p. 38.
23. This hypothesis is based on results of a study organized by Harvard Business School in 2009.
24. The full title of this treaty reads, Treaty on Principles governing the Activities of States in the Exploration and Use of Outer Space including the Moon and other Celestial Bodies, 1967. Refer UN Treaty Series.
25. Ibid, Article I.
26. Ibid, Article III
27. *K. J. Aiyar's Judicial Dictionary*, Twelfth Edition (The Law Book Company (P) Ltd), 1998, p. 465.
28. Note 23 *supra*, Article I.
29. Adapted from records of Harvard Business School relating to a debate on the subject in May. 2009.
30. The term governance, in this context, means to cover all forms of mechanisms and processes by which authority is exercised in any form, implying not only public authority, but also embracing non-government and private umbrella organizations.
31. Refer n. 3 *supra.*
32. Principles Relevant to the Use of Nuclear Power Sources in Outer Space, 1992.
33. UN Guidelines for Prevention and Mitigation of Space Debris, 2007.
34. Eric A. Posner, Law and Social Norms, Universal Law Publishing Co. Pvt. Ltd, Delhi. First Indian Reprint, 2009. Originally published by Harvard University Press, USA, in 2000.
35. Ibid, p. 3.
36. The allegation of Iraq possessing WMDs and its attack appears a congruous situation from recent history.

CHAPTER FIVE

Space Commercialisation

An Era of Responsibility and Cooperation

INTRODUCTION

Space domain is an inhospitable environment to which humans are neither genetically adapted nor bodily acclimatized. Further, activities in outer space are inherently hazardous and highly risky whether it is space walk or in-orbit satellite repairs or jumps with space parachute. Therefore, independent and self-reliant space activity, in isolation, may be beset with imponderable risks. There could be accidents and emergencies where assistance and support from other actors in space may become essential and unavoidable for health or survival. It may, at the same time, be economical to operate a common facility for medical first aid, disaster management, and engineering emergency.

Besides responsibilities incumbent on private commercial actors to ensure safety in space activity, duties relating to the welfare of the space workers is paramount and inescapable. Cooperation, apart from providing fail-safe arrangement as stand-by, may afford economies in providing common utilities and shared facilities. This illustrates the element of dependence and the extent of cooperation needed in the outer space, howsoever big and autonomous is the set-up and infrastructure. This compulsion for mutual succour compels for voluntary cooperation emanating from a sense of responsibility and desire for economy. Therefore, this impels us to highlight the character of contemporary space age of private commercialisation as an era of responsibility and cooperation.

It seems too trite to assert that international law is based on the maxim of *pacta sunt servanda* and depends on agreement and will of the sovereign state for compliance to operate within the group of state-parties. Over the years, through state practice, some of the basic principles of international law got universalized in adherence to become customary law. The latter, in turn, requires no specific treaty from new or non-party states to oblige them to accept and honour its existence and join its systemic operation. With elapse of time, and abiding state practice, some tenets of the customary international law were deemed so fundamental and close to natural state behaviour. These have so embedded themselves in the psyche of the state that these got exalted to the status of *Jus Cogens*.

The evolutionary process undergone by international law appears applicable to the tenets and regime of 'space law' *albeit* compressed in period because space law can claim barely half a century of existence. What really happened to metamorphose international law over centuries has been caused to space law to mature in decades. In fact, space law grew as an adjunct of international law and has metabolized rather fast. It is now getting metamorphosed into an independent and auto-poietic system[1] with complexities and cross linkages with other sub-systems of cognate legal regimes,[2] international jurisprudence, objects and subjects of law, their operations, and applications.

The intrinsic complexity of space law, and its operation, thus becomes discernible; its contours are gradually crystallizing to new formats and its grammar becoming more distinct and communicable. In fact, some inherent deficiencies and ambiguities of the law are also becoming apparent. There is no reductionist approach of criminality in space law; the bottom-line is either common survival or collective annihilation. This calls for ultra-responsible behaviour with amicable cooperation between space-farers because in many hazardous situations, the nature may not give another opportunity. The stakes are clear and high; and choices limited. The decision, however, is in our hand, of our volition and depends upon our wisdom and sagacity.

From another angle, Western law pedagogues and protagonists of traditional theories have, for centuries, vehemently maintained and consistently taught that international law is the law of civilized nations, thereby implying that it is the European nations[3] who practice civilized conduct in international relations and thus, their behaviour can be regulated by mutual agreements and relatively soft laws. This view becomes readily adaptable to space law, the corpus of which comprises some UN General Assembly resolutions, a couple of treaties, a few agreements, and a lot of guidelines and principles. A scrutiny of this documented law brings to clear focus the basic tenets of state responsibility and international cooperation. Based on this premise, it is proposed to establish that space law, in a comparative vein, is a regime for responsible and cooperative nations of international comity, who are able to usefully interact and responsibly cooperate to fruitfully explore and use outer space, without let or hindrance, in the outer space domain.

THE NATURE OF SPACE LAW

From primordial times, the outer space has been governed and regulated by the rule of God, laws of nature, and the principles of astro-physics. In fact, the necessity of international law arose only to regulate conduct of human activity and operation of human-made objects in outer space. Thus, the primary purpose of law has been proper governance to ensure peace and order by informing of normative behaviour and regulating human activity within prescribed limits. A Spanish proverb succinctly sums up this wisdom that it is not the fence that protects the orchard but the fear that goes with it and the respect that society accords. Thus, this element of fear is imparted and instilled by the law. If it so happens, then the law has substantially achieved its purpose of protection and consequently safety and security seem well assured.

By corollary, this principle can be safely extended to outer space where this *specialibus law* performs a vital function by its proclamations of permitted, prohibited and regulated activities. It, thus, defines the nature of activities in outer space and stipulates norms of human conduct in relation to this domain. Hence, space law seems to govern and promote public order in outer space. By and large, this specific law has succeeded in achieving this task within the outer space and from outside. The corpus of space law is a few treaties and mostly comprises of soft law. A serious study of this subject uplifts a sense of altruism reflected in the concepts of responsibility and cooperation, among space-faring nations and between signatory countries, enshrined in this law that would assure survival of humanity and improved quality of life of mankind on the earth and in outer space.

In principle, every human activity in every field needs law, not to curb freedom but to regulate its operation to make it amicable and compatible with the same or similar rights of the others. A legal doctrine '*summum jus, summa injuria*', it broadly means that absolute right may cause great injury, implies the need for reasonable restrictions on enjoyment of any right equally by all. In other words, regulation and not restraint is in the best interest of all because rights have correlatives in duties and both must coexist for the benefit of all, that is provided to all. It also seems relevant to mention that culture is the manifestation of a country's soft power and it comes crystal clear that core values which each culture cherishes, universally turn out to be cooperation and responsibility and these constitute the core fundamentals of space law.

Regulation Prior to OST

Pre-OST era was the period of cooperation between the two space-faring states voluntarily appreciating a sense of reciprocal responsibility, when treaty law did not exist. At that stage, the UN assumed responsibility and arrogated authority to regulate activities in the outer space under Article 1 (4) of the UN Charter, which enjoins that the UN shall be a nodal centre for harmonizing the actions of nations in the attainment of common ends and peaceful objectives. In pursuance to this mandate, the General Assembly took upon itself under Article 13 of the Charter to initiate studies 'encouraging the progressive development of international law and its codification'[4] relating to the outer space.

The UN General Assembly, thereafter, became active to pass Resolutions that established principles of non-appropriation in outer space and celestial bodies, freedom of exploration, extension of international law and applicability of the Charter of the UN as well as the Statute of the International Court of Justice to regulate human activities and artificial objects in outer space.[5] As part of its efforts in this direction, the General Assembly, within the framework of the UN, constituted an international body for cooperation in the study of activities in the outer space that is now called the Committee on the Peaceful Uses of the Outer Space, in short, COPUOS.[6] The importance of cooperation among states is boldly underscored here.

The next important stage in the evolution of space law dawned with the General Assembly, adopting by acclamation,[7] "The Declaration of Legal

Principles Governing the Activities of States in the Exploration and Use of Outer Space".[8] The Declaration enunciated nine cardinal principles, which later got embodied in the Outer Space Treaty[9] of 1967. The two fundamental principles underlying the Declaration were, and continue to remain, state responsibility as well as international cooperation, assistance and consultations among the states. These principles find copious references and due emphasis in the total gamut of space law spread over treaty law, agreements, principles and guidelines promulgated by the UN.

The Need for Order in Outer Space

It is wisely said that scattered and disorderly notes of sound make cacophony but the same notes put in some proper order compose a good symphony. Similarly, words in a scattered and jumbled mode make no much sense but the same words arranged in good order create poetry. Same way, a house in disarray looks a mess and may lead to accidents but when put in proper order makes it a snug home full of warmth and congeniality. To conclude the analogy, proper order to human actions makes for good life and cultured living. In analogous vein, in the outer space domain, despite the laws of nature, human activities with launched satellites and other artificial objects can be disorderly and unregulated and a sure recipe for disaster. Whereas, good governance and public order in outer space can certainly lead to human advancement, sustained growth, and better welfare in the larger interest of humankind.

THE PRINCIPLE OF STATE RESPONSIBILITY

It is axiomatic in International Law "that state as a sovereign person, can have no legal responsibility whatever".[10] Or graffiti says the king can do no wrong. But such an absolute statement of classical law is no longer tenable in modern times; and contemporary law of nations admits of wider international liability for harm caused due to acts of State or certain internationally injurious acts committed by its agents, officials or nationals so authorised, enabled or ordered.[11] A correlative of this is international duty cast by international pacts, treaties and conventions and out of these arise the *vinculum juris*, legal obligation to act within the confines of law and assume responsibility for unauthorised injuries and violation of international legal duty. It thus, "is necessary to distinguish two different kinds of state responsibility. These may be named 'original' in contradistinction to 'vicarious' responsibility".[12] The original responsibility may comprise for international delinquencies and acts of state organs while vicarious responsibility may relate to acts of private persons who are nationals of the state.[13]

The principle of state responsibility is a classical doctrine of international law and has been adhered to for centuries, only new connotations of state responsibility have gradually evolved with progressive times and changing international milieu.[14] State responsibility is a correlative of international obligation and this concept has now been embedded in space law with 'customary' legal mandate and a superior normative value. Nevertheless, its compliance is equally obligatory and attendant with sanctions. This doctrine is expected "to serve as a specific instrument of legal regulation in international relations and stimulate the functioning of international law".[15]

This tenet of state responsibility for its own acts, or of government functionaries or official organisations or its nationals, that cause international wrong, injury or damage, is a well-established principle of customary international law. This has been embodied in space law that is *lex specialis* for the outer space domain, which is so unique, hazardous and vulnerable. Till recently, space activities which bear long gestation period, involve highly complex technologies, and require huge outlays with endemic risk of failure, were undertaken by state agencies funded from the state exchequer. This trend of space exploration and use, however, is fast changing. Commercial space activities, being initiated and undertaken by private players with no dependence on public funds, is the emerging trend. However, the space-faring nations have behaved responsibly and done so voluntarily and in reciprocity, almost every time, till now. These, of course, are generalized statements that need to be buttressed with specific provisions of law and events of violation. A few such examples of law are discussed in succeeding paragraphs.

State Responsibility under International Law

The principle of state responsibility is a classical doctrine of international law and has been adhered to for centuries almost as *jus cogens*; only new extensions to state responsibility have gradually evolved with changing times and new concepts donned on sovereignty. State responsibility is a correlative of international obligation and this general principle constitutes 'customary' legal mandate of a higher normative value. States as subjects of International Law are bound by its tenets and obligated to compliance.[16] This doctrine is thus expected "to serve as a specific instrument of legal regulation in international relations and stimulate the functioning of international law".[17]

Many scholars of International Law while discussing substantive rules of rights and duties of the State assume that there exists a minimum international standard of justice and have highlighted the international responsibility of the States for breaches of duty, even by governmental authorities.[18] The scholars further assert that international wrong committed by nationals also "engages the responsibility of the State".[19] On the contrary, State also has a bounden duty to ensure safety and protection of its nationals and their assets in foreign countries in every possible manner whether legally, diplomatically or by alternative dispute redressal methods.[20] Hence, ultra-hazardous activities like space activities should need a separate legal regime with well-defined responsibility.[21]

In general terms, state responsibility refers to the legal consequences that follow upon violation or a *delictum* as an act of commission or omission relating to any international legal obligation. It is, however, immaterial whether such delinquent action has been performed by any of its legally constituted entities, juridical persons and nationals, including executive organs of governments and natural persons, whoever can be deemed as subjects of international law. It may be added for clarity that the state responsibility extends even to harmful consequences of legitimate activities by its nationals. Thus any omission, failure or detrimental effect, in turn, sets up legal liability *qua* aggrieved parties of another state, subject to the basic rule that all means of domestic protection must first be exhausted.

It is, however, pertinent to mention that in theory and practice of international law, certain circumstances and specific situations exonerate and preclude state responsibility. Some examples are, use of force in self-defence, *force majeure* in disasters apart from local laws relating to the period of limitation on actions and claims. In this connection, it is pertinent to mention of the formulation of the 'Articles of Responsibility of States for Internationally Wrongful Acts' (ARSIWA) by International Law Commission. This articulation is well respected in juridical circles and is often cited as honourable legal authority.

State Responsibility under Space Law

State responsibility is rather definitive and expansive under space law. Let's first refer to the OST, which provides a general legal framework for the scientific exploration and peaceful uses of outer space. The specific provision relevant to international responsibility is contained in Article VI. The text of the Article reads, 'States Parties to the Treaty shall bear international responsibility for national activities in outer space, including the Moon and other celestial bodies, whether such activities are carried on by governmental agencies or by non-governmental entities'. This means that corporate sector and other private 'astro-preneurs' are permitted to undertake legitimate space activities.

The next element of responsibility under space law mandates an assurance "that national activities are carried out in conformity with the provisions set forth in the present Treaty".[22] It means that activities that are not scientifically exploratory or that where the use of outer space or celestial body is not peaceful nor in the benefit of mankind would be contrary to the Treaty. Further in elaboration, the Treaty permits exploration but not exploitation and least of all for private appropriation and personal profit in contravention of the interest and benefit of all countries.

The third element of state responsibility relates to space activities by private enterprise in the form of public-private partnerships and individual ventures by billionaires and corporate conglomerates that are gradually filling the widening hiatus created by withdrawal of state patronage. These are the private actors in space activities in respect of whose conduct there is no clarity in law but all the same respective states are bound to bear responsibility for their acts. In order to properly acquit this responsibility, the State may have to regulate and supervise their activities by a specific domestic legislation or modulation of national statutes to ensure that space industry gets impetus and still causes least of injury to third party or infringement of space laws resulting in consequential international liability.[23]

Therefore, space law requires that, 'The activities of non-governmental entities in outer space, including the Moon and other celestial bodies, shall require authorisation and continuing supervision by the appropriate State Party to the Treaty'. The term, non-governmental entities, connotes a broad plexus of business models that are progressively filling the hiatus due to state withdrawal from non-strategic, non-exploratory activities. Thus, this article of the Treaty provides a normative leverage to promote and oversee space activities of private sector. The purpose of articulated stipulation for state authorisation is to establish a nexus of committed responsibility with the state; and continuing supervision mandates the need for conformance to the permissibility under the Treaty. The states have so far abided by these legal provisions but the future appears uncertain with privatisation of space activities coming of age and starting to wield its own clout in national economies.

The next aspect of responsibility binds that "States Parties...shall pursue studies of outer space, including the Moon and other celestial bodies, and conduct exploration of them so as to avoid their harmful contamination and also adverse changes in the environment of the Earth resulting from the introduction of extra-terrestrial matter and, where necessary, shall adopt appropriate measures for the purpose".[24] The nature of this responsibility ordains due regard in conduct for avoidance of negligence in actions, whether of commission or omission. So far no serious case of such dereliction has come to notice but considering the trend, exploitation of celestial resources, planetary migration, space habitations, and other multiplying applications and uses, may jeopardize sustainability of space environment and its usability by posterity.

State Responsibility under Other Space Law Instruments

The fundamental of state responsibility finds a portfolio of copious references scattered in other international instruments regulating space activities either in direct reference or by its generic variants like duty to assist in emergencies and distress or offer cooperation or engage in consultations for unusual events and potentially dangerous experiments, *et al.* These are parts of the same generic responsibility skeletally mentioned in articles VI and VII of OST. In order to correctly grasp the import and comprehend the nuances of this principle, it is proposed to adduce a few illustrations to vindicate the above statement. A few provisions from other international instruments of space law emphasising this precept are discussed in succeeding paragraphs.

For instance, take the case of the Convention on International Liability for Damage Caused by Space Objects, 1972 that amplifies the provision of responsibility and liability and outlines the procedure for incumbent claims.

Thus, an inalienable incident of responsibility arises due to *vinculum juris* that relates to liability for any damages caused by even bonafide state activities performed by its space objects, to third parties or other adjacent users in the outer space or on celestial bodies. The liability attaches to the launching state or that procures launching. Thus, "A launching state shall be absolutely liable to pay compensation for damage caused by its space object on the surface of the Earth or to aircraft in flight".[25] The Convention upholds the principle of fault liability[26] for consequential damages and compensation there for. But the element of causal fault in space activities, quite often, is difficult to establish and hence many accidents remain un-litigated and un-negotiated like the Iridium-Cosmos collision.

Another nuance of responsibility, humanitarian in character, is embodied in the Agreement on Rescue of Astronauts etc. It states, "If owing to accident, distress, emergency or unintended landing, the personnel of a spacecraft land in territory under the jurisdiction of a contracting party, it shall immediately take all possible steps to rescue them and render them all necessary assistance".[27] This duty becoming particularized and specific on such a request of the launching authority, though however, it is equally binding even without such intimation.[28]

The Moon Agreement[29] too carries a definitive and specific clause on this point. It reiterates, "States party to this Agreement shall bear international responsibility for national activities on the Moon, whether such activities are carried on by governmental agencies or by non-governmental entities..." And states shall assure that "national activities are carried out in conformity with provisions set forth in this Agreement".[30] This call for adherence to the law is loud and clear; and more so ordains a responsibility for due care and implies liability for damages caused, advertently or inadvertently.

International Responsibility Derived from National Constitution

Yet another aspect of state responsibility stems from national constitutions because international law has a symbiotic relationship and an intimate nexus with municipal laws. For example, Indian Constitution, on a higher plane, directs under article 51 'to promote international peace and security' as well as 'foster respect for international law and treaty obligations...'. This requires the government to maintain amiable inter-state relations, subject to national posturing, and geo-political strategy. Thus, the constitution directs the state to perform its international obligations under ratified treaties, even if necessary to legislate a new domestic enactment. Indeed, the language is directive, explicit and binding.

Further, Article 253 of the Constitution empowers Parliament to make suitable and appropriate domestic laws to implement the provisions and obligations under any treaty, agreement or convention adhered to by the state. This duty of international responsibility is, therefore, solemn and obligatory as well as the basic philosophy of Indian public policy. "[S]ubstantial individualism of the international community"[31] is neither approved by the Indian Constitution nor espoused by the Indian political ethos.

Responsibility Towards Humanity in General

One is impelled to allude to another relevant aspect of state responsibility that can be sublimated to *erga omnes* and this rule has since been recognised in customary international law that *pari passu* becomes applicable to contemporary space law. The legal force of this particular obligation that is owed by the states to the international community as a whole has been identified and obliquely highlighted by the International Court of Justice in the Barcelona Traction case[32] among others. As a result, this social duty of the state towards humanity at large has been accepted universally and has got deeply rooted in state practice. In fact, state responsibility *erga omnes* can be elevated to the status of *Jus Cogen* of space law and can consequently draw substantive support from the Vienna Convention.[33] Thus, such a responsibility will also be equally incumbent on states.

AN APPRAISAL

In nutshell, in the beginning, space activities were state-sponsored, state-governed, and state-funded because such activities represented advancement of technology and offered strategic advantages. While these motivations still prevail, this sole reason has somewhat eroded in its importance with private actors entering the fray. Multi-media applications, future of space transportation, possibility of celestial habitations, and viability of commercial exploitation of celestial resources are becoming prospective business propositions. As a result, states are restricting investment to strategic research only and commercial ventures are passing on to private enterprise. And, it is here that private actors find their specific niche but their considerations of business and motivation for enterprise is profit, even in contravention of international responsibilities of the state. Their benchmark is profit.

This calls for state regulation of private activities in space. The Treaty puts an incumbent rider of state regulation and continuing supervision. Wisdom ordains a holistic approach and comprehensive agenda with optimal governance. Thus, all stakeholders should responsibly strive for safe, secure and sustainable use of outer space and profitable exploitation of celestial natural resources with benefit to all countries. Collective responsibility of all actors in this fragile and hazardous domain thus becomes imperative. None can afford to be a weak link. Encouragingly, India has behaved as a responsible nation, with unblemished credentials, in its space activities and as a launching facility for the world.

THE PRINCIPLE OF INTERNATIONAL COOPERATION

Introduction

International Law is based on the maxim of *pacta sunt servanda* and depended on agreement based on the will of the sovereign state for compliance or acceptance to operate within the group of state-parties. This relational mechanism at international level and the practice of states, at best, assured a regime of co-existence and tolerance, broadly, on a principle of 'live and let live' and nothing beyond that. In improvement, the legal regime of outer space is held aloft on the pillars of state responsibility and international cooperation. There is a realisation that in the space domain total independence and complete self-reliance are difficult to achieve and reciprocal help from space-faring entities would not only be necessary but also unavoidable in distress, emergencies and disasters. Space law propagates this slogan and space-faring nations acknowledge this compulsion.

Over a period of time, through consistent state practice, some of the basic principles get universalized in adherence to become natural responses or behavioural norms of state practice. These get elevated to customary law that, in turn, requires no specific treaty or ratification from non-member or new states to oblige them to accept and honour its existence and join its systemic operation. With passage of time and cumulative *opinio juris,* some tenets of the customary international law were deemed so fundamental and universal as having embedded themselves in the human psyche as natural reaction or instinctive response and these got exalted to the status of *Jus Cogens*.

This evolutionary process undergone by international law appears applicable to the regime of space law *albeit* compressed in period. What really happened to international law over centuries has been caused to mature space law in decades. In fact, space law grew as an adjunct of international law and metabolized fast. It is now getting metamorphosed into an independent and auto-poietic system[34] with germane complexities and cross linkages with other sub-systems of cognate legal regimes,[35] international jurisprudence, objects and subjects of law, their operations and applications. As a result, most of the space law is already treated as "instant customary law" and proposals are rife to elevate some select tenets into *jus cogens* of space law.[36]

The intrinsic complexity of space law, thus, becomes discernible with new activities like exploitation of planetary mineral resources or space travel and tourism or celestial habitations. Consequently, its contours are gradually crystallizing into new formats and its grammar becoming more distinct and communicable. But compliance and adherence to law and selecting cooperation as motto is our determination and discretion. There is no reductionist approach of criminality in space law; hence the bottom-line is either common survival or collective annihilation. The stakes are clear and choices limited. The decision, however, is in our hand, of our volition and depends upon our wisdom and sagacity. International cooperation, therefore, is the mandate of space law and certainly the *mantra* for survival and sustainability, at least, for the simple reason that it finds copious repetition to impress the importance of this idiom.

A scrutiny of this documented law brings to clear focus the essentiality of the application of this basic tenet of international cooperation in the space domain. Even an ontological churning of the space law with statistical approach will throw up international cooperation as a fundamental and modal principle in space activities without adhering to which success may be limited and disaster ominous. This hypothesis is vindicated in this section by examples and illustrations from space law which in turn assures that cooperative nations of international comity are able to usefully interact and fruitfully operate without fear, let or hindrance in the outer space and on celestial bodies to carry on their competing activities.

The Mandate of International Cooperation

To put it simplistically, the principle of international cooperation pervades the spirit of space law and is interspersed in almost all instruments comprising the corpus of space law. Even the Guidelines and Principles, that are primarily non-binding normative space law, also echo this sentiment. And to top it all, there is a dedicated resolution for the purpose, namely "Declaration on International Cooperation in the Exploration and Use of Outer Space for the Benefit and in the Interest of All States, Taking into Particular Account the Needs of Developing Countries". This Declaration was adopted by the UN General Assembly on 13 December, 1996.[37] It reiterates this singular concept as intrinsic spirit of the OST.

Further, in view of the importance in developing the norms of space law and their significant role in promoting international cooperation in the use of outer space for peaceful purposes, the General Assembly and the Secretary General of the United Nations have called upon all member states of the United Nations not yet parties to the international treaties governing the use of outer space to ratify or accede to those treaties as soon as feasible.[38] The concern shown by the authorities speaks volumes on the desirability of the cooperative attitude.

International Cooperation in Outer Space Treaty

Outer Space Treaty, in particular, is replete with specific references to cooperation between states and the relevant provisions are meaningful and binding. To begin with, the Preamble to the Treaty optimistically exhorts states parties, "Desiring to contribute to broad international cooperation in the scientific as well as the legal aspects of the exploration and use of outer space for peaceful purposes". It further believes "...that such cooperation will contribute to the development of mutual understanding and to the strengthening of friendly relations between states and peoples".[39] The hope is sincere and aspiration genuine; this intention permeates all through the Treaty.

Article I of the Treaty mentions while referring to the freedom of scientific investigation in outer space and celestial bodies that, "...states shall facilitate and encourage international cooperation in such investigation". Again Article III while permitting space activities urges for "...maintaining international peace and security and promoting international cooperation and understanding". Further Article X endorses international cooperation to afford "...an opportunity to observe the flight of space objects launched by ... states". Extending the principle, Article XI emphatically commands to "promote international cooperation in the peaceful exploration and use of outer space...including the moon and other celestial bodies,...[and] to inform...of the nature, conduct, locations and results of such activities".[40]

Further, astronauts have been exalted in status and accorded the privilege of being Envoys of Mankind in outer space with intent to involve all states into this notional concept and elicit their unflinching cooperation for supporting space activities.[41] Similarly, the very basis of the Agreement on the Rescue of Astronauts, the Return of Astronauts and the Return of Objects launched into Outer Space, 1968 is essentially for cooperation and as stated in the Preamble it has been "[P]rompted by sentiments of humanity". The tenor of the emphasis is clear and explicit and seems oriented towards cooperation with humaneness and magnanimity among comity of nations.

Generic Variants of International Cooperation

Apart from the term international cooperation, the OST has used other variants and vocabulary with similar hue of meaning. For example, words like consultation, understanding, due regard, and mutual assistance have been used elsewhere with similar intent and spirit. Article IX of the OST is most relevant in this context. It exhorts that the states 'shall be guided by the principle of cooperation and mutual assistance and shall conduct all their activities in outer space, including the Moon and other celestial bodies, with due regard to the corresponding interests of all other State Parties to the Treaty'. Different lexicon connotes same meaning and purpose.

Again, in the same article in relation to a possibility of 'potentially harmful interference with activities of other states...it shall undertake appropriate international consultations before proceeding with any such activity or experiment'. It also enjoins on member-states that if it 'has reason to believe that an activity or experiment planned by another State Party in outer space, including the Moon and other celestial bodies, would cause potentially harmful interference, [it] may request consultation concerning the activity or experiment'. This article ordains cooperation in the interest of protection of space environment but has been dubbed as procedural article that does not creates any substantive obligation. Many would agree that the escape route is illusory and text of the provision is meaningful and affords a crucial option. This article, nevertheless, espouses a common objective and responsibility with affirmative duty to consult or seek consultation where in doubt or sense a necessity.

Another classic example of cooperation for intrusive inspection is contained in Article XII of the OST. It iterates, 'All stations, installations, equipment and space vehicles on the Moon and other celestial bodies shall be open to representatives of other States Parties to the Treaty on a basis of reciprocity'. The only rider is to 'give reasonable advance notice of a projected visit, in order that appropriate consultations may be held and that maximum precautions may be taken to assure safety and to avoid interference with normal operations in the facility to be visited'. This provision highlights voluntary cooperation that is expressive of an attitude of openness and willingness to share certain information mutually. The practice of exchange of visits sure seems a healthy practice to strengthen this spirit.

International Cooperation in the Moon Agreement

The Preamble of the Moon Treaty[42] is indeed visionary and functional. From the very beginning, it is "[D]etermined to promote on the basis of equality the further development of cooperation among states in the exploration and use of the Moon and other celestial bodies". It also expresses an ardent desire 'to prevent the Moon from becoming an area of international conflict'. In fact, it is a solemn pledge that cannot be accomplished without international cooperation and sincere contribution from all states.

Again in Article 2, it maintains, 'All activities on the moon...shall be carried out...in the interest of maintaining international peace and security and promoting international cooperation and mutual understanding and with due regard to the corresponding interests of all other states parties'. It echoes the sentiment contained in the OST. The tone, it will be noticed, is conciliatory and cooperative; and jurisprudentially determines a correlative duty to an accorded right.

Article 4 directs, "Exploration and use of the Moon shall be the province of all mankind and shall be carried out for the benefit and in the interest of all countries...to promote higher standards of living...".[43] It further adds, "States Parties shall be guided by the principle of cooperation and mutual assistance in all their activities concerning exploration and use of the Moon. International cooperation in pursuance to this Agreement should be as wide as possible".[44] The stress on the importance of international cooperation among the comity of nations, and in particular space-faring countries, is unmistakable.

In another aspect of cooperation, while the Agreement in Article 6 assures 'freedom of scientific investigation on the Moon by all States Parties without discrimination...[and] on the basis of equality' it also emphasises on the desirability of exchanging scientific and other personnel on expeditions to or installations on the Moon to the greatest extent feasible and practicable'. This reiteration follows the approach recommended in the OST in Article XII.

Again Article 10 of the Agreement expects that, 'States Parties shall adopt all practicable measures to safeguard the life and health of persons on the Moon'. And, 'For this purpose they shall regard any person on the Moon as an astronaut within the meaning of Article V' of the OST. It further mandates that, 'States Parties shall offer shelter in their stations, installations, vehicles and other facilities to persons in distress on the Moon'. This provision indeed oozes altruism and kindness to obligate space-faring entities to a solemn duty to collaborate for humanitarian cause. Article 12 (3) of the Agreement, in the same vein, expands and reinforces this duty to '...the event of emergency involving a threat to human life...'. The obligation so imposed is, thus, uncompromisable and admits of no denial or excuses.

International Cooperation in Normative Space Law

Such and similar expressions of advisory nature or as pseudo-obligations are repeatedly found in other normative space law documents. Because, the corpus of space law, besides treaties and agreements, comprises several guidelines and in-principle documents and codes of conduct regulating space activities and suggesting best practices for its uses. These may be contained in resolutions adopted by the UN General Assembly or other initiative and are supposed to convey an appeal to maintain public order in the respective field of activity and urge for voluntary cooperation to best satisfy individualised needs and simultaneously reap optimum benefits for mankind.

A significant example could be Principles for regulating activities in the field of international direct television broadcasting by satellites.[45] This area involves allotment of slots for geo-synchronous satellites and sharing of telecommunication spectrum and radio frequency allotments. These attempts to satisfy competing and conflicting demands of states, which "should be carried out in a manner compatible with the sovereign rights of States, including the principle of non-intervention as well as [with] the right of everyone...".[46] Further, paragraphs B, H and I of the document also encourage the same principle. In fact, paragraph D is fully devoted to international cooperation and urges "[s]pecial consideration...to the needs of the developing countries...for the purpose of accelerating their national development."[47] A large-hearted and public-spirited attitude is clearly recommended.

Other sibling document enunciating international cooperation is the Principles Relating to Remote Sensing of the Earth from Space[48] which covers a very sensitive issue, so very delicately poised in the corpus of Space law. This aspect comes in sharp relief in paragraphs stating Principle V, VIII and XIII. To illustrate, Principle V states that, "remote sensing activities shall promote international cooperation...on equitable and mutually acceptable terms".[49] This also commands generosity from the sensing states.

Another pertinent example is that of UN Guidelines for Mitigation of Space Debris, 2007 that lament the quantum of existing accumulation of detritus, particularly in the lower reaches of outer space and the almost exponential addition to the same every decade. In remediation thereof, it specifically solicits cooperation among states and coordination of technological resources for reduction in redundant satellites, scavenging of space litter, avoidance of incidental debris and conscious effort to shun advertent creation of junk in outer space.[50] Cooperation will ensure to make outer space operations safe, viable and sustainable till into the distant future and for posterity.

The Declaration on International Cooperation[51] adopted by the UN General Assembly is solely devoted to promoting and fostering the cult of international cooperation among states. The Declaration 'recognises the growing significance of international cooperation among states and between states and international organisations...' for 'efficient collaboration ...for the mutual benefit and in the interest of all parties...taking into particular account the needs of developing countries'. The sincere concern of the UN for cooperation and amity among nation for their own betterment and welfare as well as for conflict avoidance and dispute resolution in outer space activities becomes amply evident and should be taken as an obligatory plea rather than a mere exhortative rhetoric or impassioned appeal.

And lastly, the EU Code of Conduct[52] encourages for cooperation, consultation, transparency and mutual assistance to 'seek solutions based on an equitable balance of interests'. This accepts and imparts a new understanding of sovereignty and the role of governing mechanisms that is at variance from the one imbedded in traditional international law. The EU has urged nations worldwide to join and adhere to this Code to make its acceptance almost universal. Nevertheless, it remains non-obligatory and provides only "a feel-good factor"[53] with flimsy expectations. The US is also preparing a similar Code of Conduct for Outer Space. This trend, however, is proliferating to other countries, too.

One can also solicit support from the views of Goedhuis that in meeting the varied challenges of the space age man has been able to cavort and combine the forces of the social complex which provide a realisation of greater world interdependence because of limitations of technology and ultra-hazardous domain of outer space and thus necessitate cooperation. Inclusivity of all states, technically capable, or still struggling for technological competence, is inalienable and integral to the order of outer space regime. This important feature of space law reflects the gradually transforming structure of international law and reveals a process to detoxify international relations of the phantom of sovereignty and national exclusivity. It rightly brings home recognition of the compulsion of international cooperation in activities in the domain of outer space and on the celestial bodies.[54]

It is, thus, held by many scholars that space law contains stronger cooperative duties and obligation to collaboration than general international law. Rudiger Wolfrum has particularly stressed that this principle marks a significant break and a conceptual transition away from the traditional international law of co-existence to a new law of cooperation.[55] Similarly, Rudolf Dolzer holds that the structure of Space Law is based on active cooperation and mutual assistance complemented by specialised duties towards activities in and relating to outer space. This reflects concept of obligation of assistance with voluntary spontaneity and in the form of reciprocity.[56]

From the foregoing analysis, it gets amply substantiated that international cooperation is the cornerstone of space law for betterment of mankind and improvement in quality of life on the earth. International cooperation is not a peripheral issue but a strong strand that runs through the regime of space law and becomes common denominator of treaties and agreements, principles and guidelines. Therefore, this concept has been fully imbibed and internalized; and has, thus, become integral to its obligatory functioning as well as normative behaviour of all states. Thus this principle undoubtedly and rightfully assumes the status of *jus cogen.*

CONCLUSION

Civilised nations do not have to be mandated to interact with cooperation or to act in their respective and common best interests. Therefore, it behoves such nations to naturally react and behave in that manner and of course, we all claim to be civilized nations honouring the tenets of international law and cooperating in international relations. Yet history is witness to a grand fact that many world-wide and sustained wars have happened among, so called, civilized nations; and at the end of each and every war on the globe all parties, including the victor, have invariably come to the negotiating table for a final solution to compromise the very reason for war. If we were to do this after devastation and death then why not cooperate and negotiate before the catastrophe. Sagacity lies in choosing this prudent option rather than regret the holocaust *post facto*. This brings us the concept of international responsibility that has multiple resonances. And these responsibilities cannot be well discharged without cooperation of states. Hence, importance of international cooperation comes in clear focus as a cardinal principle of peaceful and prosperous living.

Space law is as yet an evolving branch of international law and within the short span of half a century, a nascent convention called OST has already assumed the status of customary law of outer space and is treated globally binding even on states that have not been party to the Treaty. Some of the salient provisions of the Treaty are taken as peremptory norms of state behaviour and conduct in outer space and hence, can logically be elevated to the pedestal of *Jus Cogens* of space law for reflexive obedience and universal compliance. International responsibility and international cooperation are two such tenets, among others, recommended by *opinio juris* to be exalted as *jus cogens*.[57]

Despite its fast growth, the architecture of space law is supported on the foundation of cooperation between nations and well-established concept of responsibility of the states for international wrongful acts. This incidentally, is also the *sine qua non* of reciprocal relations even for competing entities in the ultra-hazardous domain of outer space. Thus, just as international law is the law of civilized nations, in the same manner, space law is the law of responsible and cooperative space faring nations who understand their stakes and carry good sense to appreciate their debt to the future generations. Their relevance increases manifold on the dawn of the era of space commercialisation. The hypothesis is vindicated. *Quod Erat Demonstrandum.*

NOTES

1. Anthony D'Amato, "International Law as an Autopoietic System" in Rudiger Wolfrum and Volker Robens, editors, *Developments of International Law in Treaty Making*, Springer, Berlin, 2005, pp. 335-399.
2. For example, regimes for Antarctica, High Seas, *et al.*
3. For views on contribution of Asian states to evolution of international law, refer R. P. Anand, *Development of Modern international Law and India,* Indian Society of International Law, New Delhi in collaboration with Nomos Verlagsgesellschaft, Baden-Baden, Germany, 2005.
4. Ogunsola O. Ogunbanwo, *International Law and Outer Space Activities*, Martinus Nijhoff, the Hague, 1975, p. 11.
5. General Assembly Resolutions 1148 (xii) of 1957 and 1721 (xvi) of 20 December, 1961.
6. General Assembly Resolution 1348 (xiii) of 1958.
7. Adopted on 13 December, 1963. Note 4 *supra*, p. 14.
8. General Assembly Resolution 1962 (xviii) of 1962.
9. Treaty on Principles Governing the Activities of States in the Exploration and Use of Outer Space, including the Moon and Other Celestial Bodies, 1967.
10. L Oppenheim, *International Law A Treatise*, Vol. I, Peace, Seventh Edition, ed, Hersch Lauterpacht, London, Longmans, Green & Co. (1952) 304.
11. Ibid, p. 306.
12. Ibid, pp. 305-7.
13. Ibid, pp. 304-34.
14. The new concepts of state responsibility relate to, for example, war and aggression, coercion of minorities, denial of freedom by colonial powers and now extend to international and inter-governmental organizations.
15. Tunkin, G. I., International Law, Progress publishers, Moscow, English translation, 1986, p. 223.
16. Schwarzenberger, *International Law, Vol. I* (3rd ed., 1957), pp. 68-70.
17. Tunkin, G.I., International Law, Progress Publishers, Moscow, English translation, 1986, p. 223.

18. Charles G. Fenwick, *International Law*, Bombay, Vakil, Feffer and Simons Private Ltd (1967) 333.
19. Ibid, p. 334.
20. Michael Akehurst, *A Modern Introduction to International Law*, London, George Allen and Unwin (1980) pp.88-102.
21. C W Jenks, Liability for Ultra-Hazardous Activities in international Law, 117 *Recueil des Cours*, 99, 165 (1966). Also refer John Kelsen, State Responsibility for Abnormally Dangerous Activities, 13 HARV. INTL. L. J. 197, 238 (1972).
22. OST, Article VI.
23. G.S. Sachdeva, "State Responsibility for the Space Activities of Private Actors" in Venkat Rao and Kumar Abhijeet, eds., *Commercialisation and Privatisation of Outer Space*, New Delhi, KW Publishers, 2016, p. 13-30.
24. OST, Article IX.
25. Convention on International Liability for Damage Caused by Space Objects, 1972, Article II.
26. Ibid, Article III.
27. Agreement on the Rescue of Astronauts, the Return of Astronauts and the Return of Objects Launched into Outer Space, 1968, Article 2.
28. Ibid, Article 5.
29. Agreement Governing the Activities of States on the Moon and Other Celestial Bodies, 1979. Popularly referred to as the Moon Agreement.
30. Ibid, article 14.
31. R.A. Mullerson, "Sources of International Law: New Tendencies in the Soviet Thinking", 83 AJIL (1989), p. 508.
32. Barcelona Traction, Light and Power Co. *(Belgium v. Spain)* 1970 ICJ 3, 32 (5 February, 1970).
33. *The Vienna Convention of the Law of Treaties*, Article 53. Also refer G. S. Sachdeva, "Select Tenets of Space Law as *Jus Cogens*" in Venkat Rao, Gopalakrishnan and Kumar Abhijeet, eds., *Recent Developments in Space Law*, Springer, 2017, pp. 7-26.
34. Anthony D'Amato, International Law as an Autopoietic System, in Rudiger Wolfrum and Volker Robens, editors, *Developments of International Law in Treaty Making*, Springer, Berlin, 2005, pp. 335-399.
35. For example, regimes for Antarctica and High Seas.
36. G.S. Sachdeva, "Select Tenets of Space Law as *Jus Cogens*" in Venkat Rao, Gopalakrishnan and Kumar Abhijeet, eds., *Recent Developments in Space Law*, Springer, 2017, pp. 7-26.
37. UN Resolution 51/122.
38. The Report of the Secretary-General on international cooperation in space activities for enhancing security in the post-cold-war era. (A/48/221). Also refer the General Assembly Resolution 48/ 39, para 2.
39. Outer Space Treaty, 1967, The Preambular paragraphs.
40. Ibid. Word in parenthesis added.
41. Ibid, Article V. For a detailed analysis refer G.S. Sachdeva, *Outer Space: Security and Legal Challenges*, New Delhi, KW Publishers, 2010, pp. 89-104.
42. *Agreement Governing the Activities of States on the Moon and other Celestial Bodies, 1979.* Also euphemistically referred to as the Moon Treaty.
43. Ibid, Article 4 (1).
44. Ibid, Article 4 (2).
45. Principles Governing the Use by States of Artificial Satellites for International Direct Television Broadcasting, 1982. UN General Assembly Resolution 37/92 (annex) adopted on 10 December, 1982.

46. Ibid, Paragraph A—Purposes and Objectives of the Document. Parenthesis added.
47. Ibid, Paragraph D—International Cooperation.
48. UN General Assembly Resolution 41/65 adopted on 3 December, 1986.
49. Ibid.
50. Like testing of ASAT missile in the outer space by China and the US in 2007 and 2008 respectively.
51. Declaration on International Cooperation in the Exploration and Use of Outer Space for the Benefit and in the Interest of all States Taking into Particular Account the Needs of Developing Countries, 1996. UN Document Supplement No. 20 (A/51/20).
52. The European Union Code of Conduct for Space Activity, October, 2010. Refer Michael Listner, An Update on the Proposed European Code of Conduct, *The Space Review,* August, 08, 2011.
53. For a detailed discussion, refer Manpreet Sethi, *Code of Conduct for Outer Space: A Strategy for India*, New Delhi, KW Publishers and Centre for Air Power Studies, 2016. Also refer, Ajey Lele, ed., Decoding the International Code of Conduct for Outer Space Activities, New Delhi, Pentagon Security International, 2012.
54. D Goedhuis, An Evaluation of the Leading Principles of the Outer Space Treaty of 27 Jan 67, *NTIR*, vol 15, 1968, p. 40. Also refer Fenwick at note 19 *supra,* p. 110.
55. Rudiger Wolfrum, The Problems of Limitation and Prohibition of Military Uses of Outer Space, *ZaoRV*, vol 44, 1984 and R Wolfrum, Common Heritage of Mankind, *Encyclopaedia of Public International Law*, vol 11, 1989, p.67. Also refer Tunkin, n. 18 supra, p. 251.
56. R. Dolzer, "International Cooperation in Outer Space", *ZaöRV*, vol. 45, 1985, p. 527.
57. Refer G.S. Sachdeva, "Select Tenets of Space Law as *Jus Cogens*" in Venkat Rao, Gopalakrishnan and Kumar Abhijeet, eds., *Recent Developments in Space Law*, Springer, 2017, pp. 7-26.

Index